Praise for *In Their Own Way*

"*Thousands of potentially good learners in this country are currently being labeled as learning disabled and treated as such. In Their Own Way provides wonderfully practical advice to parents about how to appreciate and foster every child's unique individuality and way of learning. I recommend it highly.*"
—LOUISE BATES AMES, coauthor of *Your Child from Five to Ten*

"*Thomas Armstrong shows us how to use each student's uniqueness in achieving quality education for all. In Their Own Way is a book to be read by parents and teachers.*" —LAURENCE J. PETER, author of *The Peter Principle*

"*The impact of the diagnosis of serious illness on adults has been thoroughly documented. Dr. Armstrong makes a valuable contribution to the subject of the harmful effects of inaccurate diagnosis and the subsequent labeling of children.*"
—NORMAN COUSINS, author of *Anatomy of an Illness*

"*Too many educational specialists test, label, and throw their hands up. Thomas Armstrong asks us all to observe carefully, discern areas of strength, and help children to realize all of their potentials. He has written a positive and wholly constructive work.*" —HOWARD GARDNER, author of *Frames of Mind*

"*Thomas Armstrong outlines the problem so clearly and so carefully that all parents should be able to see themselves, as well as their children, in its pages.*"
—LENDON H. SMITH, M.D., author of *Improving Your Child's Behavior Chemistry*

"*This is a kind, decent, caring book—one that should help parents through their children's schooling years and support children through their growing times.*"
—HERB KOHL, author of *36 Children*

"*This book should be required reading, especially for those who make educational policy.*" —GEORGE LEONARD, author of *Education and Ecstasy*

In Their Own Way

Discovering and Encouraging Your Child's Multiple Intelligences

Revised and Updated

Thomas Armstrong, Ph.D.

Jeremy P. Tarcher/Putnam
a member of Penguin Putnam Inc.
New York

Most Tarcher/Putnam books are available at special quantity discounts for bulk purchase for sales promotions, premiums, fund-raising, and educational needs. Special books or book excerpts also can be created to fit specific needs. For details, write Putnam Special Markets, 375 Hudson Street, New York, NY 10014.

Jeremy P. Tarcher/Putnam
A member of
Penguin Putnam Inc.
375 Hudson Street
New York, NY 10014
www.penguinputnam.com

Library of Congress Cataloging-in-Publication Data

Armstrong, Thomas.
In their own way : discovering and encouraging your child's
multiple intelligences / by Thomas Armstrong.
p. cm.
Includes index.
ISBN 1-58542-051-4
1. Multiple intelligences. 2. Child rearing. I. Title.
BF432.3 A79   2000   00-029906
155.4'139—dc21

Printed in the United States of America

10 9 8 7 6 5 4 3 2 1

This book is printed on acid-free paper. ♾

Book design by Tanya Maiboroda

Dedicated to the memory of Shari Lewis

Acknowledgments

I would like to thank several people for their support and assistance during the writing of both the original edition of *In Their Own Way,* and this revised and expanded edition. They include: the originator of the theory of multiple intelligences, Dr. Howard Gardner; my wife, Barbara Turner; my original editor, Janice Gallagher; my current editor, Mitch Horowitz; my professors at the University of Massachusetts (Harold Washburn), Lesley Graduate School (Dr. George Hein, Dr. Cynthia Cole, Dr. Jill Hamilton, and Alice McKearney), and the California Institute of Integral Studies (Dr. DeLee Lantz, and Dr. Ralph Metzner); the late John Holt; Diane Divoky; Dr. Stanley Krippner; the late Dr. Louise Bates Ames; Mert Hanley; my agent Linda Allen; and the thousands of children, parents, and professional educators I've worked with over the years who have affirmed the shining principle of this book—that every child deserves to learn in his or her own way!

Contents

Chapter 1
The Worksheet Wasteland: Neglecting Talents
and Abilities in Our Nation's Schools   1

Chapter 2
Eight Ways to Bloom: Discovering Your Child's
Multiple Intelligences   15

Chapter 3
Testing for Failure: The Formal Test Trap   35

Chapter 4
Dysteachia: The Real Reason Your Child
Isn't Thriving in School   51

Chapter 5
Learning in Their Own Way: Giving Children
at Home What They May Not Be Getting at School   67

Chapter 6
Bodywise: Making Learning Physical   85

Chapter 7
The Inner Blackboard: Cultivating the
Imagination in Learning   99

Chapter 8
Teaching with Feeling: Opening the Heart
to Learning   111

Chapter 9
The Learning Network: Building Support
Systems in Your Child's Academic Life   **129**

Chapter 10
Great Expectations: Creating Positive Beliefs
in Your Child and Yourself   **141**

Chapter 11
A Patient Attitude: Honoring Your Child's
Learning Rate   **151**

Chapter 12
The Doors of Perception: Helping Children
Come Back to Their Senses   **161**

Chapter 13
The Ecology of Learning: Providing Your
Child with a Nurturing Environment   **173**

Afterword
The Learner of the Future   **185**

A Parent's Guide to Multiple Intelligences   **191**

Questions Parents and Teachers Ask
About Multiple Intelligences   **193**

Lesson Plans and Guidelines for Teaching Your
Child Anything Through Multiple Intelligences   **201**

Multiple Intelligences and Your Child's School   **215**

Teaching Your Child About Multiple Intelligences   **223**

Books for Parents   **229**

Organizations for the Eight Intelligences   **241**

Learning Materials for the Eight Intelligences   **247**

Books for Children in the Eight Intelligences   **253**

Games That Develop the Eight Intelligences   **259**

Internet Sites for Children in
the Eight Intelligences   **263**

Computer Software That Develops
the Eight Intelligences   **267**

Notes   **271**

Index   **283**

The Worksheet Wasteland

Neglecting Talents and Abilities in Our Nation's Schools

How many thinkers and creative spirits are wasted, how much brain power goes down the drain because of our archaic, insular notions of brain and education? The numbers are undoubtedly horrendous.

JEAN HOUSTON,
The Possible Human

B

illy loved to invent crazy machines. One of them caused water to run down a chute, moving Ping-Pong balls into sockets, in turn causing bells to ring and a miniature pig to spin around. This finally moved an alligator's head into which you could stick your pencil to be sharpened. Other machines did similarly creative and practical things. Yet in spite of these innovative projects, Billy was flunking out of school. He couldn't seem to do things the school's way. For example, when Billy's mother asked him to figure out the area of a room using the methods the school had taught him, Billy struggled. He tensed his body, erased frequently, and finally came up with a totally unrealistic answer.

Then Billy did it his way. According to educator and human potential consultant Jean Houston, who was working with him at the time: "Billy shut his eyes and made little rhythmic movements with his head, as if he were listening to an inner song. After a while he jotted down something on the pad, closed his eyes for some more internal business, opened them, jotted something else down, and gave us the correct answer." Asked to describe the process, Billy responded, "Well, when I close my eyes to figure something out it's like a cross between music and architecture."

Susan was a first grader who read the encyclopedia for recreation. In reading class, she had to patiently submit to a curriculum that included books with titles like *ABC and Me* and *Little Pig*. Finally, the teacher asked the class to write a story about *Little Pig*. Susan wrote: "Little Pig, Little Pig. I'll tell you what you can do with Little Pig. You can take this book and . . ."

By the age of twelve, Chris was managing two profitable businesses at home and had a one-man art show at his elementary school. At five, Justin was giving talks on the solar system, creating elaborate Lego structures, and writing and illustrating his own original stories. Marc was an eleven-year-old Dungeons and Dragons expert, widely read on the subject. He also created animated movies. All three of these boys were labeled learning disabled by their school districts and forced to attend special remedial classes at their respective schools.

Each of the children described above is a unique learner whose gifts, talents, and abilities were ignored by the schools. They're not alone. Every year millions of children across the nation are being labeled as ADD or ADHD (attention deficit disorder or attention deficit hyperactivity disorder), learning disabled, dyslexic, or simply as underachievers. Millions more seem to be making satisfactory academic progress but are secretly dying inside because their true gifts and abilities are not being drawn out by the schools. Your child may be one of them. Here are some questions to ask yourself in order to discover if this is indeed the case.

- Does your child have some hobby, skill, interest, or ability that excites him at home? If so, is he getting a chance to use that talent or ability at school?
- When was the last time your child raced home from school to tell you something important that he'd learned that day?
- Does your child like to hang around school at the end of the day, talking with a teacher, developing a project, or practicing a skill, or does he rush off as soon as the bell rings?
- When you speak with the teacher about your child, what group of words does the teacher use most: *problems, needs, difficulties,* and *disabilities,* or *talents, accomplishments, interests,* and *abilities?*
- Does your child complain of stomachaches, headaches, and anxiety in the morning before going off to school, or does he talk at the breakfast table about all the exciting things he's going to be doing that day?
- Does your child bring home lots of textbooks, workbooks, and ditto sheets for homework, or does he instead have

projects to work on that require real thought, creativity, and innovation?

The answers to these questions will give you a clue as to whether your child's school is nurturing his multiple intelligences. Over the past fifteen years, research by psychologist Howard Gardner and his colleagues at Harvard University has indicated that every child has many different ways of being smart: through words, numbers, pictures and images, music, physical expression, experiences with nature, social interaction, and self-understanding. Instead of focusing so much attention on human potential in a narrow way—as we do when we talk about a child's IQ score, for example—psychologists, educators, and parents are now beginning to look at a child's potential more in terms of their multiple intelligences. Many schools have begun to incorporate multiple intelligences approaches into their curriculum. However, your child's school may not be one of them. The truth is that schooling for millions of children across the country is bland and boring. If your child sticks out one iota from the norm—in other words, if your child shows his true individual nature—then there is always the danger that he will be discriminated against or stuck with some sort of label and treated like a category instead of a real human being. Our schools have lost the ability to respond to individual differences. The purpose of this book is to help you regain that inner dignity for your children by discovering how they truly learn best and then helping them learn in their own way.

The Nation's Schools: A Worksheet Wasteland

Einstein once wrote, "It is nothing short of a miracle that the modern methods of instruction have not yet entirely strangled the holy curiosity of inquiry." Back in the 1980s, John Goodlad, a former dean of the School of Education at UCLA, and his colleagues visited over one thousand classrooms in the United States. The picture he left us with was of a joyless wasteland of almost insufferable proportions. Goodlad wrote, "Shared laughter, overenthusiasm, or angry outbursts were rarely observed. Less than 3 percent of classroom time was devoted to praise, abrasive comments, expressions of joy or humor, or somewhat unbridled outbursts such as 'wow' or 'great.'" Less than 1 percent of the day involved students in sharing opinions or openly reasoning about some problem or issue. Virtually all of the elementary school classrooms were dominated by the teachers, with students having next to no choice in how things were run. Almost 80 percent of the day in elementary schools was taken up with the basic skills, with art taking up only 7 percent of the school week, dance only 2 percent, and drama only 1 percent.

Since that time, things appear to have only gotten worse. In spite of a spate of reforms in the 1990s, there seems to be a movement back to an even more bleak classroom landscape. Textbooks (and their accompanying worksheets) structure 75 to 90 percent of all the learning that goes on in our schools. Sales of textbooks registered the strongest gains in any category of the $21 billion U.S. book market, with elementary school textbooks increasing by 13 percent in 1997–1998 to $3 billion in total sales. U.S. schoolchildren are the most tested students in the world, taking more than 100 million standardized tests annually, and there are increasing calls for more rigorous testing at both the state and national levels. Individual states that have the most impact upon textbook construction—especially California and Texas—are moving away from more creative approaches to presenting subject matter in reading and math and are embracing phonics and back-to-basics arithmetic to an extent not seen since the early 1960s. State legislatures are implementing rigid accountability standards on school districts in their states, creating stress on administrators, teachers, and students to perform, perform, perform . . . or else! Schools are even beginning to get rid of recess, so that they can cram more academic learning into kids in preparation for the high-stakes tests at the end of the term.

What happens to the learners in this worksheet wasteland? The truth is that most of them learn to comply and remain passive and may outwardly appear to be very successful students. Other children, unable to go along with such stale fare as they're given daily in the classroom, begin slipping in their achievement but are able to keep up appearances to a greater or lesser degree. These are the underachievers that we keep hearing so much about. Lawrence Greene, in his book *Children Who Underachieve,* estimated that up to 50 percent of our nation's children are underachievers. Finally, there is a group of children totally unable to keep up with the charade, mostly because their own unique ways of learning clash so severely with the narrow way that the schools go about educating them. This group has earned a couple of unjust labels in recent years: learning disabled (LD) and attention deficit hyperactivity disordered (ADHD).

The Learning Disability Trap

On Saturday, April 6, 1963, a new disease was invented in Chicago, Illinois, which over the next thirty-five years would slowly begin to infect millions of schoolchildren nationwide. This was no simple virus or common bacteria. Hidden deep within the neurological system, it resisted detection by medical personnel, evaded clear diagnosis through testing, and had no discernible cure. The federal government would spend billions of dollars on this learning disease, and yet by 1998 it would be said to afflict 15 percent of the American population.

It was on that Saturday in April that Samuel Kirk, then a professor of special education at the University of Illinois, told a group of concerned parents about learning disabilities. He suggested that they use the term to describe "children who have disorders in development of language, speech, reading, and associated communication skills." They enthusiastically agreed and shortly thereafter established The Association for Children with Learning Disabilities.

Since that time, the learning disability (LD) movement has mushroomed, with the founding of many more organizations and the writing of hundreds of books and tens of thousands of articles. The popular media have made it a suitable subject for dramatic television shows and full-length feature films. More important, and devastating, millions of children have been labeled learning disabled, dyslexic, and a host of related terms, then sent to special programs to be treated for their "condition."

Yet, in spite of the impact of this term on the lives of children and adults around the country, the experts seem to be no closer to defining what it means, let alone to finding a cure for it. Bob Algozzine, a professor of special education at the University of Florida and contributing editor to *The Journal of Learning Disabilities*, wrote: "No one . . . has been able to demonstrate to me that a specific, distinctly unique group of behaviors differentiate LD children from many of their classmates. To build an empire on such a foundation is very dishonest." Douglas Friedrich and his colleagues at Central Michigan University studied 1,600 children referred to specialists because of suspected learning problems, and in analyzing the ninety-four formulas that had been used to diagnose for learning disabilities, sadly noted: "It seems such a shame to subject persons to the lifelong effects of the label 'learning disabled' when we really don't know what it is."

The LD movement, nevertheless, only seems to be growing stronger. Parents have been alerted to such warning signs of LD as reversals of letters and numbers, messy handwriting, poor coordination, problems telling time, confusion about right and left, and difficulty in reading. Psychologists continue to develop more intricate ways of testing for learning disabilities. Meanwhile, children with the LD label still don't receive adequate explanations from adults about what learning disabilities are and why they can't be normal like other children.

The Attention Deficit Debacle

As if one learning disease wasn't enough for our kids, mental health professionals have been spending the last few years concocting another one. It's actually a rehashing of a label that has gone through twenty-five name changes in the past one hundred years, including organic driveness, restlessness syndrome, minimal brain dysfunction, and hyperkinesis. This time around it's called attention deficit hyperactivity disorder (ADHD) or just attention deficit disorder (ADD), and it's being applied to far more children than ever received one of the earlier labels. Current estimates put the number of kids labeled ADD or ADHD at about 2.5 million in the United States. The use of Ritalin to treat this supposed disorder has skyrocketed 700 percent over the past eight years! Its "symptoms" include hyperactivity, impulsivity, and distractibility, and it's said to result from neurochemical imbalances of as yet to be determined genetic origins. One problem with the label is that these symptoms are far too general and subjective. Many kids have these characteristics for varying periods of time due to a wide range of circumstances. A child can be hyperactive for any number of reasons: because he's allergic to milk, bored with school, highly creative, severely depressed, having trouble learning to read, scared of other kids in the neighborhood, or a hundred other reasons. ADD proponents say that there are tests that can tell the difference between "true" and "pseudo" ADD, but these tests are similarly subjective. Often, parents and teachers are simply given checklists and asked to rate the child on a scale of 1 to 5 or 1 to 10 on a number of behavioral items such as "fidgets often in seat at school." Still other tests ask kids to press buttons on computerized machines to show that they are paying attention. This sounds more like Big Brother and the Brave New World than common educational sense! ADD seems like a matter of convenience to many adults who are in charge of "round kids" who don't fit into the "square holes" of home and school. The label helps a teacher get a troublesome child out of a regular class and into a special education room, helps a parent get a drug prescription to set the problem right (instead of first considering other more fundamental changes), and even helps many students get more time to take tests and complete assignments in class. Unfortunately, though, it's the child who gets saddled with the disability label and has to go through school looked upon as less normal than the other kids.

Neglecting Learning Abilities

Nowhere in this litany of deficit, disability, and disease is there the recognition that these children may learn very well *in their own way.* This is because few researchers have bothered to look at how these youngsters learn best. Mary Poplin, former editor of *The Learning Disability Quarterly (LDQ)*, comments: "The horrifying truth is that in the four years I have been editor of *LDQ*, only one article has been submitted that sought to elaborate on the talents of the learning disabled. . . . Why do we not know if our students are talented in art, music, dance, athletics, mechanical repair, computer programming, or are creative in other nontraditional ways? . . . It is because, like regular educators, we care only about competence in its most traditional and bookish sense—reading, writing, spelling, science, social studies, and math in basal texts and worksheets." The one positive article that *was* submitted to her came from Dr. Sara Tarver and her colleagues at the University of Wisconsin's School of Education. They discovered that children labeled learning disabled scored higher than so-called normal children on tests of nonverbal creativity. Tarver also noticed that the so-called learning disabled children scored higher than "normals" in first grade on verbal scores but that their creativity in this area declined in the higher grades. She speculated that "one aspect of schooling which may contribute to the relative decline of learning disabled children's verbal creativity has to do with the negative reactions of others toward their uniqueness." In other words, these children are ridiculed by teachers and students for being creative, and they soon learn to keep a low profile, stifling their individuality in the process.

Other authorities affirm the inner richness of these youngsters. Harvard neurologist Norman Geschwind, one of the leading figures in the field of learning disabilities until his death, observed: "It is commonplace to hear parents of dyslexics say that they knew that a particular child would be dyslexic because like his dyslexic siblings . . . even at the age of three . . . he was showing unusual skill in drawing, or doing mechanical puzzles or building models." With regard to attention deficit disorder, creativity researcher Bonnie Cramond, a professor of psychology at the University of Georgia, writes: "There are so many similarities in the behavioral descriptions of creativity and ADHD that one is left to wonder, could these be overlapping phenomena?" Cramond notes that the highly creative person, like the so-called ADHD individual, rejects limits imposed by others, is a risk-taker, has a broader range of interests, often likes to work quickly, daydreams, and has a high energy level.

In my own classes for the "learning handicapped," I had an amazing group of children: a boy who held the national freestyle swim record in his age group, a girl who was a model for a national department store chain, gifted artists and writers, a psychic child, expert storytellers, superior math students, and many other talented human beings.

And yet, when these children enter school, virtually all the focus of teachers and parents gets placed upon their "disability." It reminds me of the story about the animals who decided to create a school for climbing, flying, running, swimming, and digging. They couldn't agree on which subject was most important, so they said that all the students had to take the same curriculum. The rabbit was an expert in running but almost drowned in swimming class. The experience shocked her so much that she never could run as well after that. The eagle was a whiz at flying, of course, but when he showed up for digging class, he was so inadequate to the task that he got assigned to a digging remediation program. It took up so much of his time that he soon forgot how to fly. And so on with the other animals. The animals no longer had the opportunity to shine in their areas of expertise because all were forced to do things that did not respect their individual nature. In much the same way, we're doing that with our children, neglecting their gifts and talents while at the same time forcing them to waste hours of time in boring and inappropriate remediation groups and special classes. Eagles are meant to fly!

Initiation into the Lie

I'd like to give you a picture of what goes on in the life of a child with a unique way of learning, so that you can see how the schools unwittingly disengage people from their true potentials. Imagine an active and eager six-year-old girl brimming with excitement as she begins her first day of school. She's used to spending her days drawing, splashing around with friends at the local pond, playing ball on the neighborhood lot, building with blocks, and singing songs. As she enters the school on that momentous first day, she has expectations of being able to move about, explore things, sing, play, and interact with the other children. Instead, she finds herself in a world where she must sit in her seat for long periods of time, learn to decode long and complicated instructions from the teacher, and strain her eyes while looking at small squiggly numbers and letters in funny-smelling books.

When her disappointment and confusion become evident to the teacher, he refers her to a specialist for an evaluation. She is then subjected to a battery of tests that pick, poke, and prod at her inner world. The examiner dutifully records the many errors she makes. She easily catches onto the worry of her parents and teachers as they sit in conference talking about her "problems."

Finally the "experts" diagnose her as having an official problem. Perhaps they call it *attention deficit disorder, learning disability, dyslexia, hyperactivity, reading disability,* or simply *underachievement.* The specialists prescribe a fancy treatment plan that is supposed to cure her of this dreaded condition. They place her in a special program—perhaps in a small room in a remote corridor of the school or a trailer in the back of the school. Here, a teacher with special training "remediates" the learning problem using a wide range of esoteric methods and materials, including special learning kits, behavior modification, and lots of worksheets. During recess, the child hears the other children talking about "the retards in Room 103."

Returning to the special class, she feels even more confused and restless. The teacher notices this, and during the next official meeting of the school team of professionals, they decide to keep her in the special program for at least another year. In this way, the child remains stuck in a cycle of learning failure, perhaps for the rest of her school days.

The above scenario may sound like a Kafkaesque nightmare, but it's an all-too-common occurrence in the public school system. I've not only seen this happen, I've participated in it. In spite of my best intentions and educational ideals, I found myself again and again being caught up in the workings of a system that has its own life and that seeks to turn children into defective merchandise sent back to the shop for repairs.

In the regular class, this child's peers may fare no better. Forced to abandon their own unique patterns of learning ability—their gifts, talents, and interests—they learn quickly to submit to a new way of learning that substitutes abstract symbols for living images and routine assignments for dynamic play. Their new life in this barren environment recalls what Kafka himself said about education in his own day: "Probably all education is but two things, first parrying of the ignorant children's impetuous assault on the truth, and second, gentle, imperceptible, step-by-step initiation of the humiliated children into the lie."

A New Focus: Honoring Each Child's Multiple Intelligences

It's time for the schools, and parents as well, to start focusing their attention on the inner capabilities of each and every child. We've known for many years that human beings use only a small fraction of their potential. If that's true, then in even the most brain-damaged person there's a tremendous potentiality hidden within that is going untapped. John Lorber, a British pediatrician, studied one individual who, due to neurological illness, had virtually no brain. Instead of the normal 4.5-centimeter thickness of cerebral cortex, this young student had just a thin layer measuring a millimeter or so. In spite of this obvious shortcoming, he was measured as having an IQ of 126, was socially competent, and gained first-class honors in mathematics. Yet the schools persist in labeling hundreds of thousands of children with perfectly normal brains as "attention deficit disordered" or "learning disabled" when in fact teachers simply have not found a way of teaching them on their own terms, according to their own unique patterns of neurological functioning.

The part of the brain that thrives on worksheets and teacher lectures probably takes up less than 1 percent of the total available for learning. More likely, these stale methods of learning are actually what educator Leslie Hart referred to as "brain-antagonistic"—they shut down potentials rather than open them up. Too many classrooms around the country still rely heavily on worksheets and lectures and give students few opportunities to build, draw, perform, role-play, or engage in other active learning methods. In other words, the children aren't given an opportunity to exercise the vast portion of their brains devoted to new learning.

The children described at the beginning of this chapter were obviously very good at exploring uncharted regions of the brain—learning through music and architecture, words and feelings, business and film. Some people might consider them "gifted" and beyond the reach of the average schoolchild. But here they would be making the same mistake that is made by those who label children as "disabled learners." For by assigning the label of gifted to only a few select individuals, we're shutting the door to millions more who possess untold inner riches. All children are gifted. Every child is a unique human being—a very special person. Unfortunately, the schools prefer to send some kids to classes for attention deficit disorder or learning disabilities, group others according to ability, and send a small group to programs for the gifted. They've even got a category for the "learning disabled/gifted" student. When will it ever end? It will end when parents and educators decide to toss aside all of these labels and begin the task of understanding and nurturing each and every child's uniqueness so that they can begin to learn in their own way. The next chapter will present Howard Gardner's theory of multiple intelligences so that you can help your children learn in the way that is most natural to them.

Chapter

2

Eight Ways to Bloom

Discovering Your Child's Multiple Intelligences

Most people in our society, even if they know better, talk as if individuals could be assessed in terms of one dimension, namely how smart or dumb they are. This is deeply ingrained in us. I became convinced some time ago that such a narrow assessment was wrong in scientific terms and had seriously damaging social consequences. . . . I describe [eight] ways of viewing the world. I believe they're equally important ways, and if they don't exhaust all possible forms of knowing, they at least give us a more comprehensive picture than we've had until now.

HOWARD GARDNER

Peter can defeat any challenger in a game of chess. Sally spends her free time listening to opera. Ed is a superathlete. Frank entertains his peers with long-winded stories of adventure. Ann loves to draw and paint. June is always organizing a party or committee at school. David sits at home alone planning a business venture. Kimberly enjoys bird-watching and deciphering the tracks of small animals.

Although a typical IQ test might not show it, all of these children are highly intelligent. Each demonstrates a particular strength in one of eight different kinds of intelligence: logical-mathematical, musical, bodily-kinesthetic, linguistic, spatial, interpersonal, intrapersonal, and naturalist, described by Harvard psychologist Howard Gardner in his prize-winning book *Frames of Mind* and in other writings. This new model of intelligence has received worldwide recognition as one of the most innovative theories of learning and intelligence developed in the past century. Gardner's theory of multiple intelligences provides a solid foundation upon which to identify and develop a broad spectrum of abilities within every child.

Eight Kinds of Smart

Ever since IQ tests were invented almost a hundred years ago, people have thought of intelligence as some*thing* (singular) that one is born with that doesn't change very much during the course of a life. We know now that this is wrong. The work of Dr. Howard Gardner and his colleagues at Harvard University has demonstrated that there are *many* forms of intelligence that aren't measured on standard IQ tests. Gardner defines *intelligence* as the ability to solve problems and to fashion products that have cultural value. He says that psychology and education have spent too much time studying intelligence in the testing room and should be looking more at the real world for examples of how people solve problems and fashion products that make a difference in the culture. Noticing how a mechanic solves a problem with a carburetor or how an accountant solves a financial dilemma provides better examples of intelligence at work, he says, than any test results. After looking at many different kinds of abilities, competencies, and skills used around the world, Dr. Gardner finally came up with a list of seven basic intelligences (he has recently added an eighth intelligence) that he says make a good working list of the many kinds of intelligence.

Linguistic Intelligence: Word Smart

Linguistic intelligence is the ability to use words effectively. A look at the traditional 3 Rs of school life reveals that linguistic intelligence takes up at least two-thirds of them: reading and writing. Within these two activities, there are a broad range of linguistic capacities, including spelling, vocabulary, and grammar. Linguistic intelligence also is concerned with speaking ability. This is the intelligence of the orator, the stand-up comedian, the radio personality, or the politician who often use words to manipulate and persuade. In everyday life, linguistic intelligence comes in handy for talking, listening, reading everything from traffic signs to classic novels, and writing anything from E-mail messages and letters to poetry and office reports.

Logical-Mathematical Intelligence: Number Smart

Logical-mathematical intelligence involves the capacity to work well with numbers and/or to be adept at logic or reasoning. This is the intelligence that a scientist uses when she creates hypotheses and rigorously tests them against experimental data. It is also the intelligence used by a tax accountant, a computer programmer, or a higher mathematician. Of course, the rest of us need to use this intelligence to balance our checkbooks, comprehend the national debt, or understand the latest newspaper report on genetic research. Some people seem to have a knack for numbers or logic, while others moan inwardly whenever a math problem or science concept comes up.

Spatial Intelligence: Picture Smart

This is the intelligence of pictures and images. It involves the ability to visualize pictures in one's head or to create them in some two- or three-dimensional form. An artist or sculptor possesses this intelligence in strong measure, as does an inventor who can visualize new inventions before drawing them on paper. One inventor, Nikola Tesla, was said to be able to design and *test* his inventions in his mind. Einstein said he used this intelligence in coming up with his theories of relativity. We need this intelligence for everything from decorating our homes or landscaping our backyards to reading an office flow sheet or appreciating a work of art at a museum.

Bodily-Kinesthetic Intelligence: Body Smart

Bodily-kinesthetic intelligence is the intelligence of the whole body (athlete, dancer, mime, actor), as well as the intelligence of the hands (machinist, seamstress, carpenter, surgeon). Of course, you hope that the surgeon has some of the other intelligences as well! But you don't want a surgeon working on you who passed all of his logical-mathematical med school exams, but everyone in the operating room calls "all thumbs"! Our society depends on people with good fine-motor coordination in a wide range of fields, including construction workers, assembly-line workers, mechanics, plumbers, and repair people of all kinds. We also need people who "think" through the body. Einstein wrote that in addition to visual-spatial capacities, he also used "muscular" processes in working out some of his top physics problems. One of his favorite "thought experiments," for example, was riding on the end of a beam of light. He realized that this sort of thrill ride played havoc with our traditional notions of time and space and led him to come up with the theory of relativity. In the everyday world, we need to use body smart for everything from unscrewing a jar of mayonnaise and working under the hood of a car, to playing competitive sports or doing the jitterbug at a local swing club.

Musical Intelligence: Music Smart

Musical intelligence involves the capacity to carry a tune, remember musical melodies, have a good sense of rhythm, or simply enjoy music. In its higher forms, it includes the divas and piano virtuosos of culture. But while it is often associated with entertainment, there are many practical careers in life that require some degree of musical intelligence, including disc jockeys, sound engineers, piano tuners, electronics salespeople, and music therapists. In everyday life, we benefit from being musically smart whenever we sing in a choir, pick up a musical instrument, or enjoy music on TV, radio, or CDs.

Interpersonal Intelligence: People Smart

This intelligence involves the ability to understand and work with other people. Like each of the other intelligences, people smart takes in a lot of territory, from the capacity to feel empathy for another person (such as a counselor might possess), to the ability to manipulate large groups of people toward a common end (such as a political dictator or a CEO of a large corporation might have). Interpersonal intelligence includes the ability to "read people" (e.g., to size them up within a few seconds), the capacity to make friends, and the skill that some people have to walk into a room and immediately begin making key business or personal contacts. Since so much of life involves interacting with others, interpersonal intelligence may actually be more important for life success than the ability to read a book or do a math problem.

Intrapersonal Intelligence: Self Smart

This intelligence may be the hardest one to fully understand, but it also could very well be the most important of the eight kinds of smart. It is essentially the intelligence of self-understanding, of knowing who you are. It's the intelligence of knowing what you're good at and what you're not good at. Some people waste a good deal of their life trying to be something that they're not, while others recognize early in life their key talents and deliberately cultivate them to achieve success. This is also the intelligence of being able to reflect upon one's life goals and to believe in oneself. Self smart is an important intelligence for entrepreneurs and other self-made individuals who need to possess the requisite self-discipline, confidence, and self-knowledge to enter into a new field or business. Similarly, counselors, therapists, and others who work with personal emotions and motivations use this intelligence to help others develop a better sense of who they are.

Naturalist Intelligence: Nature Smart

The naturalist intelligence involves the ability to identify the natural forms around us: birds, flowers, trees, animals, and other fauna and flora. It also includes sensitivity to other natural forms, such as cloud formations and geological features of the earth. This intelligence is required in many kinds of occupations, including biologist, forest ranger, veterinarian, and horticulturist. In everyday life, we use this intelligence when we're planting a garden, camping with friends or family, or supporting local ecological causes.

It's very important to remember that *every person has all eight intelligences* and uses them in different combinations during the course of daily life. A child who plays soccer, for example, has to use body smart to run and manipulative the ball, picture smart to visualize where the ball will be after a competitor kicks it, and people smart in order to work smoothly with one's teammates on the field. The act of reading, which seems like a very "word smart" thing to do, also engages picture smart (to visually decode the text and create images of the content), body smart (if one is reading out loud), and self smart (to relate the reading material to one's own experiences).

At the same time, one must keep in mind that each person has all eight intelligences in their own way. Some people excel in several, others have special difficulties in many of the intelligences, but most of us are somewhere in between: We have one or more intelligences that we may find very easy to express, some that are so-so, and one or more that we might have great difficulty in using.

Our society generally focuses on only two of the eight types of intelligence when deciding who's smart in the culture. We look up to the highly linguistic person who reads and writes well and the logical thinker who reasons in clear and concise ways. Yet there are other equally valid forms of intelligence. What about people who sing or dance well? Or those who can paint, draw, act, sculpt, invent, design, or understand nature? And what about individuals who are great leaders or have deep empathy for others? These musical, bodily-kinesthetic, spatial, naturalist, and interpersonal learners often get overlooked in discussions about superior intelligence.

This cultural neglect spills over into the classroom. Our schools prize mainly linguistic and logical-mathematical abilities. Children with talent in these areas will usually do well in school. But children with poor verbal or logical skills will often fail, even if they're highly talented in one or more of the other major intelligences. The theory of multiple intelligences gives us a way of looking at the complete picture of a learner's potential so that these neglected abilities will be honored and developed as well.

Discovering Your Child's Multiple Intelligences

To repeat, everyone has all eight intelligences, but in different proportions. Your child may be a great reader but a poor math student, a wonderful drawer but clumsy out on the playing field. Children can even show a wide range of strengths and weaknesses within one area of intelligence. Your child may write very well but have difficulty with spelling or handwriting, read poorly but be a superb storyteller, play an excellent game of basketball but stumble on the dance floor.

As you read through the descriptions of each type of intelligence that follow, resist the temptation to categorize your child into one of the eight intelligence groups. Your child is more complex than this. You should find your child described in several of the sections. Take what seems to apply to your child in these descriptions and add to this other observed strengths and weaknesses in all eight varieties of intelligence. Taken together, these constitute your child's unique profile of multiple intelligences.

Linguistic Intelligence

Children gifted in linguistic ability have highly developed auditory skills and enjoy playing around with the sounds of language. They often think in words. They frequently have their head stuck in a book or are busy writing a story or poem. Even if they don't enjoy reading or writing, they may be gifted storytellers. They often love word games and may have a good memory for verse, lyrics, or trivia. They might want to be writers, secretaries, editors, social scientists, humanities teachers, or politicians. They learn best by verbalizing or hearing and seeing words. Check any of the following that seem to apply to your child:

❑ likes to write creatively at home
❑ spins tall tales or tell jokes and stories
❑ has a good memory for names, places, dates, or trivia
❑ enjoys reading books for pleasure
❑ spells words accurately and easily
❑ appreciates nonsense rhymes and tongue twisters
❑ likes doing crossword puzzles or playing games such as Scrabble or Anagrams

❑ enjoys listening to the spoken word (stories, radio programs, talking books, etc.)
❑ has a good vocabulary for his or her age
❑ excels at subjects in school that involve reading and/or writing

✎ List here any other linguistic abilities that you've noticed in your child:

This is the intelligence that is most commonly associated with being "school smart." However, your child may not be school smart yet still be highly linguistic: Perhaps she talks a lot at school instead of paying attention, or enjoys writing poetry at home but not doing written assignments at school, or has significant difficulty reading but is a superb storyteller. There are many different ways to be linguistic, so don't ask, "Is my child word smart?"— since every child is word smart—but rather, "*How* is my child word smart?"

Logical-Mathematical Intelligence

Youngsters strong in this form of intelligence think numerically or in terms of logical patterns and sequences, or other forms of logical reasoning. Before adolescence, these children explore patterns, categories, and relationships by actively manipulating the environment and experimenting with things in a controlled and orderly way. In their teen years, they're capable of highly abstract forms of logical thinking. Children gifted in this area are constantly questioning and wondering about natural events. These are the youngsters who love hanging around computers or chemistry sets, trying to figure out the answer to a difficult problem. They often love brain teasers, logical puzzles, and games— like chess—that require reasoning abilities. These children may

want to grow up to be scientists, engineers, computer program-
mers, accountants, or perhaps even philosophers. Check any of
the following that seem to apply to your child:

❑ computes arithmetic problems quickly in her head
❑ enjoys using computer languages or logical software programs
❑ asks questions like "Where does the universe end?" or "Why is
the sky blue?"
❑ plays chess, checkers, or other strategy games with skill
❑ reasons out problems logically
❑ devises experiments to test out things that aren't understood
at first
❑ spends lots of time working on logic puzzles such as Rubik's
cube or logical games
❑ enjoys putting things in categories or hierarchies
❑ has a good sense of cause and effect
❑ enjoys math or science classes at school and does well in them

✎ List here any other logical-mathematical abilities that you've
noticed in your child:

This is the other major intelligence that is associated with being "school smart." Sometimes kids who are highly intelligent in
this area are considered by their peers to be "nerds" if they are
not very developed in interpersonal intelligence, however they
also can be school leaders as well. Just as with linguistic intelligence, there are many different ways to be number/logic smart.
Some kids will show it through excellent science fair projects at
school, yet they may not do well on science tests. Other kids may
flunk math because the teacher wants them to show their work on
paper but they do it so quickly in their head that they don't feel
like they have to do this time-consuming work. Some kids may
have great difficulty with basic arithmetic yet be highly logical. If

someone would just show them how to use a handheld calculator, they could get over the arithmetic hump, so to speak, and get on with the higher-level problem-solving that they're really good at.

Spatial Intelligence

These kids seem to know where everything is located in the house. They think in images and pictures. They're the ones who find things that have been lost or misplaced. If you should re-arrange the interior of your home, these children will be highly sensitive to the change and react with joy or dismay. They often love to do mazes or jigsaw puzzles. They spend free time drawing, designing things, building with Lego blocks, or simply daydreaming. Many of them develop a fascination with machines and con-traptions, sometimes coming up with inventions of their own. They might want to become architects, artists, mechanics, engi-neers, or city planners. Check any of the following that seem to apply to your child:

❑ excels in art class at school
❑ reports clear visual images when thinking about something
❑ easily reads maps, charts, and diagrams
❑ draws accurate representations of people or things
❑ likes it when you show movies, slides, or photographs
❑ enjoys doing jigsaw puzzles, mazes, or other visual activities
❑ daydreams a lot
❑ builds interesting three-dimensional constructions
   (e.g., Lego buildings)
❑ doodles on stray scraps of paper or on schoolwork
❑ gets more out of pictures than words while reading

✎ List here any other spatial abilities that you've noticed in your child:

Kids who are highly developed in spatial intelligence some-times have difficulties in school—especially if there isn't an em-phasis on the arts or visual methods of presenting information. Some of these kids can be labeled as "dyslexic" or "learning dis-abled" because of their problems decoding words. They may ap-proach words in the same way that they relate to pictures—as interesting visual images—and rotate them in their minds or when writing them down. This makes perfect sense from a spatial perspective (after all, the spatial mind of the architect is con-stantly looking at pictures and buildings from different points of view), but it breaks down in the world of linguistic symbols, where a rotated or reversed letter can change its very identity (for ex-ample, "b" to "d"). It's important for parents and teachers to re-member that such kids may be actually using a highly developed spatial ability when they reverse letters and so not to think of them as "disabled" but rather help them learn to use pictures, re-buses, visualization, arts, and other visual strategies in mastering reading skills.

Bodily-Kinesthetic Intelligence

Children highly developed in bodily-kinesthetic intelligence of-ten squirm at the breakfast table and are the first ones to be ex-cused as they zoom out the door and head for the neighborhood playground. They process knowledge through bodily sensations. They get "gut feelings" about answers on tests at school. Some are primarily graced with athletic abilities or the skills of a dancer, ac-tor, or mime—they are great at mimicking your best and worst qualities. Others are particularly gifted with excellent fine-motor coordination and can excel in typing, drawing, fixing things, sewing, crafts, and related activities. Children highly developed in bodily-kinesthetic intelligence may communicate very effectively through gestures and other forms of body language. They may want to be mechanics, carpenters, actors, athletes, or pilots when they grow up. They need opportunities to learn by moving or act-ing things out. Check any of the following that seem to apply to your child:

❑ does well in competitive sports at school or in the community

❑ moves, twitches, taps, or fidgets while sitting in a chair

❑ engages in physical activities such as swimming, biking, hiking, or skateboarding

❑ needs to touch things in order to learn more about them

❑ enjoys jumping, running, wrestling, or similar activities (if older, may show this in a more subdued way)

❑ demonstrates skill in a craft like woodworking, sewing, carving, or sculpture

❑ cleverly mimics other people's gestures, mannerisms, or behaviors

❑ gets "gut feelings" when working on problems at home or school

❑ enjoys working with clay, fingerpainting, or other "messy" activities

❑ loves to take things apart and put them back together again

✎ List here any other bodily-kinesthetic abilities that you've noticed in your child:

Kids who show high levels of bodily-kinesthetic intelligence may be at risk at school to be labeled with America's newest learning disease: attention deficit hyperactivity disorder (ADHD). Such children need to be able to move, touch, and build in order to learn. If they have to sit still in school for any sustained period of time, it is like handcuffing their most natural learning ability to the desk. They need frequent opportunities for movement during the school day: strong physical education programs, stretch breaks, field trips, hands-on learning, role-playing, and other dramatic ways of learning new information. As mentioned in the last chapter, the use of Ritalin to manage the behaviors of children labeled ADD/ADHD has increased 700 percent in the past six years. If schools employed bodily-kinesthetic activities more often for all of its kids, I suspect that the use of medication to control inappropriate behaviors might probably be able to be decreased in many instances (see chapter 6 for more information on using "bodywise" strategies to help kids learn).

Musical Intelligence

Kids highly developed in musical intelligence often sing, hum, or whistle tunes quietly to themselves. Put on a piece of music and you can recognize these children by the way in which they immediately begin moving and singing along. They may already be playing musical instruments or singing in choirs. However, other musical children show this potential more through music appreciation. They will have strong opinions about the music you play on the radio or stereo. They will be the ones to lead a group sing-along on a family outing. They're also sensitive to nonverbal sounds in the environment, such as crickets chirping and distant bells ringing—and will hear things that others in the family have missed. Check any of the following that seem to apply to your child:

❏ plays a musical instrument at home or in a school orchestra or band

❏ remembers melodies of songs

❏ does very well in music class at school

❏ studies better when background music is playing

❏ collects CDs or tapes

❏ sings to herself or to others

❏ keeps time rhythmically to music

❏ has a good singing voice

❏ is sensitive to environmental noises

❏ responds strongly to different kinds of music

✎ List here any other musical abilities that you've noticed in your child:

The musical mind is something that has been virtually ignored in education outside of formal training in an instrument or music theory. But many kids bring their musical minds to school and might learn more effectively if lessons had music in them. A child could learn about the Civil War, for example, more vividly if the teacher brought in songs about the Civil War to illustrate key points. A lesson that brought in musical intervals to help teach ratios might be more successful than one that relied only on numbers. In my own classes, I began each day with singing and found that it helped set a positive mood for the rest of the morning. Parents and teachers should recognize that some kids need to rhythmically rock or quietly tap or hum while they are studying. Rather than being a nuisance, this actually helps them organize their thoughts much as cultures traditionally employed music to transmit important information from generation to generation or while engaged in their community tasks. Hopefully, over the next few years, the musical mind will receive more recognition in educational research so that kids who think musically will be able to have their inner gifts recognized as valid.

Interpersonal Intelligence

Children gifted in interpersonal intelligence understand people. They are frequently leaders among their peers in the neighborhood or in their class at school. They organize, communicate, and, at their worst, manipulate. They may know what's going on with everybody in the neighborhood, who likes whom, who's feuding with whom, and who's going to fight whom after school. These youngsters often excel in mediating conflict between peers because of their uncanny ability to pick up on other people's feelings and intentions. They might want to become counselors, businesspeople, or community organizers. They learn best by relating and cooperating. Check any of the following items that seem to apply to your child:

❏ has a lot of friends

❏ socializes a great deal at school or around the neighborhood

❏ appears to be "street smart"

❏ gets involved in after-school group activities

❏ serves as the "family mediator" when disputes arise

❏ enjoys playing group games

❏ has a lot of empathy for the feelings of others

❏ is sought out as an "adviser" or "problem-solver" by peers

❏ enjoys teaching others

❏ seems to be a natural leader

✎ List here any other interpersonal abilities that you've noticed in your child:

Highly interpersonal children may or may not be successful in school. Some "people-smart" kids show natural abilities to anticipate what the teacher wants, to cooperate in school activities, and to succeed academically even if they have specific problems with reading or math. Others may be popular with peers but have real difficulties in school with adult authorities. Remember that, even if a child is having problems getting along with others in the classroom, they may show their leadership or empathic abilities in another context, like an after-school club or even a neighborhood gang (some of the greatest criminals of society have good interpersonal skills, which, properly channeled, could make them super citizens!). On the other hand, some people struggle with interpersonal functioning all their lives, and it continually gets in the way of their being able to fit into society. If your child experiences significant interpersonal difficulties over a sustained period of time at home or school, then it's time to get them help from a licensed mental health professional.

Intrapersonal Intelligence

Children who are highly developed in intrapersonal intelligence know who they are and what they are capable of accomplishing in the world. They are often good at setting goals for themselves, and, even if they don't reach those goals, they're good at creating new ones that are more realistic. They also may have a talent for persistence and profiting from the mistakes of the past. They aren't necessarily introverted or shy, but they may have a strong need to seek solitude for reflection. Many of them have a deep awareness of their inner feelings, dreams, and/or visions. They may keep a diary or have ongoing projects and hobbies that are known only to themselves and perhaps one or two trusted friends. There may be a quality of inner wisdom or intuitiveness that accompanies some of these children through their lives. This deep sense of self can set them apart and cause them to go off on their own into uncharted territory. They may want to become writers, entrepreneurs, or even enter into religious or spiritual work. Check any of the following items that seem to apply to your child:

❏ displays a sense of independence or a strong will
❏ has a realistic sense of her strengths and weaknesses
❏ reacts with strong opinions when controversial topics are being discussed
❏ works or studies well alone
❏ has a sense of self-confidence
❏ marches to the beat of a different drummer
❏ learns from past mistakes
❏ accurately expresses inner feelings
❏ is goal-directed
❏ engages in self-directed hobbies or projects

✎ List here any other intrapersonal abilities that you've noticed in your child:

Kids who are highly developed intrapersonally may do very well in school, especially if the classroom is based upon self-directed projects, independent study, and other forms of self-paced learning (e.g., computer software programs). Their natural confidence is also a plus in weathering hard times (especially if they have difficulty with reading, math, or other academic subjects). Some strongly intrapersonal students, however, may always be at odds with the curriculum or with teachers or administrators—seeking to do it their own way rather than the school's way. In such cases, it's important for a parent to support the child's learning at home and to help the school understand the importance to society of having some "different drummers" around to provide a unique point of view. Like interpersonal intelligence, if a child is suffering from a lack of development in intrapersonal intelligence, showing low self-esteem and even anxiety or depression, then referral to a counselor or other trained mental health professional is a wise move.

Naturalist Intelligence

Kids who are highly competent in this intelligence are nature lovers. They would rather be out in the fields or woods hiking or collecting rocks or flowers than being cooped up in school or at home doing their paper and pencil homework. On the other hand, if the schoolwork involves studying lizards, butterflies, dinosaurs, stars, or other living systems or natural formations, then their motivation is likely to soar. Some of these kids feel more affiliation with animals than with human beings. They may want to grow up to become veterinarians, forest rangers, ecologists, or farmers. Check any of the following items that seem to apply to your child:

❏ relates well to pets
❏ enjoys walks in nature or to the zoo or a natural history museum
❏ shows sensitivity to natural formations (e.g., mountains, clouds, or, if in an urban environment, they may show this

ability in sensitivity to popular culture "formations" such as sneakers, CD covers, car models, etc.)

❏ loves to garden or be around gardens

❏ spends time near aquariums, terrariums, or other natural living systems

❏ displays an ecological awareness (e.g., through recycling, community service, etc.)

❏ believes that animals have their own rights

❏ keeps records of animals, plants, or other natural phenomena (e.g., photos, diaries, drawings, collections, etc.)

❏ brings home bugs, flowers, leaves, or other natural things to share with family members

❏ does well in topics at school that involve living systems (e.g., biological topics in science, environmental issues in social studies, etc.)

✎ List here any other naturalist abilities that you've noticed in your child:

This intelligence was crucial to humanity's ability to survive in early evolution (it allowed us to distinguish between poisonous and edible plants, for example). Yet it is also important to survival today. So much of our environment is endangered by technological excesses that we need people who have a naturalistic bent to provide solutions to our ecological problems. Many kids growing up today are these "earth angels," who possess a highly developed naturalist intelligence that can help protect the planet in the new millennium. It's important to provide them with "living classrooms," at home and school, that offer opportunities for cultivating gardens, caring for pets, studying how living systems evolve, and thinking about how to take better care of the natural world.

After reading through the descriptions of the eight intelligences and checking items that relate to your child, be careful not to label your child with any one intelligence. Remember that your child has all eight intelligences that come together in a unique way. If you checked only one or two items in a given category, still, those traits may represent something very significant to your child that could be part of their success in the future. And even if you didn't check items in a specific intelligence, that doesn't necessarily mean your child isn't intelligent in that area—it may simply mean that I didn't cover the area in that intelligence in which your child excels. (Each of these intelligences is like an ecosystem with tremendous diversity!) You may wish to think of other ways in which your child demonstrates competence in each of the eight intelligences (space has been provided for you to list some of these abilities). Or you might even consider other intelligences your child possesses that haven't even been covered in this book.

Gardner has been quite emphatic about not using traditional tests in attempting to identify types of intelligences in children (the above checklist is not a test, but simply a tool to help you begin to think about your child's multiple intelligences). Formal tests that require children to answer questions orally, fill in blanks, or do other paper and pencil tasks tend to favor students who are strong in linguistic and logical-mathematical abilities while discriminating against others who are weak in these areas but strong in one or more of the other areas.

Unfortunately, the schools persist in this kind of assessment. The next chapter explores this question of testing in the schools, showing how formal tests severely limit our perceptions of a child's capabilities. It presents you with sound reasons for discarding most of the standardized test results used to evaluate your child and offers practical alternatives for discovering and describing your child's learning potential and progress—in all eight kinds of intelligence.

3

Testing for Failure

The Formal Test Trap

Emile Zola got a zero in literature at the Lycee St. Louis in France and also failed in German, and rhetoric . . . The Beaux Arts rejected Cezanne when he applied for entrance . . . [Einstein] failed to pass his entrance examinations in zoology, botany, and languages . . .

VICTOR AND MILDRED G. GOERTZEL,
Cradles of Eminence

While I was a learning disability specialist, a woman from the school district's diagnostic center came one day to visit my special class. She brought with her a nine-year-old girl who shyly held her hand and hid behind her. This child had spent the previous six weeks undergoing extensive testing. "She's a nonverbal child," the lady from the diagnostic center emphatically told me. A couple of days later, Sally was a student in my class. Within two or three hours, she easily became one of the loudest, most verbal children in the room.

Why was the diagnostician so "off" in her evaluation of this child? Was it just a bad guess? I think not. I'd say instead that the lady was so wrapped up in the technicalities of formal testing that she failed to see the real Sally. In the same way, test givers across the country dehumanize millions of children by focusing on scores and percentiles instead of on their rich and complex lives.

The Tyranny of Testing

Forty years ago, Banesh Hoffmann told a shocked country about the "tyranny of testing" in his classic book of the same name. His book and others that followed stirred up much controversy, leading the National Education Association in 1976 to recommend the elimination of group standardized intelligence, aptitude, and achievement tests. However, the dust seems to have settled from this uprising, and the testing industry today appears more powerful than ever. The National Education Association has completely changed its stand and now "recognizes the need for periodic comprehensive testing for evaluation and diagnosis of student progress." No wonder, since it would have taken a major miracle to eliminate testing. Last year teachers gave over 100 million standardized tests to children across the country.

A look at some of the individual items from these tests illustrates the ambiguities that a child must confront during evaluation time. A widely used achievement test asks the child to choose the correct item: "Something you see in your sleep is a . . . dream, fairy, wish, dread." Most normal children will have seen all of the above at one time or another in their slumber. Another well-known achievement test asks the child to circle the correct word: "An idea is a . . . picture, laugh, thought." For the spatially gifted child—who thinks in images and pictures—the first response would be most natural (the word "idea" actually goes back to the Greek word ἰδεῖν, meaning "to see"), but the last word would be the only response marked as correct. One of the most well-known intelligence tests for children asks: "What are you supposed to do if you find someone's wallet or pocketbook in a store?" and gives one point for the answer "call a radio or TV station" but no points for "just lay it up on the counter" or "wouldn't take it." This test is supposed to come up with some objective measure of intelligence, but in one study, ninety-nine school psychologists independently scored the test from identical records and came up with IQs ranging from 63 to 117 for the same person.

Few people realize that the tests being used today in our nation's schools represent the end result of a historical process that has its origins in racial and cultural bigotry. Many of the founding fathers of the modern testing industry, including Lawrence Terman (creator of the Stanford-Binet IQ test) and Carl Brigham (the developer of the Scholastic Aptitude Test), advocated eugenics, or the systematic control of hereditary characteristics to achieve racial superiority. They saw testing as one way of achieving their aims. According to Harvard professor Steven Jay Gould, in his acclaimed book *The Mismeasure of Man*, these tests were influential in legitimizing forced sterilization of allegedly "defective" individuals in some states and in keeping immigrants out of the United States at a time when they were fleeing the Nazi menace in Europe during the 1930s.

Such narrow-minded thinking appears shocking to us today. Yet psychologists still use test results to argue for the intellectual superiority of one race over another. The recent best-seller *The Bell Curve* presents the argument that intelligence levels differ among racial and ethnic groups and that American society is headed down a road where a largely white "cognitive elite" must deal with the negative economic and social consequences of individuals (disproportionately of minority status) who possess low levels of intelligence. And as David Owen points out in his book *None of the Above: Behind the Myth of Scholastic Aptitude*, tests like the SAT continue to favor certain social classes even as they close the door of educational opportunity to members of other groups. On the basis of test scores, the powers that be channel students into different "tracks" that determine their educational futures and, by virtue of the training they receive, chart their ultimate vocational destiny. While competency needs to be evaluated, the question remains whether formal testing is the best way of going about accomplishing this goal.

A New Breed of Tests

Mass testing of children on achievement and aptitude tests and widespread screening of children on IQ tests have gone on for seventy years. But now a whole new breed of individual tests and diagnostic instruments have arrived on the scene that threaten to make Banesh Hoffmann's dire pronouncements of testing tyranny look tame by comparison. Over the past thirty years, hundreds of tests have come into being for diagnosing learning disabilities, attention deficit disorder, and other special educational "problems."

This new diagnostic era of assessment would be a bright spot on the educational horizon if these tests really helped children. Unfortunately, it appears that most of them are worthless in identifying learning problems. Gerald Coles, assistant professor of psychiatry at Rutgers Medical School, put it succinctly: "We don't know what these tests measure." He made that statement after examining dozens of studies that evaluated the ten leading tests for learning disabilities. His examination turned up numerous flaws in test construction, including the use of poor subject selection and faulty research design. The tests may have *looked good*, but they failed to provide any useful information about how children actually learn.

These diagnostic tests—like their kin, the intelligence and achievement tests—have little to do with the real lives of children. One test asks children to read out loud nonsense words like "twib" "expram," and "fubwit," in order to test their ability to sound out words. Another test requires children to repeat orally long lists of random numbers to get a sense of their memory skills. Still another test to diagnose ADHD asks children to push a button on a mechanical box anytime they see a "1" followed by a "9" flash on a computerized screen. Most of these tests demand that children do things they've never done before, would never choose to do on their own, and will never do again. Yet on the basis of their performance, these tests classify children as either normal or disabled learners.

It's no wonder then that children aren't crazy about taking tests of this kind. Test anxiety, confusion, and doubt are only some of the emotional snares that confront youngsters referred for an evaluation because of learning problems in the classroom. This stress is compounded when children perceive the tester as an alien force in their lives. A Maryland mother wrote me about her eight-year-old daughter's testing experience: "Tammy had a 'language-learning' evaluation yesterday. The woman was so cold and brittle in her manner that I think Tammy was positively heroic to answer questions for her for an hour and a half."

Testing is no picnic for children even when the tester is sympathetic. A New York teacher comments after giving an eight-year-old boy one of the most widely used individualized diagnostic tests in the country: "It was very obvious . . . that he did not like taking the [test] at all. Although he didn't say so, it was pretty obvious by his facial expressions that he was being pretty severely stressed. At the end, I felt a need to explain the test to him, so I explained why I had spent some time with him and asked if he had any questions. He didn't have any questions. His only statement was, 'I couldn't do it. I don't know the words.' Not crying, but very upset." By putting stress on children in this way, tests do a disservice to the deeper emotional needs of these youngsters and serve the needs of the test makers instead. For, by manufacturing disability in the assessment room, test makers are creating a whole new generation of "disabled" individuals who must now have their problems "remediated" by fancy educational programs, often created by the test makers themselves.

The Myth of the "Objective Test"

The child who shows up in the assessment room exposes himself to a host of testing side effects that may bias the results. Through a series of nonverbal cues, the tester often unconsciously manipulates the results. This testing room side effect, sometimes referred to as the *Clever Hans phenomenon,* was named after a trick horse who could perform astounding feats like computing numbers and spelling words in front of an amazed audience. It turned out that Clever Hans's trainer had worked out a complex system of gestures and cues—invisible to the audience—which the horse responded to on command.

The tester, usually lacking the awareness of a horse trainer, nevertheless may unintentionally manipulate the child's behavior for good or ill. Already having some idea of why the child has been referred for evaluation, he carries a subliminal set of expectations concerning how the child will perform. This works against the child referred for learning problems, since the tester will be on the lookout for any signs of difficulty and may unconsciously reinforce wrong answers or fail to give the child opportunities to perform well.

Whatever the outcome, it's clear that these assessments do not objectively test a child's ability. As San Diego State University sociologist Hugh Mehan points out in his book *Handicapping the Handicapped,* "Treating test results as social facts obscures the constitutive process by which testers and students jointly produce answers in individual tests." Mehan and his colleagues also observed the way learning disability specialists use a "test until find" approach in their work, where testers administer assessments to a child until they locate a suspected disability—at which time they stop testing and label the child. If they don't locate a disability after two or three tests, they administer up to fifteen or twenty other tests until they either find a disability or exhaust their entire battery. This way of working with children encourages fault-finding and minimizes the chances of discovering strengths and abilities.

In some cases, it's a practical necessity for school districts to find disabilities in their children. They receive more money from federal and state sources for a learning disabled child than for a normal child. However, state and federal guidelines also place a ceiling on the number of children who can be identified as learning disabled. So when a school district hits its ceiling, they're no longer as eager to label. Mehan observed how one school district reached a ceiling point in March, which prompted a memo from the director of pupil personnel services to "refer only severe and obvious cases." The average number of referrals dropped by almost half. This means the learning disabled child in September may not be disabled in June because the school ran out of money. Tests in this case become instruments for fiscal management rather than objective measures of a child's abilities.

The Percentile Nightmare

Tests are supposed to give parents and teachers information about how children are progressing in their learning. Instead, they tend to reduce children and all of their thoughts, feelings, behaviors, and achievements to a handful of percentiles, rankings, letter grades, and fancy-sounding labels. For example, many achievement tests have a grade point level as their final score. One of the tests I gave as a teacher—the Wide Range Achievement Test (WRAT)—had children read a list of words, spell another list of words, and do a few math problems. On the basis of this quick procedure, children received scores such as 2.5 (second grade, fifth month) or 3.7 (third grade, seventh month) for each subject. An unsuspecting observer—including many parents—would think that a child was doing second or third grade work on the basis of this test. Yet it only took five errors out of forty-one spelling words to move from 5.0 to 3.9, a drop in the mind of the parent from fifth grade work to third grade work. Such test results tell us nothing about how the child spells or misspells words, whether the child misspells words in writing compositions, if the child enjoys spelling, or any number of other important questions related to the child's actual learning experience.

The WRAT is popular because it's so simple and quick to administer. Teachers can sit the child down and in a few minutes get scores on all the basic skills. Our school district regularly used the WRAT to write specific goals for children in special education: "Johnny will improve in spelling over the next ten months from a 3.2 score as measured on the WRAT to a 4.0." This sounds good but what it really means is that Johnny will be able to spell two or three more words on this little test that he takes every year.

Some tests carry this penchant for speed to absurd limits. One popular test gives teachers the opportunity to play medical doctor by administering a neurological screening to a child in twenty minutes. Computers are also a big part of the picture in this hurry to assess. One software program assures us that a teacher with no previous computer experience will be able to create in less than fifteen minutes a complete IEP (individualized educational program) that is in compliance with federal special education laws. Administrators understandably need to be concerned with efficiency. But what are we doing to children when we reduce them to statistics and computer printout sheets?

Testing also boxes children in with convenient labels couched in scientific-sounding educational jargon. The learning specialist says that the child who is not paying attention during the testing session suffers from "attention deficit disorder." The child who has difficulty remembering test instructions has "poor auditory sequential skills." Children get saddled with diagnostic terms such as *dyslexia, dysgraphia, dyscalculia,* and the like, making it sound as if they suffer from very rare and exotic diseases. Yet the word *dyslexia* is just Latin bafflegab, or jargon, for "trouble with words." Any parent who has a ten-year-old child struggling in a first grade primer could have told you that.

Using numbers and jargon from educational testing to describe students serves another purpose as well. Coming from the mouths of psychologists and learning specialists during a parent meeting, this practice carries with it a special aura of expertise and authority. After all, who could possibly question the conclusions of a psychologist who said that "Martha has visuo-spatial dysfunction as indicated by her score of 7 on the object assembly subtest of the WISC?"

San Diego State sociologist Hugh Mehan points out that statements made by psychologists and learning specialists during parent conferences were often followed by silence—suggesting unquestioned acceptance of their conclusions. Parents who shared what they knew about their children, on the other hand, were usually pummeled with questions, casting doubt on the truth of their statements. Parents deserve better treatment than this. Yet testing continues to reinforce the school's authority by placing the almighty statistic on a pedestal far beyond the reach of all but the most trained professional. Common sense and real-life experience function like menial serfs in this educational hierarchy.

Protecting Your Child from Formal Testing

Despite the many shortcomings described above, our national confidence in testing seems to be stronger than ever. We see this unquestioning attitude in every headline that blares out, "National Math Scores Drop for Second Straight Year," or "IQ Scores Higher in Suburban Communities." What can a parent do to help counteract the dehumanizing qualities of formal testing? Given the reality of deeply rooted cultural and financial forces working to keep the testing industry as powerful as ever, you may want to consider some ways to protect your child from the worst aspects of formal testing.

Examining School Records

Don't be pushed around by test scores that teachers and administrators present to you about your child. One Vermont private school director recommended that parents of incoming children destroy all previous school test records, as these serve only to distort the child's true capabilities. While you can't exactly do this if your child is in public school, you can refuse to give these scores the sort of importance that they receive in school circles. Also, federal law gives parents the right to inspect confidential files, to request in writing that certain materials be taken out, and, if school officials refuse, to request a hearing on the matter. Parents also can insert into school records written statements objecting to the material that is there and present additional information on their child.

Alternative Evaluation Methods

Encourage your school to rely more on alternative methods of evaluation in assessing your child. Possibilities include criterion-referenced testing, informal testing, observation, and documentation.

Criterion-Referenced Testing.   These assessments don't statistically compare children to each other. Rather, they report on those skills that your child has actually mastered, as well as on those objectives your child has yet to achieve. By making test results concrete and positive (Johnny can multiply two-digit numbers, do fifty push-ups in ten minutes, use a table of contents), they give constructive information that a parent or teacher can use to take a child to even higher levels of achievement.

Informal Testing.   These are tests that you make up as you go along to find out whatever you want to know about a child. No need to purchase expensive test kits and fill out elaborate testing forms. If you're wondering whether your child can subtract or not, you don't have to go out and get an elaborate psychoeducational test battery. Just grab a piece of paper or a miniature chalkboard, write down a couple of subtraction problems, and let your child loose on them. What is particularly good about informal testing is that there is less concern for the test results and more concern for the test process.

What kind of strategy does your child engage in when he subtracts? Does he count on his fingers? Does he remember to borrow? Ask him to explain what borrowing means. Does he understand, or is he just using a rule that he memorized?

These and other questions can give you a rich collection of data about your child's problem-solving abilities vastly superior to the information that most tests give. Ask your child's teacher how much he or she relies on informal testing. During parent conferences, do you hear about your child only in terms of test scores and jargon? Or do you really receive meaningful information about the way in which your child learns? If so, the teacher probably uses informal assessment at least some of the time.

Observation.   The trouble with most of the highly sophisticated tests used by learning specialists these days is that they have little to do with the child's own personal reality. The child is diagnosed as deficient in auditory memory skills yet is able to tell you a long story that someone told him a week before. This happens because the test suggesting a deficiency involved repeating back to the examiner nonsense syllables or random digits—activities that are without meaning to the child. They ought to call deficiency in this area by another name: *auditory yawnitis dysfunction*—the inability to remember meaningless and boring information.

Observation gives a parent or teacher the opportunity to see children in meaningful contexts doing things that have a real connection to their lives. Anything observed at home or at school in the course of a day—whether it shows a strength or a weakness—can be important information. It's truly appalling how often I've looked into the school records of a child only to see endless pages of test results smothering a few vague sentences here and there describing something about the child ("Susan tries hard," or "Peter is cooperative"). Keep a daily journal of your own observations and encourage your child's teacher to do the same.

Documentation.   This method of evaluation lets you keep track of your child's school performance in concrete ways. Some of the "documents" you or your child's teacher can keep include writing samples, cassette tapes of your child reading a book, pictures your child has drawn, snapshots or videotape of your child engaged in a learning activity, or samples of things your child has made or done. These materials, when assembled as a "portfolio" of learning accomplishments, or summarized in a report, show much more of the real child than a dry collection of test scores.

Multiple Intelligences Assessments. So much of school testing involves paper and pencil performances that favor kids who are good at linguistic or logical-mathematical intelligences. When some children are asked to demonstrate what they know only through words or numbers, they don't have the opportunity to show what they *really* know about a subject. However, if they are given the chance to express their learning through some of the other intelligences, often they can really shine. One highly bodily-kinesthetic high school girl, for example, had trouble passing tests on the table of periodic elements in chemistry until she choreographed a dance that helped her remember the information. Other kids may be able to express what they know about a school subject far better through pictures, music, role-play, discussion groups, three-dimensional exhibits, or other vivid projects than through a standardized test. Here are some examples of the kinds of activities that kids can engage in at school to show competency of a subject in each of the eight intelligences:

Linguistic Intelligence: written reports, oral reports, poetry, essays, plays, written dialogues

Logical-Mathematical Intelligence: experiments, statistical charts, Venn diagrams, computer programs

Spatial Intelligence: drawings, photo essays, murals, sketches/diagrams, mind maps, videotapes

Bodily-Kinesthetic Intelligence: role-play, drama, dance, hands-on demonstrations, three-dimensional projects, exhibits

Musical Intelligence: songs, raps, chants, musicals, sound-effects performances, musical conceptualizations (e.g., showing understanding of a character in a novel through a musical performance on percussion instruments)

Interpersonal Intelligence: group discussion, peer teaching (e.g., showing competence by explaining it to someone else), debates, group simulations, interviews

Intrapersonal Intelligence: journal-keeping, self-paced software, scrapbooks, independent projects

Naturalist Intelligence: ecology projects, use of plants or animals (or pictures of them) in the assessment (e.g., for simple addition, adding two daisies to two pansies to equal four flowers), field work, nature studies

If your child isn't passing tests at school, find a way to translate the information on the test into one or more of the forms described above, and then see whether this makes a difference in your child's ability to express his understanding. The greater number of ways in which children have to show competency in a subject, the more chances they have to achieve real success.

Assessment As a Positive Experience

Whether at home or at school, see that evaluation becomes a supportive educational experience for your child. When I was in graduate school, I needed to find children on whom to practice my own testing skills. After locating some neighborhood children, I discovered that I couldn't pay them to take the tests. Their feelings about testing were too negative. The best way to make evaluation fun for children is by making it part of what they already enjoy doing. I remember having positive feelings as a child while taking the presidential fitness tests out on the playground because I was doing things that I would have chosen to do anyway—climb the parallel bars, do chin-ups, and run across the field.

If you want to know how well children read, spare them from formal reading tests. Instead, sit with them and their favorite storybook and informally assess how well they read. Instead of a test on fractions, bake bread with them and discover as they work with measurements how well they're able to compute. This method of evaluation lets you see children applying their learning in concrete ways, rather than demonstrating it in some irrelevant and disconnected way on a paper-and-pencil test.

Discussing Test Results with Your Child

Make sure your child gets direct feedback at home and at school on assessment results. Children who have trouble learning may go through a five-hour diagnostic battery at school and then end up in remedial groups or special education classes without ever being told anything about the test scores that resulted in their changing programs. Even in regular classes, children work for hours on materials they will never see again. Take time, preferably right after any assessing that you or your child's teacher has done, to discuss the results with your child. Better yet, see that your child has the opportunity to receive self-feedback, by providing her with scoring keys, self-correcting materials, or other information about where to go for the answers. Let her keep charts and graphs of her learning progress in quantifiable areas, and diaries or journals to keep track of special achievements.

Evaluation of school progress doesn't need to be tyrannical. Neither does it have to serve as a way of sorting children into various kinds of disabilities. Ideally, there should be no dividing line between testing and learning. As you teach your child anything, you gather information about what she does and doesn't know. Moreover, you use that information to determine what next steps to take in the learning process. By seeing evaluation as linked to the process of learning—and not as a way of deciding who can and can't learn—we can make it a positive force in our children's lives.

Teaching to the Tests

Unfortunately, some teachers take the learning evaluation link too literally. Pressured to show high test scores, they engage in "teaching to the tests," constructing the curriculum around the test, rather than the other way around, as it should be done. Testifying at a National Institute of Education hearing on minimum competency testing, the former principal of a nationally regarded public school in New York City, Deborah Meier, observed that reading instruction in the New York City schools actually amounted to instruction in taking reading tests. George Madaus, director of the Center for the Study of Testing, Evaluation, and Educational Policy at Boston College, commented: "In typical reading classes, students read commercially prepared materials made up of dozens of short paragraphs about which they then answer questions. The materials they use are designed to look exactly like the tests they will take in the spring. . . . When synonyms and antonyms were dropped from a test on word comprehension, teachers promptly dropped the commercially prepared materials that stressed them." This approach to testing and teaching threatens to turn our nation's children into a generation of cynical fill-in-the-blankers rather than truly independent thinkers who possess a deep thirst for knowledge. We'll explore this tragedy more fully in the next chapter when we examine how teachers bore students to an early intellectual death with textbooks, worksheets, and other stale instructional methods.

Dysteachia

The Real Reason Your Child Isn't Thriving in School

Formal education has become such a complicated, self-conscious, and overregulated activity that learning is widely regarded as something difficult that the brain would rather not do. Teachers are often inclined to think that learning is an occasional event, requiring special incentives and rewards, not something that anyone would normally engage in given a choice . . . reluctance to learn cannot be attributed to the brain. Learning is the brain's primary function, its constant concern, and we become restless and frustrated if there is no learning to be done. We are all capable of huge and unsuspected learning accomplishments without effort.

FRANK SMITH,
Insult to Intelligence: The Bureaucratic Invasion of Our Classrooms

It's been said that if we taught children to speak the way we teach them to read, we'd have a nation of stutterers. This is just another way of saying that our schools are selling millions of kids short by putting them into remedial groups or writing them off as underachievers, when in reality they are disabled only by poor teaching methods. We hear so much about the learning disabled or ADD child in the news media. It's probably truer to say that these children are "worksheet disabled," "curriculum disordered," or simply "dysteachic." And there are millions of other children out there who don't show any of the overt signs of "pedagogical illness" who secretly are suffering from teaching strategies inappropriate to their real needs.

The schools fail our children when they limit their teaching methods to lectures, textbooks, worksheets, and tests. They create learning problems when they focus on a narrow band of isolated skills representing only two of Howard Gardner's eight kinds of intelligences. They stifle the learning potential of children when they channel them into ability groups, "tracks," and special classes. They dampen the thirst for knowledge in all children by teaching them things that have little relevance to their personal lives.

The Four Ts That Kill Learning: Talk, Textbooks, Task Analysis, and Tracking

Enter a typical classroom, says John Goodlad in *A Place Called School*, and the chances are better than 50-50 that you will observe a group of thirty or so children seated at tables or desks working quietly on worksheets or workbooks, preparing for assignments, or listening to a teacher lecturing to them from the front of the classroom. These practices continue despite research that fails to support their effectiveness as learning methods. The children in our schools are victims of several widespread educational malpractices.

Too Much Teacher Talk

Children listen to teachers' explanations and lectures about one-fifth of the school day in an average classroom, according to Goodlad's study. This in itself isn't so bad, but most of this "frontal teaching" takes place in the absence of any true interaction with students. Teachers talk *at* the students, not *to* them. When teachers ask questions, frequently they're of the "fill-in-the-blank" kind, requiring specific, short responses from students. Student responses are met with impersonal or automatic replies, such as "all right." Teachers rarely ask students for their own opinions or engage them in any kind of meaningful dialogue designed to sharpen thinking abilities. Educator Leslie Hart says that teachers generally speak to only about one-third of the class anyway. Teachers need quick and accurate responses from children. In their rush to get through the material, they call on those who can produce correct answers, largely writing off the rest of the class in the process.

Overuse of Textbooks

Textbooks constitute a $1.5 billion business annually and can be found in just about every classroom across the country. They're widely used because they deliver information in a tightly controlled and highly efficient manner, perfectly designed for a bureaucracy like the schools. Whether they actually teach children anything meaningful is another matter. P. Kenneth Komoski, executive director of educational products for the Information Exchange Institute in Water Mill, New York, comments: "Most textbooks tell about a discipline in order to cover it, rather than engaging the learner in the skills and processes of that discipline to a level of mastery." There's no personal "voice" in a textbook that students can learn from since most texts are assembled by editorial committees from among numerous authors. Texts contain mainly declarative sentences, speaking "the truth" from some high and impersonal place. As a result, students get little sense of the complexities—and realities—of the topic they are studying. Since textbooks are currently under fire from all sides of the political and cultural spectrum, publishers take special pains to avoid controversy. This results in a very bland product that never really touches the actual concerns and feelings of the students they were designed to serve. The books themselves resist interaction in a very literal sense; students are not allowed to write in them and must turn them in at the end of the year. It's no wonder then that students find textbooks dull and disconnected from their lives.

Overemphasis on Teaching Specific Skills

There used to be a time when a child went to school and learned to read by reading. Nowadays, however, children may spend much of their reading time learning to master hundreds of specific skills before actually settling down to read a good book. This fragmented approach to learning has its origins in the concept of "task analysis." Followers of task analysis believe you must break down an activity into its parts and then learn the separate parts before you can master the total activity. This approach may work well for a team of electrical engineers, but it fails in the classroom. Teachers and children end up spending so much time focusing on the parts that they lose sight of the whole.

The bedrock of this educational malpractice is the worksheet or ditto. Teachers run off mass quantities of these items on duplicating machines or provide children with ready-made packages of them in workbooks. Each sheet is supposed to develop a specific skill, such as the ability to recognize the "sh" sound in reading or the capacity to add two-digit numbers in math. Students must fill in the blank, circle the correct item, draw a line from a word to its corresponding picture, or in some other way successfully complete the task. Teachers love worksheets because they provide simple and clear results of a student's progress. Yet parents shouldn't be deceived by this simplistic approach to learning. Anne Adams of the Duke University Reading Center cautions: "Parents are told that 'Johnny knows this skill, but not this one,' and they fly into a panic. What they should be looking for is independent reading as early as possible. They should have a sense that sometimes these skills lessons kill independent reading." See *Insult to Intelligence* by Frank Smith for a scathing indictment of skill teaching in America.

Overreliance on Grouping Children by Achievement or Ability

Grouping begins almost as soon as a child walks in the door on that first day of school, when the teacher begins administering screening tests to determine achievement levels. Based on the results, Betty gets into the "golden eagle" reading group and Harry ends up in the "chicken hawks." Twelve years later, Betty heads toward college in the academic track of her high school, while Harry plods along in the vocational track toward some fuzzy destiny as a busboy or burger flipper. Teachers argue that grouping by ability allows more efficient instruction and avoids frustrating either slow or fast children who aren't learning at the same rate as their peers.

Yet these justifications aren't supported by the data. Research suggests that students in ability groups don't progress as quickly as those in heterogeneous, or mixed, groups. Moreover, those children who end up in the low or slow groups definitely get the short end of the stick academically. There's less emphasis on enrichment and more focus on drill—and rote—learning in these classes. Students in the low tracks see teachers as more punitive and less concerned about them. Their self-esteem is lower, their drop-out rate is higher, and their general progress is slower than in the high tracks, where a child may advance up to five times more quickly. One might argue that this is the result of the quality of the students rather than the grouping itself, yet studies have shown that when a child of so-called average ability is placed in one of the low tracks, he does less well than if he'd been placed in a mixed group. The low group seems to function according to the laws of entropy, sucking children down to its own level of diminished expectations. More frighteningly, it shapes the destinies of schoolchildren who, given a different setting, might have gone on to develop more of their true potential.

Special Education: An Ecology of Its Own

A new kind of grouping has come into being over the past twenty-five years with the spread of special education programs for the so-called learning disabled and those labeled ADHD. There was a time when special education mainly served the needs of children with severe physical or developmental handicaps. However, it underwent a major change with congressional passage of the Education for All Handicapped Children Act in 1975. Funds then became available to schools to meet the needs of the so-called learning disabled. As a result, the percentage of children labeled learning disabled almost doubled in six years, from 21.5 percent of all special education students in 1977 to 40.9 percent in 1983.

For the most part, these programs simply heap upon children more concentrated doses of what they're already failing at in the regular classroom: more worksheets, duller textbooks, and stricter teacher control. However, LD and ADHD classes also create an entirely new ecology of their own with their own tests, their own specialized jargon, and their own educational programs. Like prisons, LD and ADHD classrooms often serve as proving grounds for misbehavior, where a small number of children referred for severe emotional problems pass along their instability to the rest of the students. Carl Milofsky, a California sociologist who spent several months in classes for the educationally handicapped wrote of his experience, "It was clear that, if anything, the special class made students more rebellious and harder to handle."

Meanwhile, special class teachers, snowed under by discipline problems, also have their hands full with all the red tape required by federal and state laws. One parent who participated in a special education conference remarked: "What I remember of that meeting was sitting there looking at all the forms she was filling out. I just thought, 'I don't see how they're getting anything done here because it seems to me all they're doing is filling out forms.'"

A more serious problem with many LD and ADHD programs is that, by removing children from the "mainstream" of regular classroom life, there's a greater likelihood that these youngsters will fall further behind their peers. Lee Ann Trusdell of the City University of New York, in a study of remedial programs in New York City, observed that many students were receiving instruction in special classes that was totally unrelated to what was being taught in regular classes. As these children become more disconnected from their homeroom classes, it becomes that much harder for them to return. In fact, many of these youngsters, initially referred to special education for minor remediation, soon make a career out of their disability and slip more deeply into the LD or ADHD labyrinth. Jeane Westin interviewed teachers in *The Coming Parent Revolution* who commented: "Few EH [educationally handicapped] children ever make it back into the mainstream of education. . . . They're gone. . . . These are the kids we don't save."

The most devastating result of the whole learning disability and attention deficit disorder myth, however, is that it has made it so much easier for teachers to toss any child who isn't learning the material in the prescribed way out of their normal classroom. As a federal study on labeling once stated, "The term learning disability has appeal because it implies a specific neurological condition for which no one can be held particularly responsible." The same could be said about attention deficit disorder (see my book *The Myth of the ADD Child* for more information).

Teachers can go on teaching in the same stale way. Children remaining in the regular classrooms get the message. Keep quiet and do your work—even though it bores you to death—or suffer the consequences of special education.

Beyond Boredom: How Children Actually Learn

While most schools operate on the basis of the "mug-jug" theory— where the teacher as jug pours knowledge into the student's mug—

the best evidence we have suggests that learning for children is like a series of small scientific revolutions. The late Thomas Kuhn, who was professor of the history of science at Princeton and author of *The Structure of Scientific Revolutions*, pointed out that a scientific revolution goes through a series of specific stages. At first, a ruling paradigm or world view—such as the belief that the earth is flat—holds sway among the people. Confirming evidence—including the observation that the world *appears* flat—is quickly assimilated into this belief system. Any contradictory evidence is viewed with skepticism and rejected. Gradually, however, contrary evidence begins to pile up until such time that it can no longer be ignored. At this moment, the revolution occurs, and people suddenly change their basic view of things—in this case, they shift their perspective and begin to see the earth as round.

Children go through a similar process. They construct what world-renowned child development researcher Jean Piaget called "schemes," or mini-world views, about a wide range of things. At first these schemes are of "the earth is flat" variety. John Holt shared one of these primitive beliefs from his own classroom experience when he observed that some children felt the higher you went up the number line, the denser or closer together the numbers got. Children do not easily let go of these beliefs. They will continue to resist new input into their fixed schemes until such time as they are developmentally ready and the evidence presented from the outside world becomes overwhelming. Piaget would say it is then that they start to accommodate or change their old beliefs so as to effectively assimilate or take in new information. The equivalent of a scientific revolution goes on inside their heads. In a word, they learn.

In order for this to happen, children need to be presented with environments that challenge their old erroneous belief systems and present them with a wide range of methods and materials for exploring new, more accurate and useful beliefs. Unfortunately, the schools generally don't do this. Instead, they tend to perpetuate fixed ways of thinking by feeding children old, tired information, providing nothing new to challenge existing beliefs. Day after day youngsters fill in blanks, answer simple questions, and listen to boring lectures. They may gain a skill here or a shred of data there. But nothing changes fundamentally in their view of the world. No real learning takes place. Harvard professor Howard Gardner's book *The Unschooled Mind* provides a powerful indictment of the failure of traditional education to provoke fundamental changes in students' thinking. He suggests many students are graduating from high school and college still holding onto concepts they developed as five year olds.

This impoverishment has its inevitable consequences in the brain. Mark Rosenzweig and Marian Diamond, at the University of California, Berkeley, startled the world several years ago when they demonstrated the impact of the environment on brain structures in rats. They set up three different environments, including a standard laboratory cage with three rats, an impoverished environment with one rat in a bare cage, and an enriched environment with twelve rats living together in a large space fully equipped with playthings that were changed daily. All rats received adequate amounts of food and water. After they had lived in these environments for a time, their brains were dissected and measured. The rats in the enriched environment had a richer network of dendrites than the rats in the impoverished or normal cages. (A dendrite is a part of a brain cell that receives chemical information from other brain cells.) Marian Diamond has recently written an excellent book entitled *The Magic Trees of the Mind* (a reference to the dendrites in the brain, which branch out of individual neurons or brain cells like trees), where she provides up-to-date information on the implications of this research with children and provides scores of enriching activities that parents can use at home to help their sons and daughters essentially "grow" new dendrites.

Children seem to have an intuitive sense of what kind of enriched environment they need to support their own neurological development. In Goodlad's study, they identified their preferred learning activities as building or drawing things, making collections, going on field trips, interviewing people, acting things out, and carrying out independent projects—in other words, participating in activities that engage all eight of the basic kinds of intelligence. Unfortunately, these activities were rarely observed in visits to over 1,000 classrooms.

How to Get the Best Education for Your Child

The picture of education presented so far in this chapter is not a rosy one. Yet, parents can still get a high-quality education for their children if they are willing to inform themselves about the options available and then take positive steps toward providing their children with a schooling environment that allows them to learn in their own way.

Look at your child's current educational setting and ask yourself whether it's providing what he really needs. To make this assessment, you need to visit your child's classroom, speak with his teacher, and spend some time talking with your child about his school experience. Here are some questions to ask:

About the Classroom
- Does it appear lively and energetic, or dull and lethargic?
- Is it filled with lots of inviting learning materials—art supplies, science materials, things to touch, stroke, manipulate, and wonder about—or is it bare except for a few dusty textbooks and ancient posters on the walls?
- Are children building, drawing, reading, collecting, writing, relating, experimenting, and creating, or are they working on skill sheets, studying textbooks, and listening to the teacher lecture?
- Are there a variety of spaces in the classroom for group discussion, physical movement, quiet study, and creative "messing around," or are there straight rows of desks, a few tables, and little else?
- Is a lot of emphasis placed on standardized testing to determine if kids are learning, or is there instead a belief that assessment is an ongoing process that is intimately linked to instruction?

About the Teacher

- Does he invite opinion and dialogue or require quick and short answers to teacher-directed questions?
- Does he move around the classroom helping individual students or spend most of the time at the front of the room talking at everybody?
- When you speak with the teacher about your child, do you hear more about the accomplishments or the problems?
- Does he seem to have a wide range of methods for teaching any given topic, or does he instead rely mainly on workbooks and textbooks?

About Your Child

- When you talk to your child about the class, do you feel his own sense of excitement toward learning, or do you instead get a feeling of quiet desperation or passive compliance?
- Does he seem to be learning for learning's sake or to earn prizes, grades, stars, or praise?
- Is he getting an opportunity to express his unique strengths, talents, and abilities during the school day, or is there a lot of emphasis on his mistakes, disabilities, and underachievement?
- Is he treated like a human being with a personal way of learning, or is he expected instead to learn in the same way as everybody else?

Parents' answers to these questions, and others like them, will help to determine whether or not their children are getting an education based on their individual needs. If you find your child's school environment is lacking—and many of you probably will— then consider some alternatives.

Five Options for Schooling Your Child

Option 1: Work to Create Change Within Your Child's Current Schooling Situation

Meet with your child's teacher and discuss your concerns about the classroom. Be an advocate for your child, pointing out specific abilities, talents, or strengths that are being neglected at school and suggest ways in which these might be incorporated into the classroom day. Offer to serve as a volunteer in the class. Bring in innovative learning materials to enrich the classroom. Above all, work cooperatively and diplomatically. Teachers are under a lot of pressure these days and may feel like your sincere attempts to help your child are just another problem they have to confront. If the teacher sees your offers of assistance as an opportunity to lighten her own load, then you will probably succeed in changing the status quo for your child. However, if your efforts are met with stubborn resistance, consider another option.

Option 2: Move Your Child to Another Classroom, Another School, or Another District

If your child should happen to be in a "brain antagonistic" classroom, and all your efforts to change things fail, then just as you would transplant a withering plant into more fertile soil, you might consider a more hospitable climate (friendlier teacher, more exciting classroom) within your child's present school or at another school in the area. In their classic book *The Myth of the Hyperactive Child*, Diane Divoky and Peter Schrag report how in one community the parents of a young boy get a note from the school nurse: "Your son is hyperactive. He doesn't sit still in school. Please see a physician." The parents send the child to another school with another teacher, and the "problem" is never mentioned again. In a suburb in Cleveland, a boy referred to a class for the learning disabled performs even worse in the judgment of the teachers than he did in the regular classroom; in desperation, they send him to another regular classroom and he begins to read. Giving your child a new start in this way may help him to avoid being caught in a vicious cycle of learning failure.

Option 3: Send Your Child to a Private Alternative School

There are thousands of alternative schools around the country that honor individual learning styles and provide rich environments addressing all eight kinds of intelligences. Two approaches that account for many of these schools are the Montessori and Waldorf systems. Montessori schools were developed in the early 1900s by an Italian physician, Maria Montessori, and number in the thousands worldwide. They emphasize sensory-motor experience, practical and academic learning based on the use of concrete learning materials, and a real respect for the integrity of the child. Waldorf education, founded by German philosopher Rudolf Steiner in the 1920s, uses an artistic approach in teaching reading, history, math, science, and literature. Also, it provides instruction in crafts, dance, drama, and music.

Hundreds of other independent alternative schools exist around the nation that allow children to learn at their own pace and in their own way. One mother told me how her first grade child was referred to a special education class in a public school for learning and behavioral problems. "Then the behavior problems at home started. Suddenly Tim didn't want to go to school anymore, hated school, was miserable at school. He hated the teacher. One morning during that year he ran away." At the end of first grade, she took him out of the public schools and placed him in a private school that emphasized both Montessori and Waldorf approaches. She comments: "They took all the pressure off. He was like a different child. He loved school, he loved learning, he couldn't wait to get to school. It was as if we were looking at a different child." While alternative schools can be expensive or inconveniently located, they may be worth the extra cost and time if they save you the hassle of living with a frustrated or dissatisfied learner. You also might consider banding together with other parents to create your own cooperative alternative school.

Option 4: Consider Teaching Your Child at Home

A growing number of parents whose children have suffered at the hand of public or private education are discovering that the best thing they can do for their children is to educate them at home. Home schooling has become popular in the past few years largely through the efforts of individuals such as the late John Holt, author of *Teach Your Own*, and David and Micki Colfax, authors of *Homeschooling for Excellence*. Current estimates of home schooling parents around the country range from ten thousand into the hundreds of thousands.

I've heard from many parents who've experienced success with this approach. One mother in Georgia writes: "My oldest child was in sixth grade and couldn't read. After home schooling her for two years, she now reads adult-level books." A New Hampshire mother whose fourteen-year-old daughter failed in several different programs in public school wrote me after a few months of home schooling: "Her mind started getting more creative, she demonstrated more patience in her projects, and now she loves to read." While this option is impractical if both parents work outside of the home, increasingly families are discovering that it may be worth it to modify their lifestyles so as to provide a better education for their kids.

Option 5: Use the Special Education Laws to Your Child's Advantage

Current federal law states that every handicapped child in the country has the right to an appropriate education. Many parents whose children aren't learning in the schools have chosen to have their children tested and declared "learning handicapped" to make them eligible for special LD or ADD programs. While there's often nothing "special" about these programs, and they frequently cause more problems than they solve, occasionally it happens that the most exciting classroom in a school is the resource room or "special class." This can be a viable option for some parents, since the ratio of teacher to students is small and teachers have been instructed to work with individual learning styles. However it should only be used as a last resort in my opinion, since it requires stigmatizing your child with a handicapping label.

On the positive side, the laws favor parent and child. By law, parents have the right to participate fully in every stage of the process that leads to placing their children in special programs. They have the right to an independent evaluation if they disagree with the school's diagnosis. They can request that specific approaches or materials be used in teaching their children. They can take their case to a court of law should the school fail to provide the kind of education they feel their children need.

If you choose the special education route, make sure you inform yourself fully beforehand of all the procedures and potential pitfalls. The book *Negotiating the Special Education Maze* by Winifred Anderson, Stephen Chitwood, and Deidre Hayden may be helpful in guiding you through this labyrinth.

Beyond these suggestions, there are more far-reaching things you can do to improve the lot of children in the schools. Get involved in your local PTA, attend school board meetings, and support school board candidates who favor child-centered approaches to education. Finally, even if you feel you can't change the way your child is being educated at school, you can still have a tremendous impact at home during the eighteen hours that your child *isn't* in school every day. The next chapter will suggest ways in which you can create learning activities at home tailor-made to your child's specific learning needs.

Chapter

Learning in Their Own Way

Giving Children at Home What They May Not Be Getting at School

The widespread acceptance of the notion that parents become incapable of looking out for their children's interests and education once they reach the age of six or seven is perhaps a carryover from an earlier time, when many parents were illiterate or immigrants who themselves lacked the skills their children would need to function in modern industrial society. But today most parents possess the ability to teach their own children, and to do a better job of it than [many teachers].

DAVID AND MICKI COLFAX,
Homeschooling for Excellence

O ne of the greatest shortcomings of the schools seems to be their inflexibility when it comes to teaching a subject or skill. Teachers present the material in one way—usually through some combination of lectures, blackboard lessons, textbooks, and worksheets—and if children don't get it, then it's *their* problem, not the teachers'. But as we've seen, children learn in a number of ways and need to be taught *their* way if it's really going to sink in. Let's explore how you can create an optimum learning environment in your home suited to your child's particular learning needs.

Finding the Right Way to Motivate Your Child

Many parents and teachers feel that all you need to do is "motivate" children in order to get them to learn. This is quite true, but just knowing that doesn't tell you how to go about doing it. As you'll see from the many ideas in this chapter, there are many ways to do this, depending upon your child's profile of multiple intelligences.

Before you read further, go back and reread chapter 2, making sure to review the descriptions of the eight types of intelligences to help you identify your child's own unique profile. Remember that every child possesses all eight kinds of intelligence to varying degrees. As you read through the rest of this chapter—with its many practical activities, techniques, and methods for learning—don't make the mistake of identifying your child as, say, a "spatial child" and use only those suggestions. Your child may benefit from specific activities found in all eight of the intelligence groups.

Learning the Word Smart Way

Children strong in this area learn best by saying, hearing, and seeing words. The best ways of motivating them at home include talking with them, providing them with lots of books, records, and tapes of the spoken word, and creating opportunities for writing. Supply them with tools for word-making, including tape recorders for oral language, and typewriters, word processors, label-makers, and printing sets for writing activities. As a family, read books together, have evenings of storytelling, and maybe even create a family newsletter that they can edit. Take them to places where words are important, including libraries, bookstores, newspaper bureaus, and publishing houses.

Learning the Logical-Mathematical Way

Children strong in this variety of intelligence learn by forming concepts and looking for abstract patterns and relationships. Provide them with concrete materials they can experiment with, lots of time to explore new ideas, patience in answering their probing questions, and logical explanations for the answers that you do give. Supply them with games like chess and Go, logical puzzles, science kits, and computer software games that include logical reasoning as part of their focus (for example, Where in the World Is Carmen San Diego?). They may also enjoy creating collections of things they can classify and categorize (stamps, coins, toys, and so on). As a family, play mystery games like Clue that require deductive logic and go to places that encourage scientific thinking, including science museums, computer fairs, and electronics exhibits.

Learning the Spatial Way

Children who excel in this area learn best visually (although it's possible to be blind and still be highly spatial). They need to be taught through images, pictures, visual metaphor, and color.

They can best be motivated through media such as films, slides, videos, diagrams, maps, and charts. Give them opportunities to draw and paint. Provide them with cameras, telescopes, compasses, and three-dimensional building supplies such as Lego blocks or D-stix. As a family, engage them in visualization games, tell vivid stories, and share dreams together. Visit architectural landmarks, planetariums, art museums, and other places where spatial awareness is highlighted.

Learning the Bodily-Kinesthetic Way

Kids talented in this type of intelligence learn by touching, manipulating, and moving. They need learning activities that are kinetic, dynamic, and visceral. The best ways of motivating them are through role-play, dramatic improvisation, creative movement, and activities of all kinds involving physical activity. Provide them with access to playgrounds, obstacle courses, hiking trails, swimming pools, and gymnasiums. Give them opportunities for fixing machines, building models, and getting involved in hands-on art activities such as carving wood and working with clay. As a family, play physical games together, participate in activities that involve lots of touching, visit sporting events, go on camping trips, and engage in other vigorous and interactive experiences.

Learning the Musical Way

Youngsters with musical intelligence learn through rhythm and melody. They can learn anything more easily if it is sung, tapped out, or whistled. Use metronomes, percussion instruments, or musical computer software as ways to help learn new material. Let them study with their favorite music in the background if it seems to help. Provide them with access to CDs and tapes, musical instruments, and music lessons if they request them. As a family, sing and make music together, talk about the words to favorite songs, and go to places that highlight musical intelligence, including operas, concerts, and musicals.

Learning the Interpersonal Way

Children gifted in this category learn best by relating and cooperating. They need to learn through dynamic interaction with other people. Give them opportunities to teach other children. Supply them with games of all kinds that they can share with their friends. Let them get involved in community activities, clubs, committees, after-school programs, and volunteer organizations. Have frequent family discussions and problem-solving sessions. Work together on group projects. Go together to family-oriented retreats and political, cultural, or social events of all kinds.

Learning the Intrapersonal Way

Children inclined in this direction learn best when given the opportunity to set goals, choose their own activities, and pace themselves through whatever project attracts them. These youngsters are self-motivating. Provide them with the chance to pursue independent study, self-paced instruction, and individualized projects and games. It's very important for them to have their own private space at home where they can work on hobbies and interests undisturbed and spend time in quiet introspection. Respect their privacy, let them know that it's okay to be independent, and provide them with the resources they need to help them pursue their particular interests. As a family, go on long quiet walks, read about heroes who stand out from the crowd, and worship or meditate together.

Learning the Naturalist Way

Kids who have a naturalist's bent come alive when involved with experiences out in the great outdoors. Provide them with access to woods to hike in, rivers or lakes to swim in, hills or mountains to climb, caves to explore, and meadows to roam free in, and they'll often use their time to observe the living things that make their residence in each place. To help them in their research, provide them with naturalist's tools, like a set of binoculars, a magnifying glass, goggles for underwater exploration, or a hiking pack for collecting samples during a trek. If they can't be outdoors, then make sure they have the opportunity to explore nature inside through an ant farm, terrarium, aquarium, or simply through having a pet or two around that they can care for and raise. As a family, go on nature walks together and talk about the living things you see and hear, practice ecological awareness, watch nature programs on TV together, and visit natural history museums, zoos, and other places where the wild things are.

Now that you have a sense of some general principles regarding the different intelligences, let's put that knowledge to work and apply these ideas to specific things that you'd like your child to learn, beginning with reading.

Eight Roads to Reading Success

In 1955, Rudolf Flesch wrote a book that shocked millions of parents and sent ripples of alarm through American education. His book, *Why Johnny Can't Read,* indicted the nation's schools for teaching reading in a way that, he said, left many children confused and illiterate. Flesch observed that the schools primarily used the "look-say" method of instruction, requiring children to memorize whole words as a way of learning to read. According to Flesch, this approach was difficult for many children and an ineffective way of cracking the English code. What was his solution? Phonics. Rather than learning whole words, children needed to learn the sounds or *phonemes* that make up whole words. Now, forty-five years later, his book is still in print and continues to be immensely popular.

During this same period of time, phonics has gone in and out of fashion with the times. Currently it is undergoing a resurgence in popularity after a decade of quietude. Despite its popularity, however, it is unlikely that phonics alone will ever be enough to help many children read. The fact of the matter is that phonics generally works just fine with many children gifted in certain aspects of linguistic intelligence. Many of these kids are auditory-verbal learners who are very sensitive to the discrete sounds or phonemes of language. A reading approach based upon subtle sound differences (sh, th, f, . . .) capitalizes on their learning strengths. However, phonics alone may not work as well with children who have difficulties with sound recognition and yet are strong in other types of intelligence. That's why it's important for parents to understand that there's no magic formula for reading success that will apply to all children. The right reading program for your child is the one that makes best use of her multiple intelligences, and there are at least eight approaches in addition to phonics that you can choose from.

Helping Your Child Learn to Read Linguistically

Some children are strong in the oral aspects of linguistic intelligence. They're great storytellers but may have trouble with the auditory demands of phonics or may find all those phonics workbooks and readers too deadly dull. Oral learners need to approach reading through their own spoken language. Sit down with them and ask them to tell you a story, describe their day, recount a television program, or talk about anything else. Write down every word they say. If you wish, you can tape record the session and later transcribe it on a word processor or typewriter. Then print out the story in easy-to-read block letters. Staple the pages together with extra blank pages inserted for illustrations and sturdy cardboard sheets at the front and back for covers. If your child wants a more professional appearance, take the "book" to a copy store that does simple binding and have it bound for a dollar or two. These bound volumes of your child's oral language can become her very own personalized readers. If you've made a tape recording of the original text, then let her listen to the tape as she reads along.

Helping Your Child Learn to Read Logically-Mathematically

Children with strengths in this area enjoy looking for patterns and regularities. Hence, reading programs based on word patterns ("the rat sat on the mat") may appeal to these children if they're given an opportunity to actively explore these patterns and create their own. Provide them with dice on which individual letters of the alphabet have been pasted, a flannel board with cloth letters, or a metal board with magnetic letters, and show them how words can be changed by shifting the letters around. Expose them to computer software programs that teach reading in a logical way.

Helping Your Child Learn to Read Spatially

Children who are highly developed spatially need to have pictures and images brought together with words in learning how to read. One approach is to create rebuses for certain words (a picture of a bee for the word "be," an eye for "I" etc.) or by elaborating certain words with spatial features (for example, putting beams around the word "sun," or making the word "tall" very long and skinny). You might create your own little rebus readers for your child or have him create his own. Software programs that teach reading through animation would also be appropriate. See chapter 7 for specific reading activities you can use that capitalize on the imagination—another strength for spatially gifted children.

Helping Your Child Learn to Read Bodily-Kinesthetically

Youngsters strong in this intelligence need to write before they read. They must involve their bodies in the creation of letters and words before they can read them in a purely auditory and visual way. Provide them with frequent opportunities for free drawing, modeling, and painting before beginning more structured writing activities. Then, let them create letters and words in clay, sand, and paint, and use the typewriter or a computer since these tools capitalize on their heightened tactile sensitivity. Chapter 6 offers many other ideas for using the body in reading.

Helping Your Child Learn to Read Musically

Children with highly developed musical intelligence will learn to read if you find simple songs that they love and type or write out the lyrics in large print to use as their basic primer just as you did with the linguistically inclined child. Also select simple poems and stories they can read or sing rhythmically. Buy book and cassette packages that combine story with song.

Helping Your Child Learn to Read Interpersonally

Reading for highly social children should take place in an interpersonal context. They need to be involved in group reading activities. Their friends should take turns with them in reading individual words, sentences, pages, or entire stories. Ask them to read to some younger children they know. Hold reading parties and invite all the kids in the neighborhood.

Helping Your Child Learn to Read Intrapersonally

For highly intrapersonal youngsters, provide high-interest reading materials, a quiet and cozy reading space in the house, and plenty of time to read leisurely at their own pace, letting them ask you about any words they need help with. They might want to keep a special book of their favorite words for reference in reading and writing stories. They will often teach themselves. High-pressure reading groups at school can easily create reading difficulties, so make sure they're able to have some quiet reading time there as well.

Helping Your Child Learn to Read Naturalistically

Kids who are naturalists need to read books in their areas of interest: bugs, butterflies, lizards, plants, flowers, ecology, clouds, and more. Magazine subscriptions to *National Geographic* and *Ranger Rick* also make sense for the nature-loving kid. Think, too, about using the outdoors as a reading setting. Perhaps your child has a special place outside (a tree house, a fort, a place under a willow) that makes an ideal setting for reading. Even learning the alphabet can take place in the natural world, as you look for letter shapes in nature's mysterious fingerprints (e.g., in leaves, twigs, flowers—one naturalist photographer even created a "butterfly alphabet" from the natural markings he found on the wings of butterflies).

Exposing children to a "brain-compatible" reading approach may be one of the best things you can give them academically. When they experience the pleasure that comes with success during the first stages of learning to read, they gain positive associations to academic learning that they carry with them for the rest of their lives.

Chasing Away the Times-Tables Blues

Many children find that trying to master the multiplication tables is a frustrating experience. The constant barrage of drills and tests in school leave many children wondering why they have to learn these "stupid" facts in the first place. Children strong in linguistic intelligence often have an easy time memorizing the tables but sometimes don't have a grasp of what multiplication actually means. Youngsters with logical-mathematical gifts may master the concept but have trouble remembering the facts. Children who have difficulties in linguistic or logical-mathematical intelligences but are strong in other intelligences may really be in trouble, since the schools generally cater to the linguistically and logical-mathematically inclined. However, all children can master both the rote and the reason behind multiplication as long as someone teaches them this skill according to their multiple intelligences. Here are some ways of reaching children by way of all eight kinds of intelligence.

Multiplication the Linguistic Way

Since linguistically gifted youngsters learn best by reading, writing, and speaking, use word problems and worksheets from conventional programs, oral drills that enable them to practice reciting the times tables in order, and flash cards that give them an opportunity to orally repeat individual answers. Let them also create their own word problems, either in written form or by speaking them into a tape recorder and then transcribing the text. Tell them stories that illustrate the concept of multiplication (see chapter 7 for the story of "The As Much Brothers"). Storytelling also helps the highly spatially developed child as well.

Multiplication the Logical-Mathematical Way

Use pebbles, matches, or toothpicks and set up situations where children group them by twos, threes, fours, and so on, letting them discover the principle of multiples through exploratory play. For example, three piles of pebbles with four pebbles in each pile equals twelve pebbles, or $3 \times 4 = 12$. Let them keep charts of their discoveries as an aid in memorizing the facts. Or alternatively, put a sequence of numbers, such as the 3's, on a piece of paper (e.g., 3, 6, 9, 12, 15, 18, 21, 24, 27, 30) and explore with your child as many different logical patterns as he can discover (e.g., adding 3 to get the next number; an odd/even pattern; adding the 1 and 2 in 12 to get 3, the 1 and 5 in 15 to get 6, the 1 and 8 in 18 to get 9, and then the pattern repeats itself).

Multiplication the Spatial Way

Give children a "hundreds" chart—a piece of paper on which are written the numbers 1 to 100 in ten columns horizontally or vertically. Then ask them to color in every second number. This will give them a visual pattern for the 2's. Then give them another hundreds chart and ask them to color in every third number for the 3's and so on. Each sheet will provide a different, colorful, and graphic depiction of that particular multiple and will give them both a picture of the concept and a mnemonic aid in memorizing the facts (or they can use only one hundreds chart and use a different color for the 2's, 3's, 4's etc. and see where colors come together).

Multiplication the Bodily-Kinesthetic Way

Ask your child to walk in a straight line counting out loud with each step, "1, 2, 3, 4, 5, 6." Then say, "Okay, now we're going to clap our hands on every second number: 1, **2**, 3, **4**, 5, **6**, 7, **8**, 9, **10** . . ." This can be followed by clapping on every third number and so forth. Ask them what they'd like to do besides clapping (possibilities include jumping, skipping, crawling, or doing a somersault). In this way, they will begin to internalize the concept of the multiples in their bodies.

Multiplication the Musical Way

Select a song that has a natural and even rhythm. Simple folk songs or other songs that are popular with children work well. Then have your child chant or sing the times tables with them to the rhythm of the song ("2 times 2 is 4, and 2 times 3 is 6, and 2 times 4 is 8 . . ."). If you can't find an appropriate piece of music, use a metronome to keep time. Alternatively, count out loud ("1, **2**, 3, **4**, 5, **6** . . ."), singing, shouting, or whispering every second number, every third number, and so on.

Multiplication the Interpersonal Way

Teach them the basic concept of multiplication through any of the above ways, and then ask them to teach it to a friend. Give them some flash cards and suggest that they organize a group flash card competition in the neighborhood. Make a board game out of a manila folder with a winding road drawn in magic marker and times table problems (2 x 3 = ?) written on individual squares.

Buy some dice and game pieces and invite all the kids in the neighborhood to come and play.

Multiplication the Intrapersonal Way

Let your child work independently on a group of problems. Provide her with a key for checking her answers, a self-correcting workbook, or a computer software program for learning the times tables on her own. Let her work at her own pace, allowing her to check her answers when she needs to, so that she can get immediate feedback on her progress.

Multiplication the Naturalist's Way

Observe the multiples in nature, from the buds on a flower, to the swirls of a pine cone or a seashell. Use these natural objects as hands-on materials for doing multiplication problems (e.g., if this flower has five buds and there are three petals on each bud, how many petals are there?). Look at patterns of reproduction in animals, where the word *multiplies* (especially for rabbits) has special meaning!

How to Teach Anything Eight Different Ways

Once you get the hang of this eight-fold teaching method, you'll be able to teach anything eight different ways. If your child isn't getting it one way, then you have at least seven more tries. All it takes is a little creativity and some elbow grease.

Let's say you want to assist your child in learning the names of the fifty states. Here are eight different ways you can help out:

- **Linguistic:** practice quizzing her orally on the names of the states
- **Logical-mathematical:** help her classify the states into different categories—by first letter, geographical size, population, entry into the union, and so on

- **Spatial:** get a multicolored map and help her associate the names with the different colors or shapes of the states
- **Bodily-kinesthetic:** find a relief map that she can feel or a puzzle map that she can take apart and put back together and assist her in identifying tactile features for each of the states to use in memorizing their names
- **Musical:** teach her the different state songs or a song that names all fifty states (if you can't find one, make one up!)
- **Interpersonal:** play a card game, such as Concentration, where players must match pairs of overturned cards; in this case the name of the state matched with its outline
- **Intrapersonal:** suggest that she write to the state governments of all fifty states (use postcards, they're cheap!) for information she can keep in a scrapbook (or, alternately, visit state government sites on the Internet)
- **Naturalist:** find out the state bird, animal, or flower for each state and use these as cues for remembering the fifty states

What about homework? If you're lucky, your child's teacher gives your child choices at least some of the time for doing an assignment. Let's say your child comes home with an open-ended homework project to complete for a unit on bird study. Here are eight ways of going about completing the task:

- **Linguistic:** book reports, oral presentations, writing compositions, tape recordings
- **Logical-mathematical:** collecting statistics about birds, answering the basic question: "How does a bird fly?"
- **Spatial:** charts and maps of a bird's migration patterns, pictures of birds
- **Bodily-kinesthetic:** hiking to a bird's natural habitat, building a replica of a bird's nest
- **Musical:** finding records or tapes of bird calls and learning to imitate them

- **Interpersonal:** interviewing a local bird-watcher about his hobby
- **Intrapersonal:** creating a special place of solitude in nature for bird-watching
- **Naturalist:** volunteering in a community project designed to safeguard the welfare of the local bird population

Finally, there's that eternal question parents are always asking: "How do I get my child to behave?" Thousands of books have been written on the subject, and nobody seems to agree on what to do. Maybe that's because different folks need different strokes. Here are eight strokes for starters:

- **Linguistic:** sit down and have a good chat with your child about why she's misbehaving or ask her to tape record or write down what's bothering her
- **Logical-mathematical:** reason with your child—show her the logical consequences of her actions (Rudolf Dreikurs based an entire discipline system on this approach)
- **Spatial:** tell your child an imaginative story illustrating her misbehavior and its possible causes and/or solutions (for a child who lies, tell "The Boy Who Cried Wolf")
- **Bodily-kinesthetic:** ask your child to act out the misbehavior and then act out the appropriate behavior and compare the two
- **Musical:** find a piece of music that contains the message you want to give to your child or use music as a relaxing influence for an out-of-control child
- **Interpersonal:** use group problem-solving activities
- **Intrapersonal:** use one-on-one counseling, goal-setting, and contracting
- **Naturalist:** observe how young animals behave with their own parents (in nature or on nature TV shows)

Want more examples? See "A Parent's Guide to Multiple Intelligences" beginning on page 191.

Bridging the Quality Gap in Education

It would be great if every classroom across the nation used this varied multiple intelligences approach to help kids learn. Imagine what it would be like to walk into any classroom in the country and see some children clustered around computers, a few reading by themselves in a corner of the room, several others busily drawing or modeling with clay, and still others at work building models or machines. Every child would be learning in the way that was personally easiest and most natural to them.

The reality is that in too many classrooms across America, students focus on the same boring activities. Even the so-called individualized programs all too often have children working on the same mindless exercises in workbooks, only at different levels. The casualties of this gap between what education is and what it could be are several million children mislabeled learning disabled or attention deficit disordered and millions of other kids who sit in class bored and tuned out, going through the motions and barely surviving in a system that has little meaning to them.

I sometimes wonder what would happen if we took all the billions of dollars we're pouring into learning disability and ADD research, standardized testing, special education, and worthless textbooks and put them instead into enriching the regular classroom—bringing in more varied types of enrichment materials, more energized and informed teachers to provide individual assistance, and more training to help teachers expand their own teaching repertoire. If we did this, I believe that millions of so-called learning disabled, ADHD, and underachieving youngsters would lose their disability, and millions of other children would begin to realize more of their true potential in learning. I'm sure of it. Yet I'm also certain that this won't happen overnight—if indeed it ever occurs. What do we do in the meantime? Here are a few suggestions for carrying this approach into your child's school.

Teaching to a Different Intelligence Each Day

Suggest that teachers approach every important skill eight different ways. Naturally, you should also be prepared for their probable reply: "Sounds great! But it's totally impractical in a class of thirty kids." If they tell you this, point out that they don't even have to treat each child differently. Tell them to go on teaching to the whole group if they'd like, but *teach a different way every day*. Suggest that they spend a few extra minutes after the regular reading unit supplementing the traditional program with techniques from this book and other books listed in the resource section. Encourage them to build into the lesson plan activities that make use of the body, the imagination, interaction between students, and music. If they teach to a different type of intelligence every day, at the end of eight days, they'll have given a little something to everybody in the class.

Pointing to Positive Change

Share examples of other schools around the country that teach across the spectrum of abilities. Mention Craddock Elementary School in Aurora, Ohio, where principal Linda Robertson put together a school fair that celebrated learning in all of its colors. This fair included a math arcade, a gymnastics and physical fitness demonstration, an art show, a talent show, and an individual investigations display. Tell them about the Key Renaissance Learning Community in the Indianapolis Public School System, one of the first public schools in the country to apply Howard Gardner's theory of multiple intelligences directly to the curriculum. Suggest that they take a look at the McWayne Elementary School in Batavia, Illinois, where multiple intelligences are integrated with reading, writing, and math in a way that makes use of the latest findings in the neuropsychology of learning. These schools are living evidence that positive change can and does occur in our nation's schools.

Creating Changes in the Classroom

Volunteer to help implement Gardner's eight ways of learning in the classroom. You can take children to an unoccupied room in the school and use some of the activities suggested in this book. Or you can work with the teacher to create "activity centers" around the classroom that focus on the eight varieties of intelligence: a listening center for musical intelligence, a book nook for linguistic intelligence, a math and science lab for logical-mathematical intelligence, a large open-space area for bodily-kinesthetic intelligence, an art center for spatial intelligence, a quiet corner for intrapersonal intelligence, a round table for interpersonal activities, and an ecology center for the budding naturalists. Let the battle cry of "eight different ways!" go forth into the schools. Our classrooms have become too one-dimensional. They're stilted by the limited vision of curriculum manufacturers, administrators, and teachers who live in the past. And if the schools resist your battle cry, don't despair. You can still give your child at home what he's not getting at school by following the kind of approach described in this chapter. The next two chapters will help you focus on two of the intelligences that have been most seriously neglected by the schools: spatial and bodily-kinesthetic.

Chapter

6

Bodywise

Making Learning Physical

The words or the language, as they are written or spoken, do not seem to play any role in my mechanism of thought. The psychical entities which seem to serve as elements in [my] thoughts are certain signs and more or less clear images . . . of visual and some of muscular type.

ALBERT EINSTEIN

Peter was driving his teacher to distraction. Instead of sitting at his desk and concentrating on the lesson, he would get up from his seat and roam at will. His grades plummeted as his teacher's blood pressure rose. Yet one day, Peter's teacher learned an important lesson of her own. She had forgotten to water the plants that morning, and so during the reading lesson she asked him to go to the back of the room and quietly do this for her. Afterward, she questioned him about the material she'd been teaching and was surprised to discover that he'd absorbed the whole lesson. She began to understand that Peter was a student who needed to *move* in order to learn. She thought of other chores that he could do around the classroom while she taught her lessons, and from that time on, Peter's performance in school began to improve.

In many other classrooms around the country, Peter would have been labeled as ADHD and might even have been medicated. Peter's teacher recognized what other parents and teachers around the country are beginning to realize: Many children need to *learn through their bodies* in order to make sense out of academic subjects. These *bodily-kinesthetic learners* often become frustrated when they have to sit for long periods of time in confining desks doing tasks that involve minimal physical activity. There are many practical ways of teaching academic subjects through physical activities. I will describe some of these alternatives later on in the chapter. Before I do, however, let's explore some of the reasons why the body needs to be brought back into children's learning.

Intelligence Begins in the Body

Child development pioneer Arnold Gesell frequently emphasized that "mind manifests itself in everything the body does." Jean Piaget reinforced this when he pointed out that the highest forms of logical intelligence can be traced back to their origins in the body. From the first days of life, an infant's body is actively exploring the world and building a preconceptual framework that serves as the foundation of all later thought. For example, an infant's ability to grasp an object that has been moved away from him demonstrates his capacity to act consistently toward an object despite its changed appearance—in this case, its different location in space. This early capability prepares the way for a later development in middle childhood when children can internally represent objects from a variety of perspectives. They're able to mentally place themselves in the shoes of another person and imagine how an object looks from that point of view. This ability is fundamental to many higher mathematical processes.

In some individuals, thinking retains certain visceral characteristics even at the highest abstract levels. Philosopher and psychologist William James commented on a particular tactile quality to his thought: "I am myself a very poor visualizer, and find that I can seldom call to mind even a single letter of the alphabet in purely retinal terms. I must trace the letter by running my mental eye over its contour in order that the image of it shall leave any distinctness at all." James's "mental fingers" may go back to experiences he had as a young child tracing puzzle pieces or alphabet blocks. In any case, he seemed to have retained this early trait and used it to help him in his creative work (he was one of the founders of modern psychology).

Before humans communicated their ideas through abstract symbols, they used physical movements and gestures. For thousands of years, humanity passed on knowledge from one generation to another through a mixture of chanting, singing, dancing, and drama. Even with the development of written language, this unity of mind and body remained intact for hundreds of years. Dom Jean Leclercq, a Catholic scholar, suggested that monks in the Middle Ages saw reading as a physical activity. He observed that the Latin words *legere* and *lectio* (which, in part, translate as "to read") have a kinesthetic meaning: "When *legere* and *lectio* are used without further explanation, they mean an activity that, like chanting and writing, requires the participation of the whole body and the whole mind. Doctors of ancient times used to recommend reading to their patients as a physical exercise on an equal level with walking, running, or ball playing." How different this is from our idea of reading today as a mental task based on the "distance senses" of seeing and hearing.

Putting the Body Back into Learning

We seem to have lost this connection between learning and the body in our society. We expect children to sit still in their seats and read, write, or compute silently. Parents and teachers often tell students who fidget while they work to settle down. All too often these days, parents and teachers refer these kids for testing and they're labeled with ADHD. Children who move, speak, and fidget while they work may need to study in this physical way in order to make any meaningful contact with the lifeless symbols in front of them.

We're told that children who need to move while they learn sometimes have neurological problems. The ADD and learning disability experts warn us about the neurological problems underlying some children's need to move while learning. While a few of these kids may have specific identifiable neurological difficulties stemming from previous diseases or accidents (which can be identified by a qualified physician), it is, I believe, truer to say that many kids who are being labeled ADD or LD today in fact don't have *neurological dysfunctions* as much as they have *neurological differences* that predispose them to higher activity levels than other children. These psychobiological differences may be a deficit in a classroom that expects every child to sit quietly in their seat for hours at a time, but it can be a real asset in an environment where kids are allowed to change activities frequently, interact with hands-on materials, and engage in meaningful movement as a part of learning. And in a school that supports a strong physical education program that involves running, jumping, dancing, hiking, juggling, swimming, martial arts, outdoor games, or other forms of physical expression, these kids will often be much more likely to outshine the more fragile "bookish" kids in the quiet classroom.

Eliminating Bodily Stresses During Academic Study Periods

Michael Gelb, a bodyworker assisting in British schools, noticed that youngsters experiencing difficulty in schoolwork often tightened up their bodies and restricted their breathing. Teachers added to this tension by pushing harder for answers. Gelb helped these students become aware of their twisted positions and tensed breathing patterns. He encouraged them to open up and expand their breathing and posture. Often this alone would help them see the correct solution or remember the right answer to a particular problem or question.

You can help your child feel more comfortable while studying at home. During her homework time, notice how she sits. Does she appear relaxed and centered or tight and distraught? Ask her to describe the feelings in her body. Then suggest that she experiment with other ways of sitting, or propose that she even try studying in a standing or prone position. Jeffrey Barsch, a California educator, found that his students were able to read and listen better when they were lying down. Each child has her own best way of studying. The strongly bodily-kinesthetic child often needs to tap feet or change positions several times in the course of a few minutes. One teacher custom-built a special worktable for such a child that included an old sewing machine foot lever attached to the table leg, so that the youngster could move his foot rhythmically while he studied.

Bodily-Kinesthetic Teaching Strategies

Traditionally, physical education has been limited to P.E. classes and vocational programs in school, but it really can permeate every aspect of learning. Finding ways to help students integrate learning on a "gut" level may be critical to their mastering important concepts. Here are a few simple bodily-kinesthetic strategies that parents and educators can use to help kids "get physical" with learning.

Body Answers

This is actually a very common strategy in schools. The teacher asks students a question and they raise their hands. That's a body response! Such an experience requires students to activate a physical part of their brain and connect it to academic subjects. The only problem is that hand-raising is relied upon too often as a strategy and soon becomes quite boring. I'd like to suggest other creative ways in which kids can respond physically to questions, both at home and at school. Instead of raising hands, students could smile, blink one eye, hold up fingers (one finger to indicate just a little understanding, five fingers to show complete understanding), make flying motions with their arms, and so forth. During homework sessions, a parent might say, "If you understand the material, put your finger on your temple, if you don't understand, scratch your head." The children can make up their own unique physical codes to represent different states of understanding from the "aha!" experience to absolute confusion. A parent or teacher can also tailor a body answer directly to the material being studied. For learning about parallel construction in grammar, for example, you might say: "If you think this sentence has parallel construction, I want you to raise your two hands high like a referee indicating a touchdown; if you think it's not parallel, put your hands together over your head like the peak of a house."

Homework Theater

This strategy can help bring out the actor or "ham" in your child. When involved in homework with your child, suggest that he or she enact the texts, problems, or other material to be learned. For example, your child might dramatize a math problem involving three-step problem-solving by putting on a three-act play. Homework theater can be as informal as a one-minute improvisation of a reading passage, or as formal as a one-hour play that sums up your child's understanding of an end-of-semester project or assignment. This strategy can be done without any materials or can be accomplished with homemade costumes and props. If your child feels shy about performing, you might suggest using puppets and a puppet theater made out of a large cardboard box. Similarly, for learning about history, you might consider using miniatures to dramatize the event (e.g., showing how a battle was fought by putting miniature soldiers on a plywood battlefield and moving them around to show troop movements). For help on getting warmed up or into an improvisational mood, see Viola Spolin's landmark book on dramatic improvisation, *Theater Games for the Classroom.*

Kinesthetic Concepts

The game of charades has been a favorite of kids and party-goers for decades because it challenges participants to express concepts and ideas in unconventional ways using bodily-kinesthetic intelligence. This strategy works very similarly to charades by introducing kids to concepts through physical illustrations or asking them to pantomime academic concepts or ideas. Here are a few examples of concepts that might be expressed through physical gestures or movements: soil erosion, cell mitosis, political revolution, supply and demand, subtraction (of numbers), the epiphany or turning point in a novel, biodiversity in an ecosystem. You might start by illustrating a few concepts yourself without words (e.g., for soil erosion, you might start wiping your arms and legs until you gradually lose strength; for political revolution, you might act out growing frustration until finally bursting forth in outrage). This can be a good strategy to use when helping your child learn new vocabulary words. Words that are acted out—that are internalized in the body—will be far more likely to be retained in the mind than those simply repeated verbally.

Hands-on Thinking

Instead of simply asking your child to tell you what he knows about a particular subject in school by talking about it or writing about it, why not ask him to tell you through his hands: by building something that illustrates the concept? This is exactly what architects, sculptors, and designers do when thinking through concepts. Many educators have already provided these types of opportunities in math instruction (using blocks, rods, or other "manipulative" materials to learn about logical and numerical relationships), and in science through hands-on lab work. This approach also has been used in schools that use thematic teaching, where students may, for example, build adobe huts to learn about Native American traditions, or in building dioramas of the rain forest to learn about ecosystems. You can extend this general strategy into your time with your child at home, too. In helping your child learn spelling words or special terms in any academic subject, suggest that he form them in clay or with pipe cleaners. Similarly, in learning more abstract concepts, like "deficit" (in economics) or "democracy," creating simple hands-on models using clay, wood, paper, or other household materials can provide a three-dimensional projection of your child's thinking processes that can form the basis for further discussion and study.

Body Maps

Just as clay and pipe cleaners or blocks and wood can be used to create models of academic concepts, so too the human body itself makes a great springboard for jumping into higher learning. Albert Einstein was once observed at a banquet explaining to a neighbor his latest theory of the universe. He was using his rib cage and spinal cord as a model and starting point for his discussions. Einstein was using "body maps" as a strategy. Kids who count on their fingers in math are using the body-map approach as well (there are several highly sophisticated systems, such as Chisanbop, for rapidly computing numbers on the fingers). There are many other creative ways to use the body to map out concepts. In geography, for example, the body might represent the United States (if the head is the Northern United States, then where is Florida?). The body also might be used to map out a problem-solving strategy in multiplication. For example, in multiplying a two-digit number by a one-digit number, the feet could be the two-digit number, and the right knee could be the one-digit number. A child could then perform the following actions in remembering the specific steps to go through in multiplication: tap the right knee and the right foot to get the first product (indicated by tapping the thighs); tap the right knee and the left foot to get the second product (indicated by tapping the stomach); tap the thighs and the stomach (to indicate adding the two products), and tap the head (to indicate the final product). In reconstructing the plot of a story, a child can remember the different events by mapping them out on his body (e.g., "It all begins at my feet, where the hero gets lost in the woods, then at my knees, he gets rescued, then at my belly button, he discovers a new country, then at my chest, the people there make him king, and finally, at my nose, he marries and lives happily ever after.").

Using the Body to Teach the Three Rs

The general picture we get of children in the act of school learning is of them sitting at desks looking up at the blackboard, looking down at their textbooks, or writing in their workbooks. In this scenario, muscular movement is pretty much restricted to the neck, eyes, and hand muscles. For learning to really sink in, however, it also needs to involve complex movements in the large muscles of the arms, legs, and torso.

Body Reading

When your child reads at home, have him take little "muscle breaks." These might include jogging, aerobic-type exercises, or traditional calisthenics like neck rolls and leg lifts. You can also encourage him to read *while* moving. Some exercise bicycles, for example, come with a book-holder device that allows for reading and bicycling at the same time. When your child meets with an unfamiliar letter or word, suggest that he imagine it to be a miniature playground and invite him to get involved. For example, with the word "put," he could act out crawling through the loop in the p, sitting astride the horseshoe u, and climbing up the t or sliding down its shaft. He also can make the letters with his own body or create entire words with other children and adults.

Give your child opportunities to act out what he reads instead of merely telling you about it. Reading comprehension is frequently a dull activity for kids because they feel no connection to what they're reading. If they put on plays or in other ways dramatize their reading material through pantomime, dramatic recitation, or dance, the meaning will become encoded in their bodies and remain with them for a long time.

Body Writing

As mentioned in chapter 5, bodily-kinesthetic learners usually do better when they learn to write before they read. This is because writing involves direct interaction between the body and letters, whereas reading as typically taught only uses the distance senses of seeing and hearing. A lot of children are rushed into writing activities requiring the use of only the small motor movements of one hand. These youngsters need to begin their writing experience with large body movements.

Before your child even starts to write letter or number symbols, he ought to have a lot of experience with freestyle art activities, including painting, collage, and working with clay. Then, when he shows an interest in letters and numbers, suggest that he try some of the following alternatives to the usual workbook routine in practicing numbers and letters:

- Writing on huge sheets of butcher paper in large strokes with thick crayons, magic markers, or a large paint brush
- Writing on the concrete pavement of a driveway or playground with sturdy pieces of white or colored chalk

- "Writing" with a flashlight or "light saber" in a darkened room or closet
- Creating words in water on the side of a house using a squirt gun, garden hose, or spray bottle
- Drawing letters and numbers in the mud or sand outside with a long stick
- Saving old toothbrushes and using them as writing implements with finger paints
- Making letter shapes with molded clay

Supply your child with large textured letters so that he can feel each individual letter shape before writing it down. Buy sandpaper letters from a toy store or educational supply store or make an alphabet from some of the following materials: sandpaper, bread dough, macaroni, rice, pipe cleaners, yarn, glue, seeds, glitter, clay, cloth, toothpicks, straws, bottle caps, twigs, or wire.

Body Spelling

Spelling drills are usually dull affairs for children ("Repeat after me, DOG, *D-O-G*, DOG"). There's no real interaction going on for these youngsters beyond staring blankly at the word to be memorized. To involve the body, suggest that your child perform any of the following activities while spelling a word: jump while saying each letter; alternate standing up and sitting down—A (up), N(down), D(up), AND; alternate jumping and squatting; clap loudly while shouting each letter; lie down on the floor only when repeating the vowels. Ask your child to make up his own sequence of body movements.

Body Math

An excellent way to learn mathematical concepts kinesthetically is through math manipulatives. These are concrete materials—such as blocks, rods, dice, and chips—that kids actively touch, move, stack, and maneuver to explore relationships at the heart of basic mathematical operations. One commercial brand of math manipulatives, Cuisenaire rods, give children the opportunity to compare and contrast differences in length between several sizes and colors of thin wooden blocks. In playing with the rods, they learn, among many other things, the principle that there are several ways of combining small rods to equal the length of a larger rod. For example, it takes a white rod plus a purple rod to equal the length of a light-yellow rod. A dark-yellow rod plus an orange rod *also* equals the length of a light-yellow rod. This discovery paves the way for a later symbolic understanding that there are several ways of adding numbers together to create the same sum (for example, $3 + 3 = 6$; $4 + 2 = 6$; $5 + 1 = 6$). Children experience this principle with their hands first and their minds later on.

Manipulatives don't work with all children. Some kids are turned off to them because schools often use them in the same coercive way they use worksheets. Other kids must go more deeply into kinesthetic learning and rediscover numbers in their whole bodies. In a sense, they need to explore the meaning of numbers just as they were originally developed in the course of human history. A measurement such as the foot, for example, was originally based on the length of the king's foot. Our base ten system of place value goes back to the use of ten fingers in counting.

Here are some suggestions for building the body directly into your child's basic math program:

- let your child use her fingers to add, subtract, multiply, and divide
- draw a number line in chalk on the sidewalk or driveway; then have your child practice doing arithmetic problems by walking, running, jumping, or skipping along the number line
- help your child measure her height and weight, the length of her arms and legs, the area of her skin, and other bodily measurements; show her how to use her own body to measure other things—for example, the length of a room in human "feet"

- help her explore different geometric shapes through creative body movements (for example, by actually making a triangle with her whole body)
- assist her in telling time by drawing a large body-sized clock face in chalk on the sidewalk and then have her lie down on it using her arms as the clock's "hands"
- suggest that she act out math word problems instead of simply trying to figure them out in her head

For other ways of learning through the body, see the books *Teaching the 3 Rs Through Movement Experiences* by Anne G. Gilbert, *Unicorns are Real* by Barbara Meister Vitale, and *Minds in Motion: A Kinesthetic Approach to Teaching Elementary Curriculum* by Susan Griss (all listed in the resources section at the back of the book).

The Body as an Adjunct to Learning

There are many other ways of bringing the body into learning. At school, simulation, role-play, field trips, improvisation, and hands-on activities provide the basis for teaching virtually any subject. One biology teacher had his students learn the rudiments of molecular bonding by assigning to them the roles of atoms. The hydrogen atom could only bond to other student-atoms with one hand, the oxygen atom with two hands. In this way, they learned how different compounds and molecules form. Another teacher taught American history by having students spontaneously act out the roles of newly arrived immigrants from England to colonial America.

At home, you don't have to look far to find areas where kinesthetic learning takes place. Simple chores such as cooking, cleaning, gardening, and helping to fix things around the house develop body-knowing. So do hobbies including carpentry, weaving, knitting, nature study, art activities, and sports of all kinds. In the same way dance, massage, wrestling, skateboarding, karate, juggling, and model-building develop a number of important physical abilities, including eye/hand coordination, left-right orientation, balance, reflexes, body awareness, manual dexterity, and other psychophysical abilities important to academic learning. The point is that these activities are worthwhile in and of themselves, and not simply as exercises to "remediate learning dysfunction" or "develop your child's intelligence." Take care not to use them in this way. Children often resent having adults foist these special "learning activities" on them and tend to learn best when engaged in activities for their own sake. It may seem ridiculous to say this, but children take their bodies with them wherever they go, whereas they're more likely to leave their workbooks and folders behind. As more parents and teachers begin to recognize the importance of the body in learning, we're likely to see a sharp decline in the number of so-called ADD/ADHD children (as well as Ritalin prescriptions) and a corresponding increase in real learning capacity and enjoyment among millions of children nationwide. It is equally important to recognize the value that imagination plays in the learning experiences of kids. The next chapter explores the importance of fantasy and "visual thinking" in the lives of children.

The Inner Blackboard

Cultivating the Imagination in Learning

If a Hopi and an English-speaking person were watching a person running across a field, both might say, "He is running"; thus both would be operating from a direct observational basis . . . Later on, however, when the runner was gone, it would be appropriate for the English-speaking person to say "He ran away." The Hopi would say something like, "He runs in my memory."

BOB SAMPLES,
The Metaphoric Mind

 *aydreamer.* When parents hear this word used to describe their children in school, they begin to worry. Yet daydreamers may turn out to be highly imaginative children who simply don't have any outlets in the worksheet wasteland for their marvelous powers of fantasy. The schools allow millions of imaginative kids to go unrecognized and let their gifts remain untapped simply because educators focus too much attention on numbers, words, and abstract concepts and not enough on images, pictures, and metaphors. Many of these children may be ending up in LD and ADD classes and many more may be wasting away in regular classrooms, at least in part because nobody has been able to figure out how to make use of their talents in a school setting. Imagination forms an integral part of every child's development and deserves to be nurtured in practical ways in order to teach youngsters what they need to learn in school.

Seeing Is Conceiving—From Image to Abstract Thought

Growing evidence points to the importance of the formation of mental images as a crucial step along the way toward higher abstract thinking for the young child. As we saw in the last chapter, thinking really begins in the body. However, as the child grows, thinking becomes clothed in the rich fabric of inner imagery. In the first few months of life, problem-solving is focused on the body. A baby attempts to get a toy back that has dropped out of sight by swinging his arms to and fro, mimicking the movement that originally led him to acquire the toy. After the first year, however, a child becomes capable of holding an inner image of a lost toy and can use this mental map to help search for it. Many years later, as a teenager, he may rely on purely logical relationships as clues to the possible location of a lost possession. Development moves from the body to the image to the abstract concept. Jerome Bruner, a former Harvard professor and one of the founders of cognitive psychology, refers to these three levels of representation as *enactive* (through the *body*), *iconic* (through the *image*), and *symbolic* (through the *concept*). The iconic level is the critical link between purely physical expression and totally conceptual representation. As such, it is really the bridge between body and mind.

While iconic representation may appear developmentally before symbolic knowledge, this doesn't mean that image is inferior to reason. Mental imagery seems to make up the very substance of so-called higher forms of thinking. George Lakoff and Mark Johnson, authors of *Metaphors We Live By*, point out how much of our everyday language is saturated with metaphors having a visual basis; for example, in the world of high finance, commonly used terms include *liquid assets, cash flow,* and *hard cash*. One theorist, Rudolf Arnheim, professor emeritus of the psychology of art at Harvard University, goes so far as to say that all thinking—no matter how theoretical—is visual in nature. Even concepts as abstract as "democracy" and "future" have some basis in image, according to Arnheim. The images may not be readily apparent or easily described. However, if one takes the time to reflect, the connection with image will surface. Arnheim cites the case of early twentieth-century psychologist E. B. Titchner, who attended a lecture during which the speaker made frequent and emphatic use of the monosyllable "but." Titchner came to associate the word with "a flashing picture of a bald crown, with a fringe of hair below, and a massive black shoulder, the whole passing swiftly down the visual field, from northwest to southeast." We all appear to carry subliminal visual associations like this one that we associate to commonly used words and concepts.

In a more practical vein, culture owes many of its most advanced scientific and technological discoveries to the workings of fertile imaginations. Elias Howe, the creator of the sewing machine, struggled for many months to come up with a workable design for his invention. Finally, one night he had a dream where he was captured by natives who demanded that he finish his invention or die. On his way to the execution, Howe noticed that the spears of the natives had holes near the points. He suddenly awoke with the realization that the needle of his own machine needed to have a hole near the tip. His struggle ended, and a new era of sewing convenience began. Eugene S. Ferguson, professor of history at the University of Delaware, points out that many objects of daily use—carving knives, chairs, lighting fixtures, and motorcycles—as well as everything from pyramids to cathedrals to rockets had their design and function determined by technologists using pictorial forms of thinking.

The Flowering and Withering of Imagination in Childhood

Geniuses don't have a monopoly on creative imagination. Most children before the age of seven or eight are highly imaginative. They have the ability to take a simple household object such as a matchbox and transform it, through fantasy, into a car, a house, a piece of furniture, an animal, or any of a thousand other objects. They experience dreams vividly and sometimes wake up feeling uncertain about whether their nighttime adventures have actually occurred or not. They look at smudges on walls and swirling clouds and see marvelous scenes. They spontaneously weave fanciful stories with the skill of a master storyteller.

Unfortunately, this rich imaginative world begins to fade as children enter school—with its demands on imageless thinking, pictureless facts and concepts, and abstract-symbol systems. Imagination has little or no place in schools. Imaginative answers on most tests receive no credit. Teachers discourage fantasy-oriented responses because they take up valuable class time. Budget constraints and the need to cover more "academic" objectives impel administrators to cut back or eliminate entirely subjects such as art and creative writing that allow the imagination to flourish.

I believe that many cases of so-called learning disability or "dyslexia" that we see now in the country result from this rupture of what should be a natural process of transition from the image to the symbol. Spatially intelligent children who have a flair for imaginative experience enter school and become strangers in a strange land of barren symbols and ciphers. Since no one makes use of their imagination to teach them the skills they need to learn in society, this resource atrophies just as it does in their more successful peers. The potentially creative visionary becomes the bored daydreamer. Fortunately, though, there are ways of bridging this gap between image and symbol and feeding the imagination of all children.

Use Pictures and Images
to Introduce Words and Letters

Too many children enter the first grade classroom with high expectations, only to find a barren world of meaningless symbols on workbook pages, in basal readers, and on the blackboard. Research suggests that most first graders see the alphabet with the posterior regions of the right hemisphere of their brain, where much of one's spatial intelligence is processed. They see letters as pictures. An *A* is a couple of slanted lines with a horizontal line in the middle or a picture of a tepee or a mountain peak. In later grades, however, children begin to shift their perception of letters over to the auditory-linguistic area of the left hemisphere and learn to regard the letter A as an abstract symbol associated with a group of sounds.

Some kids, however, *don't* make this shift. These often tend to be highly imaginative children with strong spatial intelligence. Because they regard letters as pictures or spatial symbols, they aren't that concerned about directionality. A picture of a horse, after all, remains a picture of a horse whether the horse's nose is facing toward the right or left side of the page. It even remains a picture of a horse if it is turned upside down. From the standpoint of the highly spatial child, the more different perspectives one can get of a subject, the richer one's knowledge of that subject becomes. This "three-dimensional mind" is a decided asset when designing Lego structures, fixing machines, or working with sculpture. However, when a picture-smart child such as this encounters linguistic symbols in the classroom, then his marvelous intelligence for shape-shifting runs into serious difficulties. For example, if he looks at a lowercase b and wishes to rotate it in his mind, it turns into a d or even a p or q. This can be awfully confusing. Parents and teachers look at the child reversing letters in reading and writing and instead of paying attention to their high levels of spatial intelligence, they begin to worry and think about getting him tested.

Oftentimes, such a child ends up with the label "dyslexic" or "learning disabled" (and increasingly also ADD or ADHD). Everyone is looking at what is "wrong" with the child rather than celebrating the wonderful spatial gifts of the child. It's interesting to note that many artists, architects, and designers reported having had great difficulty in school, especially when they were beginning to read and write. For some of them, it was only when they got out of school that they were able to do the things that really made them successful in life. What highly imaginative, picture-oriented, 3-D learners need are adults who will recognize the unique ways in which they think (remember Billy at the beginning of chapter 1), and design educational approaches that will help them make the transition from spatial image to linguistic symbol in a natural way. Parents and teachers who are helping kids learn to read can help highly spatial children bridge the gap between image and letter by presenting the alphabet pictorially. To introduce the letter S, for example, tell a story about a snake. Let them draw pictures of the snake or make the snake in clay. Finally, draw the snake yourself so that it begins to look more and more like the letter S. Point out how the sound a snake makes ("sssssss") is the sound the S makes as well. Use your own imagination to create pictures out of the other twenty-five letters of the alphabet. See the book *Alphabatics* by Suse MacDonald for suggestions on how to get started. In addition, show your child how to draw pictures out of the letters of words to illustrate their meaning. Draw the word *rain,* for example, with little droplets falling off of it, or the word *sun* with an aura of yellow light around it. Write the word *short* squashed down and fat in very thick letters.

This technique was used with children who were having a hard time learning to read by conventional methods. Barry was a Florida youngster failing the sixth grade in all subjects except mathematics. Standard remedial techniques resulted in little progress. Finally, educator Barbara Cordoni and her colleagues recognized something that no one else noticed in earlier efforts to teach him: Barry loved to draw. They decided to give him the opportunity to create pictures out of his spelling and vocabulary words. For the word *street* Barry hung lamps from the t's to illustrate a community street scene, drew wheels onto the loops in the word *bike,* and made pictures out of many other words from his schoolwork. During the course of the semester, Barry's grades jumped from Fs to As.

Traced back far enough into the ancient past, the alphabet was once a picture language, or series of ideograms. Several current languages have kept much more of their connections to pictures, including Chinese and the Japanese script known as *Kanji.* In Japan, children learn three different scripts: *Kanji,* and two forms of *Kana,* which is a phonetic system that is more consistent than English in its correspondences of sound and symbol. With two alphabets to lean on, children in Japan have both visual-spatial and auditory-linguistic ways of learning the language. As a result, reading disabilities are rare.

Chinese ideograms have been used as a way of teaching reading to so-called dyslexics in our culture. Some Pennsylvania psychologists took a group of non-Chinese second grade inner-city schoolchildren with severe reading difficulties and taught them to read English material written as thirty different Chinese characters. They wrote: "Children who had failed to master the English alphabet sounds in over one and a half years of schooling immediately understood the basic demands of the task and were able to read sentences in the first five or ten minutes of exposure to Chinese." It appears that these children benefited from this approach because their teachers tapped these youngsters' highly developed spatial abilities.

Use Storytelling and Metaphor
to Convey Facts and Concepts

Children love to be told stories. Their enthusiasm comes from a very deep place in their psyches, reaching back to ancient times when the history and values of culture were passed on through an oral tradition rooted in imaginative myths and legends. Nowadays, storytelling seems to only happen on Saturday afternoons at the public library, but it continues to be a powerful way to communicate knowledge from one generation to another. In an age when television and technological toys seem to leave little room for the imagination, storytelling provides an opportunity for children to supply their own inner images to match those in the tale. This feeds their powers of visualization.

Storytelling ought to be a regular part of your child's life at home and at school. You can make up your own stories or get them from books. However, don't restrict storytime to reading from books. While this is valuable as a preparation for getting your child interested in reading, kids also love to hear stories told spontaneously. If you rely on books for your source of stories, read the story several times first, becoming thoroughly acquainted with it in your own imagination. Practice telling it out loud in an empty room if you wish. Then tell the story to your child.

Storytelling is an activity worthy of doing simply for its own sake. However, it also happens to be a great way to teach children academic material. The following illustrates how I used storytelling to teach the concept of multiplication. (Note: Daughters can be substituted for sons in this story.)

The As Much Brothers

Once upon a time there was a man named Mr. As Much who lived alone in the forest. He was walking along one day when he heard a voice crying out in the distance. He hurried to the scene of the voice and came upon a deep hole in the ground. Seeing a man trapped below, he threw down a rope he was carrying and hoisted the man to safety. The man wept with joy and said, "Thank you! Thank you! I am the good magician in these parts. An evil wizard knew I had no magic for getting out of deep holes so he laid this bear trap for me. To thank you, I will foretell your future. You will marry and have three sons. Name your sons Just, Twice, and Thrice. Then when each comes of age, teach them these rhymes. Teach Just the following rhyme, 'Whatever I choose to touch will give me just as Much.' And whatever he touches will become his. Teach Twice the following rhyme, 'Whatever I choose to touch will give me Twice as Much,' and whatever he touches will double and become his. Teach Thrice, 'Whatever I choose to touch will give me Thrice as Much,' and whatever he touches will triple in quantity."

Sure enough, the man did marry, did have three sons as the magician predicted, and when they came of age he taught them the magic rhymes.

- -

At this point, I usually stopped telling the story and asked the children questions like: What would happen if Twice As Much touched two gold coins? (He'd get four gold coins.) What would happen if Thrice As Much touched four diamonds? (He'd own twelve diamonds.) The children drew pictures illustrating the story, on one side of the page showing one of the sons touching something and on the other side showing the result. In this way, they began to develop images for each of the multiplication facts.

You can use storytelling to teach just about anything. Get your child interested in reading by telling him stories from classic children's literature and having the books available should he ask for them. Make up stories using words from his spelling list. Then have him retell the story in written form, making sure he includes the spelling words. Read his history or social studies textbook and make up stories together that incorporate the places, names, and events described so that they come alive pictorially. Encourage him to create his own stories as a way of making sense out of the material he learns.

Stories often employ metaphor or images that have multiple meanings. Psychologist Robert Samples says that the mind of the child is innately metaphoric and requires an approach to learning that is interdisciplinary, multileveled, and nonlinear. Metaphors, thus, make wonderful seeds to sow in a child's mind. (To use a metaphor!) The possibilities are endless. For example, instead of passing on dull science concepts, create images for these processes. A. C. Harwood, a Waldorf educator, points out that it's senseless to explain the laws involved in the formation of rain to a young child in purely scientific terms. "But if you make a picture of God as the great gardener who wishes to water all the fields and plains and forests of the earth, and takes the water from the seas as a man takes water from a well, and lets the water fall so gently that it does not harm even the tenderest flower, and is yet so careful of the water that, when all the plants and creatures have drunk, it all runs pure and sweet back into the sea—if you speak in this manner, the child will see the world in terms he can understand."

The use of metaphor is extremely important in conveying through picture-language ideas that would have no meaning to children in a more rational form. W. J. J. Gordon and Tony Poze, two educators in Massachusetts, devised an approach to learning they call "synectics," which uses metaphor in teaching a wide range of academic subjects. In American history, they'll ask: "How is the conflict Roger Williams had with the authorities of the Massachusetts Bay Colony like the splitting of an amoeba?" or "If the colonies were the cheese, who is the rat?" In teaching about soil erosion, they'll paint a picture of a "cheerful, happy-go-lucky mountain stream" and ask the child to become this image while telling the story of its journey from the mountains to the sea.

If more educators used imagery and metaphor in teaching academic facts and concepts, we'd have a lot fewer "disabled" learners and bored students on our hands.

Inner Visualization as a Key to Memorizing Facts

Many children have highly developed visualization skills that they could use to help learn spelling words, math facts, and other forms of information—if parents and teachers only knew how to show them the way. Studies indicate that up to half of all young children produce *eidetic imagery*. This refers to the ability to experience mental pictures as clearly and vividly as perceptions of external objects. Children with eidetic imagery can look at an object, close their eyes, and scan their mental image for additional details not seen during the original perception of an object. Even children who don't appear to have eidetic imagery skills may be able to develop this capacity. E. R. Jaensch, a pioneer in the field of eidetic imagery, felt that this phenomenon was latent in everyone.

Visualization of this kind can come in very handy during a spelling test. Tell your child that he has an "inner blackboard" in his head on which he can write his weekly spelling list. Tell him to leave the spelling words up on his inner blackboard when the teacher erases the spelling words from the "outer blackboard." Then, after the spelling test has begun, all he has to do is copy the words from his inner blackboard onto a sheet of paper. It's like having a crib sheet inside of his head! He can use this technique to memorize the times tables, remember history facts, learn vocabulary words, or retain countless other bits and pieces of information.

Visualizing Success in Learning

Some children use their imaginative gifts in a negative way—they hold pictures in their mind's eye of themselves as failures in school. These pictures often come from actual memories of being laughed at by peers or criticized by parents and teachers. Over time, these memories turn into horrific images of humiliation and degradation. These images need to be countered by even more powerful pictures of confidence and self-esteem. The following are some exercises you can use to help your child visualize self-confidence and success.

A Happy Learning Time

Picture a time when you learned something that was easy and that made you happy inside. Maybe it was learning to ride a bike, paint a picture, play a game, or something else that you do well now. Experience that time all over again. Notice how happy you feel. See how easy it is for you to learn.

The Successful Student

Picture yourself at school as a successful student. You feel smart. You're confident about learning in every subject. See yourself reading easily and quickly. Notice yourself in class being the first one to answer all the questions. Picture yourself taking a test and writing down all the correct answers. The teacher comes by and puts an A on your paper. Kids come up to you after class and ask you to help them with their homework. When you go home your parents praise you for doing a great job in school. You feel wonderful for being such a good student.

Modify these activities to suit the particular needs of your own child. Allow her imagination free reign. Tape record the exercises so that they can be played back whenever she wants to hear them. Create your own versions of them and engage her in telling her own positive learning images.

Too many children suffer from "imagination deficit disorder" (IDD)—the dulling of the mind by numbers, words, abstract concepts, and social cliches. Ironically, it's the successful students who may suffer most from this condition. Many of these youngsters sacrifice their imaginations to succeed in the worksheet wasteland. We can help these children regain their image-making capacity by building visualization, storytelling, metaphor, and picture-language into our learning methods. When we do this, we're also nurturing their affective development, since inner images often have an emotional charge. The next chapter focuses on emotions and emotional intelligence, seeing how feelings serve either to hinder or to help the learning process that takes place in your child.

Chapter

8

Teaching with Feeling

Opening the Heart to Learning

It seems to me that children dig themselves foxholes in school, that their fumbling incompetence is in many ways comparable to the psychoneurotic reactions of men who have been under too great a stress for too long . . . There are very few children who do not feel, during most of the time they are in school, an amount of fear, anxiety, and tension that most adults would find intolerable. It is no coincidence at all that in many of their worst nightmares adults find themselves back in school.

JOHN HOLT,
How Children Fail

Ed burst into the classroom in a fury. He'd just gotten into a fight during recess and couldn't think straight. During class he simmered. He wadded his writing assignment into a little ball and threw it at a classmate. We stopped the lesson and talked about what happened out on the playground. I suggested that he tell me his side of the story—in writing. He spent the rest of the afternoon working on the assignment.

Roger was a physically and emotionally abused youngster. He came into my class and did very little reading. Instead, he worked with clay—making little houses that he lit up with batteries, wires, and bulbs. He spent hours absorbed in fascination—creating a little village of security for himself that he could never find at home. Almost overnight, he skipped ahead two years in reading achievement.

Sarah entered my special class from a very efficient and competitive classroom where she was overlooked and failing at math. In my class, she lined up the puppets in the math corner and began lecturing them sternly. Slowly her own math started to improve.

Each of these stories comes from my teaching experiences in special education classrooms. In each case, a child's feelings were getting in the way of learning. At the same time, each child's feelings also held the key to their academic success. Ignored or hidden from view, these emotions sabotaged their efforts to succeed. Acknowledged as real and given an opportunity for appropriate expression, emotions paved the way for effective learning to occur.

The Inner World of Stress

Many children carry around a deep inner turmoil that remains carefully hidden from view to all but the most trusted of companions. This secret stress has many sources. At home, separation or divorce, sibling rivalry, illness, parent criticism, loneliness or boredom, family financial difficulties, and neighborhood violence all fuel the stress syndrome. At school, stresses include pressures to conform academically, being humiliated by the teacher or laughed at by students, intense competition in class or during after-school sports, being excluded from group activities, getting low or failing grades, and the threat of bullying.

Some children bear their burdens well and may suffer no clearly observable effects. Other children seem to buckle under the weight of the load and show visible signs of stress, including headaches and stomachaches, restlessness, problems concentrating, irritability, aggressiveness, tight muscles, anxiety, and depression. Many of these youngsters end up in remedial classes or programs for the learning disabled, ADHD, or emotionally disturbed. Many others seem to be outwardly successful in school, yet experience no joy in learning. To help all of these children reach their full academic potential we need to provide them with ways to cope with the stresses in their lives—both the inevitable ones that come up as a natural part of learning and growing and the sudden crises that require more intensive care.

A key to helping children cope with stress is to understand the role of emotions in their lives. Rudolf Steiner called the years from seven to fourteen "the heart of childhood," because the feeling life—as symbolized here by the heart—predominates over the mind. Every moment of time at this age offers an opportunity for the emotions to be expressed. Sympathy for a wounded pet, laughter at a funny joke, tears after a fight with a friend, and a hundred other emotions come up every day in the life of a child.

Children at this age *need* to experience the poles of feeling—happiness and sadness, hope and fear, jealousy and compassion—in order to have a solid foundation for their later emotional life. A child who's too protected—with only the positive side emphasized—becomes vulnerable to stress when life becomes hard. Yet a child who's exposed to physical or emotional abuse at home, constant doses of violence from exposure to the media, and chronic threat from peers and school becomes burned-out before he's even learned how to cope.

Real learning can't take place in the absence of positive *and* negative emotions. First, there are the old feelings that get stirred up from the past—the fear of starting something new, the humiliation at having tried and failed, the rage toward a world that seems cold in the face of one's own impotence, and the apathy one feels after a string of defeats. But there are also the peak moments—the joy of having conquered what one thought were impossible obstacles, the exhilaration of mastery, and the pride at displaying for others one's newfound skill.

To ignore this complex web of feelings is not simply unwise, it is impossible. Yet this is often what we try to do when helping youngsters at home or school. We attempt to deny their emotional lives and, in so doing, cut them off from the source of energy that connects them to their own natural powers of learning. This compounds the stresses that they have to face. At school, specialists set up behavior modification programs to control behavior without any recognition of the inner emotions that drive it. Meanwhile, counselors and school psychologists are too busy with testing and administrative paperwork to be of much help to children with emotional needs. At home, parents often are too wrapped up in their own problems to have the time and inclination to sit down and listen to their children. In either place, emotions become intrusions into the lesson plan or homework time instead of motivators that can spur the student on to success in academics.

Children need to have permission to express their joy and anger freely while learning so that the vitality locked up in these emotions can be transformed into the mental activities associated with academic progress. This doesn't mean that you need to let your kids run roughshod over your life, doing whatever they want. It *does* require, however, that your child's honest expression of emotion in all of its colors be acknowledged and that your child be given opportunities for channeling his true feelings in a number of positive directions—directions that are detailed later on in this chapter. Let's take a look first, though, at the neuropsychological evidence supporting the central role that the emotions have in learning.

Emotional Intelligence: The New Basic Skill

We tend to think of learning—at least academic learning—as a highly abstract process quite distinct from more primitive emotions. Yet recent evidence from the brain sciences suggests that the emotions are vital to higher abstract thinking processes. A recent best-seller has even suggested that the emotions are so important that they deserve to be called an intelligence. In *Emotional Intelligence: Why It Can Matter More than IQ,* Daniel Goleman, a former Harvard professor and *New York Times* journalist, points out that the real world is full of examples of people with low IQ scores in charge of people with high IQ scores. The low-IQ leaders possess a high EQ (emotional quotient). They demonstrate the capacity to empathize with others, to pick up on social cues, to show individual persistence and ambition. On the other hand, those with high IQ scores who have difficulty getting along with others, who lack self-understanding, have problems with impulse control, or are emotionally illiterate (i.e., have difficulty identifying what they are feeling at any given moment in time) are more likely to have difficulty in life, even if they did well in school.

In the brain, emotional intelligence is shaped in part by an intricate dance that happens between the deep emotional centers of the limbic system underneath the neocortex (which are responsible for feelings of rage, fear, joy, and other strong feelings) and the prefrontal lobes of the neocortex (just behind the forehead), that act to help to modulate these strong emotions through inhibition, reflection, analysis, and other defusing strategies. Emotional intelligence is really the capacity to have access to a large palette of options in how to deal with strong emotions. Goleman writes: "When an emotion triggers, within moments the prefrontal lobes perform what amounts to a risk/benefit ratio of myriad possible reactions, and bet that one of them is best. For animals, when to attack, when to run. And for we humans . . . when to attack, when to run—and also, when to placate, persuade, seek sympathy, stonewall, provoke guilt, whine, put on a façade of bravado, be contemptuous, and so on, through the whole repertoire of emotional wiles."

Goleman suggests that it is essential that emotional intelligence be taught in the schools, so that kids have the opportunity to acquire skills that will help them become more resistent to depression, eating disorders, unwanted pregnancies, violence, and other pitfalls that can sabotage the most promising student. Such skills include the ability to identify, label, express, and manage feelings; to control impulses; to reduce stress; and to delay gratification. In one study cited by Goleman, preschoolers who showed the ability to delay gratification—by refusing to eat a marshmallow immediately so as to get two marshmallows a few minutes later—turned out to be more socially competent, personally effective, and, most amazingly, had SAT scores in adolescence that were on average 210 points higher than kids who ate the one marshmallow right away rather than wait for the two later on.

Goleman's concept of emotional intelligence is very similar to Gardner's personal intelligences (intrapersonal and interpersonal). Other theorists have come to similar conclusions about the unity of knowing and feeling. According to Paul MacLean, former director of the Laboratory of Brain Evolution and Behavior at the National Institute of Mental Health in Bethesda, Maryland, we have not one brain but three: a "rational brain," a "reptilian" brain, and an "emotional" brain. The rational brain is represented by the neocortex, which, as we saw above, is responsible for many abstract thought processes, including goal planning, analysis, inhibition, and reflection. The reptilian brain, consisting of the pons, the medulla oblongata, and a few other structures, controls some of our deepest and most instinctive behaviors, such as territoriality and assertiveness rituals (for example, prancing, preening, and posturing). It expresses itself most directly in the actions of mobs and gangs. The "emotional brain," according to MacLean, is the limbic system, which surrounds the reptilianlike brainstem (limbic means "forming a border around"). As we noted above, the limbic system controls many of our emotional responses to the environment, including rage, fear, grief, and joy. Since the limbic system sits right in the center of the brain, it functions as a sort of crossroads for much of what goes on within the central nervous system, uniting emotional impulses in the "lower" brain with rational thought patterns in the "higher" brain. "We have been brought up being told the neocortex does everything," says MacLean in the journal *Science*. "We try to be rational, intellectual, to be wary of our emotions. But the only part of the brain that can tell us what we perceive to be real things is the limbic brain."

Psychiatrist William Gray proposes a model of the mind which says that "ideas are rooted in emotional codes." He calls these codes "feelingtones." Gray says that these emotional tones are embedded in neuropsychological processes and serve as vehicles through which rational ideas are remembered, associated, and reported. Another way of saying this—in terms of the lives of children—is that youngsters often get more out of the *way* something is being taught than from *what* is being taught or the specific content of the curriculum. If someone teaches a fact to them with anger, enthusiasm, lethargy, or sadness, this stands out much more in the minds of children than the particular facts or ideas contained in the lessons. Jerome Bruner, author of the book *Actual Minds, Possible Worlds*, refers to a colleague of his who suggested that we "perfink" or perceive, feel, and think all at the same time.

Learning problems occur when this unity breaks down. Leslie Hart, an educator and science writer, pointed out that many so-called learning disabilities actually result when stress causes a child to "downshift" from neocortex or rational functioning to lower brain processes associated with the limbic and reptilian systems. The child who charged angrily into my classroom after a fight couldn't think straight because he was operating primarily under the influence of the lower brain systems. When given a chance to settle down and focus on an assignment that made him think about his feelings, he was able to begin the process of reestablishing those all-important connections between rational and feeling brains.

It's really this balance between feeling and thinking that's most important in the education of the child. Kids are highly sensitive to the world around them. Given the opportunity, they respond to learning materials, ideas, and techniques spontaneously.

("That's bo-ring!" or "Hey, this is fun!") Teaching that disregards the feelings and focuses totally upon the rational mind fails to acknowledge these important undercurrents, seriously damaging any chance for real learning to take place.

I've seen this happen too many times in my own classroom and in scores of classrooms that I've visited. I've observed children working quietly—too quietly—and only appearing to learn. In their obsession with silence, administrators, and many parents as well, might be fooled into thinking that a lot of serious learning is going on in these places. Yet, I'm reminded of what John Goodlad said in his study of 1,000 classrooms: "The emotional tone is neither harsh and punitive nor warm and joyful; it might be described most accurately as flat." Emotionally flat classrooms fail to teach because they neglect the emotional brain.

On the other hand, feelings can also *interfere* with learning. I've seen a lot of learning time wasted in my own classrooms because students' emotions overran the lesson plans. My students brought in so much anger, rage, and humiliation from past learning experiences that these deep feelings constantly blocked pathways to new ideas and skills. In this case, I had a surplus of emotion—too much of the "downshifting" that Hart spoke of above—and needed to focus on building a bridge between the limbic system and the neocortex.

The rest of this chapter focuses on practical activities you can use to make emotions work for you and not against you in your efforts to help your child learn. The first group of ideas tells you what to do when there's too much emotion. The second group of suggestions shows you how to bring the limbic system into academic work that's become too dry and cerebral.

De-Stressing the Learning Environment

When a child's stress levels are too high or the emotional climate is too strong, you need to focus attention on directly relieving stress or working with the actual source of emotional conflict before you can even begin to think about academics.

Centering Activities Reduce Stress

Relaxation techniques help your child feel more at ease. Several ways of releasing tension and centering awareness—including biofeedback, yoga, and meditation—have been used successfully to help lower anxiety levels in children, freeing up emotional reserves for new learning. Stephanie Herzog, a California teacher, related a story about Nick, a second grader with poor concentration and few reading or math skills. After three months of centering activities, Nick went up to his teacher and said, "Teacher, I really felt it today; I felt the relaxing feeling going down my body." From then on, he was able to focus during the centering time and started to make progress in his academic learning. By third grade he was reading at a fifth grade level.

You don't need to wire up children for biofeedback, turn them into pretzels with yoga, or sit in the lotus position in order to help them unwind. Relaxation experiences can be very simple. Try the following exercises yourself first. Then invite your child to become involved. You might want to modify the exercises to meet your child's individual needs. For each exercise, sit comfortably in a straight-backed chair with eyes closed, feet on the floor, and hands folded in your lap or outstretched on your thighs. Alternatively, lie down flat on a carpeted floor with your hands at your side.

The Balloon

- Breathe normally for a minute or so, paying attention to each breath you take.
- Now you're a balloon. Take a deep breath. Let the air come into you so you get really big. Hold in the air while you count silently to four and then let all the air out.
- Repeat two more times.
- Breathe normally for a minute or two before you get up, noticing the relaxing feeling that's come into your body.

The Body Builder

- Sit quietly for a minute, focusing on the feelings and sensations in your body.
- Stiffen the muscles of both arms as if you were a body builder flexing his muscles, counting silently to four while you do this. When you reach four, let your arms go totally limp like wet noodles. Repeat this stiffening and releasing routine with your legs, head, neck, back, chest, stomach, and finally with your whole body.
- Remain seated or lying down for two or three minutes before getting up.

My Favorite Place

- Empty your mind of all thoughts.
- Imagine yourself going to your favorite place, a place where you feel totally safe, happy, and relaxed.
- Spend some time in your favorite place, doing the things you most enjoy doing there. Take as much time as you need.
- When you feel you're ready to come back, imagine yourself returning and feel the contact your body makes with the floor or chair. Slowly begin to open your eyes. Remain seated or lying down for a minute or so before getting up.

Other ways of relaxing include listening to a peaceful musical selection, taking a quiet walk out in nature, or hugging and touching. Your child may want to engage in his own activities, including spending time with pets, being with friends, getting involved in sports, or playing a favorite game. All of these experiences help to promote relaxation if they're done in a gentle and noncoercive way.

Transforming Feelings Through Art

Create opportunities for expression through art, music, dramatic play, or physical movement. The arts channel bothersome feelings into constructive pathways, helping to reduce overall stress levels. Children who show their anger or fear in red and black paint, by noisily banging on a drum, or through jumping up and down in rhythm to a musical piece drain off excess emotion that may have clogged up their own learning arteries. Artistic expression opens the heart to new learning, allowing children to gain control over their feelings and letting them transform strong emotions into new and creative energies.

Provide your child with materials for artistic expression: paint, clay, or collage supplies for visual art; simple and sturdy musical instruments for rhythmic expression; puppets for dramatic play; or music and space for creative movement. Offer a few basic rules about the use of the materials and let your child do the rest. See *Windows to Our Children* by Violet Oaklander for other ideas on bringing out emotional expression in safe and therapeutic ways.

Easing Your Child's Load at Home and School

Help remove some of the daily stress factors that get in the way of effective learning for your child. Sometimes youngsters are saddled with too much responsibility—care of younger siblings, household chores, extracurricular activities, homework—and they get stressed out from the load. Stress's wear and tear on children may show up in learning performance before it begins to affect physical health. You can help by lightening the load where possible and encouraging your child's teacher to do the same. Ask your child which extracurricular activities he'd like to eliminate so that he can have more time for free play. Perhaps homework assignments might be reduced or modified to reflect his current interests. Finally, since change is associated with stress on many levels, try to regulate your family's daily routine with consistent meal and sleep schedules, minimizing abrupt shifts in the rhythm of your child's life.

Providing Self-Help Skills to Combat Stress

Talk with your child about the emotional conflicts that may be at the heart of a learning problem. It seems that with all the recent attention given to learning disabilities and attention deficit disorder, we've forgotten about emotional blocks to learning. An expert in the field of self-esteem education once told me about a fourth grade child who was still experiencing problems in learning how to read. Working with the child individually, he asked the child to close his eyes and report on what he experienced. The child said that he heard his second grade teacher yelling at him and telling him how he'd never amount to anything in life. The man had the child speak to this imaginary teacher, pouring out the rage he felt at being humiliated in this way and affirming his own ability to succeed. This experience was enough to help move the child past his reading frustration toward school success.

You may be able to accomplish similar results simply by sitting down with your child in a nonthreatening atmosphere and talking with her about a teacher, a low grade, a troubling paper, or a bothersome classmate. Ask her to identify the problem, the feelings that come up for her around that problem, and finally a possible solution. In being a facilitator rather than a judge or arbitrator, you can help your child come up with answers to her own problems and provide her with important self-help skills in coping with stress.

Getting Expert Help When You Need It

Professional counseling may be necessary to help your child cope with acute stress factors. Sometimes the problems a child confronts are too emotionally charged or deeply rooted to be easily dealt with in face-to-face conversations between parent and child. Physical abuse, the death of a parent or sibling, personal illness, divorce, or severe inner turmoil of unclear origin may call for the presence of a trained counselor, psychologist, or psychiatrist. Make sure in such a case that you work with a licensed professional who has specific training and experience in your child's particular area of difficulty. That doesn't mean you should turn complete responsibility for helping your child over to the experts. Work cooperatively with your counselor or therapist to develop self-help skills you can use to assist your child at *home*.

From Rage to Reading: Learning the Emotive Way

Once children's emotional lives settle down to the point where they don't overwhelm the learning environment, it's time to begin using that affective voltage to charge their learning batteries. This isn't always easy to do in the beginning—it's a little like trying to catch a stampeding elephant with a butterfly net. Yet there are many techniques for motivating a stressed-out learner that are vastly superior to Ritalin, behavior modification, or plain old-fashioned shouting. These methods work because they tranform raw, unbridled emotional energy into productive academic activity.

Use Writing and Drawing to Release Emotion

If your child is angry or in conflict, get her to write about or draw the experience. The Italian psychiatrist Roberto Assagioli said that writing is a wonderful catharsis. He recommended writing nasty letters to people you are angry with, and then not mailing them. You can use this approach with a child who is mad at a parent, peer, or teacher. At times like these you must be especially tolerant and allow free expression, both in what words are to be used and in the final appearance of the writing. By letting her discharge emotions in this way, you're helping her transform rage into reason.

Use creative writing as a means of emotional expression. New York poet Kenneth Koch successfully used this approach with stressed-out children in urban school systems. He discovered that these kids could easily speak about the problems in their lives when they used the fluid medium of unstructured poetry as a means of expression. Letting young people talk in simple unrhymed patterns about their own inner worlds gives them the opportunity to bridge the gap between verve and vowel. Here, for example, is a short poem written by a student in one of my own classes who was coping with a number of anxiety-provoking stresses in his life:

Spiders are ugly. They live in your mouth. They are very scary. And they drink your blood. And they crawl in your ear.

Koch's book *Wishes, Lies and Dreams,* as well as the very fine *Whole Word Catalogue,* produced by the Teachers and Writers Collaborative in New York City, provides many wonderful ideas and themes for children to use as starters in expressing their inner lives.

Reading with Feeling

Let your child build a reading vocabulary from words that have an emotional charge. Sylvia Ashton-Warner called this method "organic reading" and wrote about it in her acclaimed book *Teacher.* Every day, ask your child for a word that she would like to learn how to read. Print each word on a 3x5-inch index card and let her keep the completed cards in a recipe box or use a spiral notebook where all the words beginning with A are kept on the first page, all the B words on the second page, and so on. Don't worry about whether the words are too difficult for your child. Since they come from her own interest and experience, they are probably surcharged with "feelingtones" and are likely to be remembered. Kids in Ashton-Warner's classroom came up with words like *ghost, kiss, daddy,* and *kill.* After your child accumulates several words, help her build sentences and stories from her collection. She can write down these stories in a homemade book and illustrate them with colored pencils, crayons, or paints.

Choose reading materials that stimulate emotional responses. Psychoanalyst Bruno Bettelheim and educator Karen Zelan point out in *Learning to Read: The Child's Fascination with Reading* that a major contributor to reading failure in our schools is the sheer banality of the reading material to which most children are exposed. Children are emotional beings and often can only be reached by books that have an affective charge or that acknowledge their feeling lives in some real way. For those youngsters who are having trouble learning the code, simply written books on affective themes may serve to unite the lower and higher brains. Books such as *Where the Wild Things Are* by Maurice Sendak and *There's a Nightmare in My Closet* by Mercer Mayer speak to the dark side of a child's inner life, but in a way that's made safe for them. *The Temper Tantrum Book* by Edna Preston and *I Was So Mad!* by Norma Simon acknowledge anger as an important part of the child's life. *Helping Children Cope: Mastering Stress Through Books and Stories* by Joan Fassler is a wonderful guide for parents in choosing literature for children dealing with specific emotional traumas such as divorce, illness, or death. Children themselves will tell you through their own enthusiasm which books have meaning for them and which books leave them flat. Pay attention to those responses. Properly nurtured, a child's early excitement about books will pave the way for a lifetime of enjoyment in reading.

Choosing to Learn

Children often find themselves in situations where they have little or no control over what they learn. No one pays attention to what *they* feel about their educational lives. Teachers evaluate them, determine what their needs are, and give them teaching materials and techniques that will supposedly help them learn. The children have little input into this process and even less once the program has begun. They receive workbooks and assignments to complete, texts to read, and tasks to perform—but nobody seems to notice the feelings aroused within them from this whole dehumanizing process.

Such neglect of children's emotional worlds leads to inner frustration and effectively blocks learning. If they become apathetic, then they might quietly fade away into a corner of the classroom, where they may continue to stagnate until high school graduation. Perhaps they will join the million or so students annually who leave school functionally illiterate. If they respond

with rage and anger, then they could end up with the label "emotionally disturbed," "behaviorally disordered," or ADHD and have
an entirely new program drawn up for them, again without opportunities for negotiation.

Children have a right to participate in choosing the kinds of
materials, techniques, and approaches to be used in their educational careers. Because they've lived with their multiple intelligences all their lives, they are usually the best ones to talk with
about how they learn best. It's only reasonable that their own feelings be taken into consideration during the process of developing
an educational program.

Involving Children in Educational Planning

**Allow your child to be present during school meetings, parent
conferences, and informal discussions that involve her educational future.** Insist on it, even if the teacher resists. Let your child
know she can make suggestions, give input, and have an important say in the planning of her educational future. Don't merely
give lip service to this offer but practice it all the way down the
line. I've participated in too many conferences where children
were ushered into a tense meeting-room atmosphere only to be
offered a token opportunity to speak. I never saw a child say a single meaningful thing that reflected an inner belief or emotion in
this context. Yet in a one-to-one relationship or in a small, informal group where there was trust and positive regard for the child,
this same youngster would make it very clear what her feelings
were about being moved from one classroom to another or about
some other educational change.

**Give your child choices in the setting up of any learning ex-
perience.** Consult her as much as possible concerning what is to
be learned, the way in which a requirement is to be met, and the
kinds of materials to be used for any learning activity. I found children's reading performance to be far better when I gave them a
choice in what they read to me than if I simply assigned them
a book. At home, allow your child to set her own time and place

for doing homework and encourage her teacher to provide options in the assignments he gives.

These suggestions are a beginning in allowing emotions to take a central place in your child's learning. However, they can't replace the single most important factor in her emotional well-being, and that's your own relationship to her. We'll explore that topic in the next chapter.

Chapter

9

The Learning Network

Building Support Systems in Your Child's Academic Life

Two are better than one, because they have a good reward for their toil. For if they fall, one will lift up his fellow; but woe to him who is alone when he falls and has not another to lift him up . . .

ECCLESIASTES 4:9–11

aven't you done your homework yet?" "Do you call that mass of scribbles a book report?" "Hey, dummy, when are you going to shape up and be like the rest of us?" These are some of the phrases that too many kids hear at home or school—phrases that cripple the learning process for kids who desperately need encouragement from the significant people in their lives. At home, parents nag them about low grades, poor study habits, or uncooperative behavior. At school, teachers criticize them for illegible assignments, not following directions, or having a poor attitude. On the playground, peers taunt them for not following the crowd, being in special programs, or saying and doing things in a different way. Their learning network sags in the middle. It fails to give them the encouragement they need in order to feel like competent, successful human beings. As a result, they tend to stay locked in a pattern of learning failure—or, in the case of achieving students, "learning doldrums"—rather than discovering the truth of their multiple intelligences.

No child learns in a vacuum. Beginning in infancy, a baby's efforts to master the environment are mediated by those around him. Grasping for a toy, the infant finds his performance ideally facilitated by encouraging family members who help to arrange the situation so that it is neither too easy nor too difficult for him to attain his goal. On the other hand, an infant who is told harshly not to touch, is given the toy without expending any effort, or is surrounded by anxious onlookers, never experiences the joy that comes from having his own efforts rewarded. These patterns get laid down early in life so that by the time the child enters school, he finds himself involved in a complex series of mutual interactions with the world that either carry him into school with confidence or cause him to doubt his own self-worth.

Far too many children fall onto the negative side of the learning ledger. Living in a world where people regard their uniqueness as unacceptable, they either quietly submit and spend much of their lives attempting to be as bland and normal as possible or they go on the defensive and end up in a perpetual battle with those who might otherwise help them learn. What children need, beginning in early life, is a trusted ally, someone who believes in them and supports the way in which they learn best. They need an ongoing relationship with at least one competent adult who can serve as an advocate for them in the world. This positive learning relationship can then be a model for how other interactions in their lives might take place. Even in the midst of a choppy sea of criticism and contempt, this relationship can serve as a bright beacon that guides them toward constructive learning later on in life.

If you're a parent, you're in a good position to take on the role of trusted ally to your child in the world of learning. Spending more time with your child than anybody else, you have the best chance of discovering and effectively working with the bright spots in his educational life. Teachers have their hands full with many other children, making it difficult for them to provide the closeness that this special relationship requires. Moreover, children often end up seeing several teachers a day, so they don't have the opportunity to form a close bond with any one adult in school. This chapter will focus on ways in which you can use your relationship with your child to improve academic learning and to create a setting for success in his life. Teachers, therapists, or friends of children also can apply these principles to their relationships with the children in their lives.

Symbiotic Learning: How You and Your Child Can Teach Each Other

Any truly meaningful learning experience that you engage in as a parent with your child benefits both you and your child. While it's clear that adults transmit culture to the younger generation, adults have a lot to learn from children as well. King Solomon said: "None is so great that he needs no help, and none is so small that he cannot give it." When you take part in a learning experience with your child, you have the opportunity to gain insight into how *you* learn, and you may be surprised by how much your child can teach you. It's important to recognize this creative symbiosis. If you feel you have nothing personally to gain from helping your child, you'll be less inclined to put yourself entirely into the learning process. On the other hand, if you see yourself as the "all knowing" parent, you may find your child resenting this attitude and closing off possibilities for further learning. A balance is needed, so that you can open yourself up to new experiences as a learner and, at the same time, feel the joy that comes from teaching your child something new.

Make Homework Time a Mutually Enjoyable Experience

In my workshops, I've heard from so many parents that they've given up helping their kids with homework because every time they try, the kitchen table turns into a battlefield. Doing homework together can be one of the best ways to create a positive learning bond with your child. These sessions often go wrong because they're perceived by parents and children as power struggles. Parents may be overly critical of their children's mistakes and lead them to make even more errors. Children may get frustrated, angry, or bored, and stimulate these same emotions in parents. If study time is to succeed, it needs to be, above all, a cooperative and positive experience voluntarily undertaken by both parent and child. Here are some pointers for making it a success:

Let your child set the agenda for the study session. Some kids like to start at the beginning of an assignment and work sequentially through each problem or step of an assignment until reaching the end. Other children begin with the easiest part of the assignment and move toward the hardest sections (or avoid them altogether). Still others use nonlinear methods for getting homework done. It's important to honor each child's personal strategy for studying, since this approach comes from personal choice and is likely to be backed up with enough motivation to get the job done.

If your child has trouble knowing where to start, you can guide him by asking: "What do you need the most help with now?" Focus on one problem or step at a time. If your child has forty difficult problems to do, select a representative sample and work on it together. Ask her to verbalize what is confusing, difficult, or unclear. Listen carefully, acknowledge the difficulty, and respond clearly in a way that helps.

Avoid using rewards and punishments. Bribing kids with privileges and prizes communicates the message to them that learning is not worth pursuing in its own right. Punishment is even worse since it causes your child to associate learning with pain. Use verbal praise as a reinforcement only when you genuinely feel it. Praise should be a natural outcome of your own excitement and joy at seeing your child do well.

Give clear, nonjudgmental feedback. If your child is having problems with a subject, she's likely to be hypersensitive to criticism in that area. So don't say: "You mean you still don't know how to regroup in addition?" but suggest instead "I see that regrouping is difficult for you." Focus on specifics in giving feedback (not "You're wrong," but "I noticed you added 15 and 19 and got 24"). Ask her to describe the steps she went through to get a particular answer. In this way, she can often learn to give herself feedback and use important self-correcting strategies in her schoolwork.

If you don't know how to help with a particular problem or skill, be honest and say so. Sometimes parents would rather bluff their way through children's questions or assignments rather than admit ignorance. Yet your child will usually suspect this and may benefit more from your own honesty during the homework session, since this shows him that it's okay not to know something. Together you can go to a third source—a spouse, a friend, a reference work, or a teacher—and discover the answer.

Avoid power struggles. Your child may begin to feel pressured, judged, or smothered by your attempts to help and actively resist these efforts with any number of ingenious manipulations, including whining, refusal to work, changing the subject, leaving the room, arguing, and intentional mistakes. These are your child's attempts to experience a sense of control in a situation that makes him feel helpless. Whenever you begin to feel as if the session is turning into a power struggle, you can take a deep breath, say the word *relax* silently, and ask him if he would like to continue. (You may want to use some of the relaxation exercises suggested in the last chapter as an aid in de-stressing the atmosphere.)

Beyond Homework: Learning Together in Real Life

Don't limit your learning times together to homework sessions. Learning occurs all the time in the hundreds of interactions that take place between you and your child every day. Remember that your child learned one of the most complex skills in the world— the English language—just by listening to you and your friends speak and practicing the patterns he heard. There are many activities you can share with him that will naturally provide rich opportunities for academic growth. Games, for example, are excellent learning tools. Word games such as Scrabble and anagrams teach spelling and vocabulary skills. Strategy games, including chess, checkers, Go, and many card games, stimulate logical problem-solving capabilities. Games like Monopoly offer opportunities for arithmetic computation. Other activities such as cooking, carpentry, gardening, shopping, and animal care provide the basis for learning hundreds of skills and competencies. It's important to keep in mind, however, that these activities should be engaged in for their own sake—because they're intrinsically worthwhile—and not because they teach specific academic objectives. Pressuring kids to learn in this way, or even pointing out to them in the course of an activity that they are learning something, may sour them to future experiences of this kind. Trust that these activities help your child learn, and focus your energies on seeing to it that he is engaged and excited, not on whether he's getting the skill or objective you want him to learn.

Practice What You Teach

You influence your child's learning on many different levels—seen and unseen. On an unconscious level, you transmit your own values and attitudes about learning. If you had negative school experiences of your own, then your child all too easily absorbs these feelings. That's why it's especially important for you to work on developing your own deep love of learning. *It's the single most important thing you can do to help him academically.* If you worry about his reading progress yet rarely pick up a book, then what kind of example are you providing for him? On the other hand, if you actively practice the skills you want him to learn, then you provide a model he can emulate. A Wisconsin mother wrote me about how she made this principle work for her in helping her children with their homework:

> I noticed recently that when I was helping my kids with their reading that I sometimes found myself getting up and doing household chores, in which case I did not hear their requests for help or I would try to put them off until I was finished with what I was doing. On the other hand, if I sat right by them and watched what they were doing, I found myself jumping to explain things that they could surely have figured out and worse yet, becoming bossy and impatient. Quite by accident I found the perfect solution one day when I was engrossed in a novel that I couldn't put down and they wanted help with their workbooks. I just sat close at hand and continued reading. I was right there and available when they wanted help, but not so bored that I was sticking my nose into their business all the time. Best of all, there I was actively enjoying the very skill that they were working to master. Now I really look forward to sitting down with them to work on reading.

This is the way most knowledge was transmitted from generation to generation until very recently. A child would learn a skill by being in the presence of a competent adult who actively practiced that skill, whether it was hunting, fishing, carpentry, printing, sewing, cooking, reading, or writing. It's only recently that culture appointed a number of "specialists"—called teachers—to pass on its most important skills. Jim Trelease, author of *The Read Aloud Handbook*, suggests that children learn to read, not from reading drills and phonics worksheets in classrooms, but from sitting in the lap of a trusted adult and listening to stories from early childhood on. This method works because parents model the behavior that they want their children to learn in a comfortable and relaxed setting—the home.

A parent's workplace is also an excellent "classroom" to show children new possibilities and teach them new skills. Other times it's a parent's hobby, a sport, or a volunteer activity in the community. Children will often pick up a great deal simply through observation and imitation. More important, they're seeing parents doing what they love to do. It's that zest for learning that ultimately impresses children the most and becomes part of their own belief system about learning and growing. Allow your child to see you in the act of learning something new, whether it's figuring out the instructions from a do-it-yourself kit, trying a new cooking recipe, or learning a dance step. Don't be afraid to show your own inadequacies. Letting him see an adult who can face challenge without giving in to frustration provides him with something he can refer to during his own difficult times in learning.

Don't overlook the possibility of bringing in members of the community to help your child learn something that you don't know how to do. Apprenticeships used to be the primary method of education for teenagers and young adults. Nowadays, many kids are wasting away in school when they could be actively learning a skill or trade in the community that might net them an income. If your child is interested in fixing things, see if she can't spend some time every week at a mechanic's shop. If she likes to cook, give her a chance to work in a restaurant. If her interest is animals, see if there's a veterinarian in town that could take her under his wing and offer some small jobs around the clinic. Start looking at the members of your community as a valuable resource and make their expertise a part of her learning network.

Working Together with Your Child's Teachers

If your child sticks out in any way from the norm, then the chances are that at one time or another there's been friction at school between a teacher and your child. Unfortunately, as we've observed throughout this book, many teachers expect all children to learn in roughly the same way, with little allowance for diversity in the way in which they learn. A child who requires a different approach may prove to be quite an irritant. If he is in a special education classroom, the teacher is often more sensitive to individual differences. However, in these settings the teacher may tend to view him as handicapped or disabled rather than as a child with a unique combination of multiple intelligences. You need to be resourceful in either setting and come up with strategies that will help smooth out the relationship between him and his teacher.

When school difficulties arise, arrange for a meeting with his teacher to talk about constructive solutions to the problem. Include him in the discussions, attempting to smooth out any communication breakdowns that may fuel the problem. Perhaps the teacher has a strong linguistic intellect while your child is more inclined toward bodily-kinesthetic or spatial ways of problem-solving. In such a case, you may need to diplomatically suggest ways in which his needs for movement and touch or pictures and images can be satisfied in the classroom through specific learning activities. It could be that your child holds a grudge against the teacher for being unfair on a test or withholding privileges because of classroom misbehaviors. In this case, you may need to help your child express these feelings to the teacher so that the teacher can clarify test items or more clearly communicate class rules for appropriate conduct.

Avoid creating an adversarial relationship with the teacher that can only subvert your efforts to improve the relationship between teacher and child. Teachers are wary of overbearing parents and may resent what they perceive as any pushiness on your part. Yet, at the same time, serve as a strong advocate for him and be wary of attempts by a teacher to mystify you with educational jargon or unclear judgments. Don't accept: "Your child has auditory discrimination problems" when the teacher really means "Ed doesn't like listening to my lectures." Help your child communicate his own needs for learning directly to the teacher—books he would like to read in class, subjects he would like to study, projects he would like to pursue. If, after your best efforts to work out communication snags, there is still a residue of negativity between teacher and student, then consider some of the alternatives listed in chapter 4 for schooling your child elsewhere.

Learning Among Friends: The Power of Peer Teaching

Nineteenth-century British educator Joseph Lancaster once taught more than 1,000 children at a time using children to teach small groups of other children. Young people seem to have an uncanny knack for tuning into the needs of their peers. They tend to avoid some of the pitfalls that you may encounter with your child, including feeling inferior to a powerful adult. At school, encourage your child's teacher to use peer-led reading groups, study sessions, and games involving lots of social interaction. Ironically, children may not grasp a new idea or skill until they have a chance to teach it to somebody else. A Georgia mother comments:

> I have noticed that "LD" children have a more complex system for understanding than "normal" kids do. For example, my thirteen-year-old daughter Louise ("LD") was unable to understand the concept of borrowing in subtraction or carrying in addition—no matter how many different ways I tried to demonstrate it to her. I finally gave up. I started to teach her eight-year-old sister Patsy ("normal") the same concepts. She was learning well, but still a bit confused. Louise took over and was able to show

Patsy clearly how it was done. Only then, while teaching, did it make sense to her.

Your child may be particularly effective in teaching other children (or in being taught by them) if she has strengths in interpersonal intelligence. If there are younger siblings or neighborhood tots about, you might suggest to your child that she teach them a simple skill. This not only clarifies her own thinking but also gives her the opportunity to experience learning success with another person.

By now you should have a sense of the important contribution that social interaction makes to your child's academic performance. Your own attitudes toward learning and the time that you spend with your child in learning activities may have a greater impact on his academic success than all of his teachers combined. All it really takes from you is a simple expression of interest, some positive times together, and a genuine effort to bring others into his learning life in a constructive way. Beyond this aim is an even subtler factor—the positive expectations that you have for your child's success. It's to this "hidden factor" in learning that we now turn in the next chapter.

10

Great Expectations

Creating Positive Beliefs in Your Child and Yourself

Treat people as if they were what they ought to be and you help them to become what they are capable of being.

GOETHE

he proverbial senti-
ment on the previous page, attributed to the great German
thinker Johann Wolfgang von Goethe, is sadly lacking in much of
our educational work with children. Children need megadoses of
positive experience in learning. They need to be surrounded by
people who see the best in them. Instead, many children learn to
conform to the limits that parents and teachers subtly place on
them. This chapter will explore the powerful impact that your expectations—both positive and negative—have on your child's
learning progress and potential. While expectation is an invisible
phenomenon, it represents a potent influence on your child's educational career, so read this chapter especially carefully.

School Labels: Let the Buyer Beware

It can begin almost imperceptibly. A parent reads a book about
learning disabilities, underachievement, or ADHD in children
and answers the questions these books invariably ask: "Does your
child have trouble paying attention?" "Does he reverse letters?"
"Is he always late in getting his school assignments in?" This gets
the parent thinking, "Oh yes, I remember a time when Johnny
had that problem." A syndrome begins to emerge out of previously dislocated bits and pieces of information. Before you know
it, Johnny has a label.

We now know that the expectations adults have for a child's
learning capacity can greatly influence scholastic performance.
Harvard psychologist Robert Rosenthal demonstrated what he
called the *Pygmalion effect* in a series of remarkable experiments
many years ago. Rosenthal and his colleagues went into a public
school district at the beginning of the academic year and tested
children using, among other tests, an obscure measure of intelligence. After scoring the results, Rosenthal presented teachers

with a list of students in their classes who promised to be "late bloomers" based upon their performance on that particular test. In truth, this test had absolutely no validity at all, and the list of favored children had been picked at random from the whole group. At the end of the year, Rosenthal tested all the students on several measures of achievement and intelligence and discovered that the late bloomers made greater gains than any of the other kids in class. He hypothesized, on the basis of these results, that the teachers' expectations caused the so-called late bloomers to progress as much as they did. The teachers seemed to expect more from these kids, and they got it.

Unfortunately, the Pygmalion effect works in reverse as well. In one experiment, two groups of elementary school teachers were shown a videotape recording of a fourth grade boy engaged in different activities. Before the showing, one group was told that the child was normal while experimenters informed the other group that he was learning disabled. After the presentation, both groups filled out referral forms for the boy. The group informed that the child was learning disabled rated him more negatively than the control group. Another study had psychiatrists from different cultures looking at the behaviors of a child. The psychiatrists from the more restrictive societies (China and Indonesia) were more likely to see "attention deficit disorder" in the child than the other psychiatrists. A third study showed that when first grade teachers perceive a child to be "at risk" for learning and behavior problems, they are three times as likely to criticize the child in class. Constantly criticized children don't learn as well as those who receive a balance of praise and constructive criticism. Teachers don't expect as much from "disabled" learners, don't challenge them as much as "normal" children, and don't provide them with the positive attention they need to thrive as successful students.

It's no wonder, then, that self-concept scores of children labeled learning disabled and ADHD tend to be consistently lower than those of nonlabeled kids. The belief "I am a disabled learner" may limit a child's learning potential far more than whatever was causing the original learning difficulty. Psychologists are now identifying a new phenomenon in these youngsters called *learned helplessness.* These children believe that their own efforts to learn will inevitably result in failure. When they succeed, they tend to attribute their triumphs to luck—something outside themselves. When they fail, they tend to blame themselves and their own lack of ability. After a while they just stop trying. And the label provides them with another "excuse" for their failure.

All children—not just those labeled learning disabled or ADHD—are sensitive to negative suggestions from parents and teachers. In a sense, the subliminal expectations that parents and teachers silently implant in children represent a very subtle form of hypnotic induction. Former Stanford professor Ernest Hilgard observed that children between the ages of seven and fourteen are highly susceptible to hypnotic suggestion. Thus, at the age of greatest vulnerability, kids are most likely to receive negative messages about their learning abilities and school performance. What this means is that our children are being brainwashed into thinking about themselves as poor learners before they even have a chance to reach adulthood and think things through for themselves.

Informal attributions such as "Suzy's lazy" or "Melvin just doesn't measure up to his father" eat away at these kids' self-esteem, sabotaging their learning potential and turning them into cynical or closed-off students. Psychoanalyst Erik Erikson characterized the elementary school years as a struggle between the forces of industry in the child ("What I produce is really worth something") and inferiority ("Whatever I do is no good"). Children who move through their school careers having to listen to parents and teachers subtly tear them down or measure them up against an impossible standard face the prospect of emerging from this important developmental period with a conception of themselves as inferior people.

The Alchemy of Expectation

Parents and teachers *can* change their current expectations so that children really learn to believe in themselves as competent learners. Like the alchemists of old who specialized in turning lead into gold, you can transform your own invisible beliefs about your child—beliefs that may be dragging him down academically or personally—into high, yet realistic, expectations for learning success. The rest of this chapter will explore concrete ways that you can do this.

Viewing Learning Behaviors as Positive Traits

Stop using negatives in describing children and their learning behaviors. Some might think this is impossible to do with children, but, in truth, most so-called symptoms of learning difficulty can be reframed into positive developmental signs of growth. If you don't think so, take a look at Table 10-1, which matches common negative traits of children to those same traits viewed in a more positive way. You might be thinking that these "golden" terms are nothing but euphemisms for describing some clearly troubled or troublesome children. Yet we've seen from studies of teacher-child interactions how the terms we choose to focus on can make a crucial difference in a child's growth and learning.

TABLE 10-1: TURNING LEAD INTO GOLD

Lead *A child who's judged to be . . .*	Gold *Can also be considered . . .*
learning disabled	learning different
hyperactive	energetic
impulsive	spontaneous
ADD/ADHD	a bodily-kinesthetic learner
dyslexic	a spatial learner
aggressive	assertive
plodding	thorough
lazy	relaxed
immature	late blooming
phobic	cautious
scattered	divergent
daydreaming	imaginative
irritable	sensitive
perseverative	persistent

Discovering Skills and Interests

Instead of dwelling on the problems your child is having at school, try to discover his talents and abilities. I tell parents and teachers to become "strength detectives" and locate as many talents and abilities as they can. This isn't easy to do because there are so many books out on the market giving us "warning signs" and so many tests available to find out what's wrong with people, that we just haven't had enough practice doing this. Here's a simple series of questions you can ask in guiding your own discovery of your child's abilities.

Acquired skills. What does your child already know how to do? Ask your child's teacher what skills he already possesses, what he gets the highest test scores in, and what learning competencies he's displayed. If the teacher doesn't know, find another classroom for your child.

Personal interests. What excites your child? Look around the house and notice what kinds of hobbies she has, what kinds of games and toys she plays with, what TV programs and movies she enjoys, and what sorts of books or pictures she likes.

Special talents. What actual or potential talents does your child have? Use Howard Gardner's model of multiple intelligences as a guideline. Remember, a talent may not be something that has yet developed, but be on the lookout for any sign of its budding. Yehudi Menuhin loved the sounds of the San Francisco Symphony Orchestra as a three-year-old and asked his parents for a violin and violin lessons for his fourth birthday. They gave him both. Albert Einstein traced his interest in physics back to a time in childhood when he was given a small compass and became fascinated with the magnetic dial. Maybe your child sits down at the piano and becomes absorbed in making different sounds. Or perhaps he begs for a watercolor set or a basketball. Maybe he makes huge messes in the basement with a chemistry set or has an engine out in the backyard that he loves to tinker with. Take these things seriously. Your child may be telling you about a special talent or ability that deserves cultivation.

Positive qualities. What inner characteristics does your child have? This is the most subtle of the four areas but ultimately the most important. Note any of the following traits you've observed in your child: compassion, patience, persistence, loyalty, generosity, courage, faith, honor, ingenuity, creativity, friendliness, wisdom, intuition, will, playfulness, wonder, curiosity, adventurousness. While most of these attributes can't be measured by standardized tests, they may be the "secret ingredients" that carry your child into life as a successful person—if, that is, they're recognized and nurtured by an understanding adult.

Nurturing the Positive

Once you've identified a long list of positive qualities in your child's life, go to work highlighting them at home and at school. This will help to reverse the vicious cycle of learning failure or learning boredom—where negatives are in the foreground and positives are hidden. Shift the focus away from the disabilities, deficiencies, dysfunctions, and deficits in your child's learning life and concentrate on the abilities, assets, accomplishments, and advantages. There are many creative ways to do this. Make sure your child has a special place at home—a bulletin board, shelf space, or section of a room where special achievements such as awards, trophies, photos, school papers, and projects can be proudly displayed. Take time at dinner to listen to your child share the positive events that occurred that day.

More important than any specific activities you do with your child, however, is the attitude you have toward her capabilities as a learner. If you truly believe that there's something wrong with her brain, that she's a handicapped learner, or that she'll never be the great student her Aunt Judy was, then you'll get the performance and behavior to match your beliefs. Kids are very good at complying with our expectations. On the other hand, if you really believe in her, there's no telling how far she can go.

Steering Clear of Excessive Praise

Avoid lavish positive reinforcement of a child's special talents.
This could make your child feel just as uncomfortable as when
everybody was pointing out his shortcomings, especially when
done around his peers. Psychologist Stanley Krippner reports of a
teacher who noticed a boy's exceptional artistic talent and pro-
ceeded to put up many of his drawings, only to have the other
boys in the class dismiss his abilities as "sissy." He never drew after
that. Kids also get suspicious when parents or teachers suddenly
begin pouring on the praise and may pick up on the fact that
they're using it as a new "technique" to enhance self-esteem.
Make sure your praise is genuine and be sensitive in how you express it.

Using Interests and Abilities as Learning Tools

**Make the strengths you've identified work for your child in learn-
ing things that are difficult for him.** I once tutored a child who
could not remember his math facts. He happened to be obsessed
at the time with becoming a big-league basketball player—he was
only nine years old—and spent hours on his backyard court making free throws. So, instead of hunching over flash cards and
worksheets, we went outside and he dribbled the ball, counting as
he bounced, and shot a basket every sixth step until he reached
sixty. In this way, he began to learn the 6s of his multiplication
tables.

If your child loves cars and hates to read, find books about
cars. If she plays the piano and can't add, use the keys of the piano as a number line for doing mathematical computations. If
she wants to be a movie star when she grows up and avoids writing, help her write a little movie script to practice. One word of
caution here. If there's even the slightest hint that your efforts in
this direction are backfiring and she begins to avoid an activity
that she previously loved, then stop what you're doing immediately! Children don't like to be coerced, and your child might resent your efforts to get her to do something she hates by mixing it

with a favorite hobby or activity. But if you introduce an area of need into her personal world of interests and abilities in small doses and discover signs of excitement and progress in learning, you can rest assured that you're on the right track.

The Myth of Normality

Don't expect your child to learn according to some universal "norm." The main point of this book is that each child has his own unique combination of multiple intelligences in learning, which must be honored and nurtured. Parents often want and expect their kids to be normal. But the more we learn about individual differences, the more we realize that there is no such thing as a "normal" child. This concept of normality comes from such statistical artifacts as the bell-shaped curve that psychologists use to plot test scores. Educators and psychologists construct tests to conform to this all-holy curve—where most people must score in the average range (the high point of the curve) and fewer people score at the extremes.

When IQ tests were first being developed, it turned out that girls consistently scored higher than boys on many of the items. In order to make things equal, testers threw out items that favored girls until a normal bell curve was attained for all children. Diane McGuinness, a University of South Florida psychologist, says that there are basic neuropsychological differences between the sexes. Boys tend to change activities more often, enjoy hands-on learning more, and pay attention to nonverbal sounds, while girls are more focused in learning activities, more sensitive to verbal sounds, and more involved in interpersonal relationships. She suggests that if the test makers took these gender differences into account when constructing their assessments—instead of making the data conform to some statistical ideal—"overnight millions of disabled boys would become normal readers" and many boys labeled as ADHD would be seen as displaying gender-appropriate traits (what used to be called "all-boy" behavior).

It's also important to point out that in addition to gender differences, there are many other variables that make the concept of universal normality a myth. Who is to say that one child's blend of abilities/disabilities is any more or less normal than another child's? Ridding ourselves of these unreal concepts of normality allows us to see children as they really are and not in terms of some artificial standard.

Letting Children Bloom in Their Own Way

Don't make your child "live up" to your expectations. Your high expectations for your child may have more to do with your own ambitions than his. Perhaps you were a poor math student. You may want him to attain success in mathematics and reach a goal you were never able to achieve. On the other hand, you may be an avid book lover and expect him to read at an early age. The German psychoanalyst Alice Miller points out in her book *The Drama of the Gifted Child* how destructive it can be when parents try to live out their own lives through their children. Miller calls this a subtle form of emotional child abuse.

You need to believe in your child *on his own terms*. In many cases, his hopes, dreams, ambitions, loves, and abilities won't coincide with yours. In fact, it may be difficult for you even to recognize his talents because of this very fact. That's why you need to gather information from a wide range of sources—teachers, relatives, your child's friends, professionals, and neighbors—digesting what you learn as objectively as possible.

Ultimately, it's your child himself who will tell you what he is capable of and how he learns best. Listen carefully to his deepest self-expressions, and you will discover who he really is and where he wants to go in his life. Then it's up to both of you to work toward these goals—to help your child learn in his own way. In the next chapter, we'll explore the importance of helping children move along this inner pathway in their own *time*, as well, and we'll look at how destructive it can be when parents expect too much, too soon from their late-blooming children.

A Patient Attitude

Honoring Your Child's Learning Rate

TEACHER: "Monitors are you ready yet? . . . All ready girls, you have no time to waste. Now I'm waiting. . . . All right hurry up, you take too long on these problems. It should only take you about five minutes."

FROM ANTHROPOLOGIST JULES HENRY'S
FIELD RESEARCH IN AMERICAN CLASSROOMS

Forty years ago, American anthropologist Jules Henry observed that "American children work almost constantly under the lash of time." Henry's words are even more true today. Time rules not only the school day of American schoolchildren but also their entire developmental history. Beginning at their child's birth, parents start the clock, nervously awaiting the time when she first sits up, crawls, walks, and says her first words. They read child-development books that give the ages at which a normal child acquires skills, and they compare notes with their friends and relatives concerning the rate at which other children are achieving these same milestones. Any delay from the norm is viewed with alarm. To hedge against this, parents flock to programs that promise to "teach your baby to read, write, and do math" in the belief that earlier means better.

When children enter kindergarten, the curriculum—a Latin word meaning "racetrack"—begins. "Readiness" programs prepare them for reading, writing, and math skills. Then, somewhere in the middle of first grade, parents (and now, too, teachers) check their watches again. If their children are not reading or not paying attention, a little buzzer goes off saying "Something's wrong!" and programs for learning disabilities or ADHD enter the picture. Parents and teachers rarely consider the possibility that children may have their own internal clocks, ticking to the tock of a different timetable.

Concern is growing among child-development researchers that we're forcing our children into academic work even earlier than kindergarten or first grade. A joint statement issued by the National Association for the Education of Young Children (NAEYC) and the National Association of Elementary School Principals urged preschools to reduce their heavy emphasis upon academically oriented and teacher-centered education. David

Elkind, a former president of NAEYC, points out that the push over the past three decades to maximize a child's potential at an early age has created a situation where preschool children are being given a watered-down version of the first through third grade curriculum. This often results in premature learning problems due to inappropriate teaching methods. Yet children don't realize this and blame themselves for their failure to learn. In his best-selling book *The Hurried Child,* Elkind emphasizes the importance of letting children grow in their own time, with plenty of opportunities to engage in free play, fantasy, and sensory-motor experiences, activities that provide the basic building blocks for *later* academic work. This chapter will underline what Elkind and others have said about the "hurried child" syndrome in our country and will suggest practical ways that parents can help their children become achievers without rushing them into academics before their time.

Slowness as a Virtue

We live in a culture that worships speed. From fast cars to fast food, velocity is the American way of life. We esteem the individual who can make "snap judgments." We refer to intelligent people as "quick." In the schoolroom, we favor children who have their hands up first, are the first done on a test, and are the first to read, write, or compute. To be slow in our culture is to be dumb or, literally, retarded.

The reality, however, is that different children learn at different rates. Some children learn to read at age three while others don't learn until age nine or later. Unfortunately, our society considers six or seven—and increasingly now even four or five—to be "the age" at which reading must occur. The child who learns to read "on time" is accepted as normal. However the "late bloomers" are in serious trouble. For although they may develop in a perfectly acceptable way in accordance with their own particular patterns of development, they will be the ones to earn the labels learning disabled, ADD/ADHD, or underachiever.

In other cultures, slowness is a virtue. The person who acts quickly is regarded with disdain in many Eastern cultures where businessmen sit for days contemplating a business decision before taking any action. It's a sign of bad manners to be on time for a meeting in some Middle Eastern countries. Even in Western Europe there's a slower pace of life than in the United States. Anthropologist Edward T. Hall wrote: "Many of my European subjects observed that in Europe human relationships are important whereas in the United States the schedule is important."

These cultural differences are reflected in the classroom. In a comparison of beginning reading methods in fourteen countries, the United States had the narrowest "critical period" during which a child had to learn to read or be considered a disabled learner. Such countries as Norway, Sweden, and Denmark provide much greater leeway in this critical period and as a consequence have fewer problem readers.

The Advantages of Being a Late Bloomer

Most American classrooms expose six and seven year olds to the fine print of blackboards, basal readers, and worksheets; require them to listen to teacher instruction for several hours a day; and confine them to desks for long periods of time. Yet, many of these children simply aren't ready for this. The late Dr. Louise Bates Ames, who served for many years as associate director of the Gesell Institute in New Haven, Connecticut, suggested that if we would let children enter first grade based on their own developmental readiness, rather than according to when they were born (the usual method of determining placement) we might eliminate up to 50 percent of all learning disabilities in this country. Many normal kindergarten and first grade youngsters don't have the thinking skills to adequately perform the tasks given to them by their teachers. Jean Piaget pointed out that children go through four fundamental stages of cognitive development as they mature: sensorimotor, preoperational, concrete operations, and formal operations. Children cannot understand certain academic skills—including arithmetic—until they have achieved at least the concrete operations stage of cognitive development. In many children this occurs around six years of age. Different children, however, arrive at this developmental milestone at different ages. During the 1960s, when American educators debated about how schools could accelerate children through these stages, Piaget humorously referred to this urge for speed as "the American question." He emphasized that it was not important to him *how fast* children went through these stages but, more important, how thoroughly they became engaged at each step along the way.

Some educators even go so far as to say that *most* children would be better off if they postponed academic learning until later on in their school lives. Seventy-five years ago, Rudolf Steiner, the founder of Waldorf Education, criticized the tendency of parents and teachers to rush the teaching of reading and writing. Steiner observed: "Reading and writing as we have them today are really not suited to the human being 'til a later age, in the eleventh or twelfth year, and the more one is blessed with not being able to read and write well before this age, the better it is for the later years of life."

Parents will, of course, balk at the idea of their children not reading until the age of eight or nine, to say nothing of eleven or twelve years of age. Yet, in some cases, they have no choice but to wait, since attempts at remediation before that time will often bear little fruit. A Wisconsin mother wrote me about her seven-year-old child. This boy couldn't read, wrote many words backward, and had coordination problems. Rather than put him in a special education program—he'd been in one as a four-year-old—they decided to homeschool him. By the age of nine, he'd developed a fascination with reading, became an ace in badminton, and, according to his mother, could "never get enough math problems to work." Another mother took her son out of a special education program—where he was miserable—and put him in an alternative school that didn't put a great deal of importance on early reading skills. Her son went through the second and third grades without learning to read. She sometimes became worried about this. The school reassured her: "I remember being told, 'Look, some kids don't learn how to read until they are in third or fourth grade. That's just the way it is. You can't push it.

Then they hate reading whenever they do learn to read.' Well, by the end of the fourth grade, miraculously, Ricky could read."

Some students won't even learn to read until they leave school. A. S. Neill, the founder of the well-known alternative school Summerhill, gives this account of one student who had severe reading problems: "There was Jack, a boy who could not learn to read. No one could teach Jack. Even when he asked for a reading lesson, there was some hidden obstruction that kept him from distinguishing between *b* and *p*, *l* and *k*. He left school at seventeen without the ability to read. . . . Today, Jack is an expert toolmaker. He loves to talk about metalwork. He can read now. . . . He mainly reads articles about mechanical things—and sometimes he reads works on psychology."

The Art of Patience: Some Guidelines

Given that some children won't naturally learn to read, write, spell, or do math until after first grade, the big question for parents becomes: "What do I do in the meantime?" This is a crucial question, since most school systems don't stop to watch kids smell the roses along the way, but instead cling to timetables for achievement and deposit those kids who aren't keeping step into programs for handicapped learners or remedial groups in regular classrooms. Many parents have relatives and friends breathing down their necks as well, wondering why David can't do the things that *their* Julie can do. It isn't enough to simply say, "Leave him alone, he'll grow out of it" and let it go at that. This is the easy way out for parents and teachers faced with a difficult dilemma. The truth is that he *will* grow out of it, but *only* if he's given the proper support and nurturance at home and at school.

The Importance of Faith

Trust that your child really will learn in his own time. Because late bloomers do not bloom at the age or time they are supposed to, doubt may creep into the minds of the gardeners/parents that their children will never bloom. Parents need to have an almost sacred faith in the processes of life and growth, especially when they feel anxiety, frustration, or intense impatience because their late-blooming children are not developing according to their standard of progress.

You wouldn't sit in front of a plant and get angry at it for not growing faster. So why do the same thing to a human being? To parents who truly despair, I offer this wonderful little passage from the Sufi musician Hazrat Inayat Khan: "And when a person says, 'Oh I have waited and waited and waited but my ship never comes' he is keeping his ship back, . . . But the one who does not even see the ship but says 'It is coming, it is coming' is calling it and it will come." Remember from the last chapter how important our hidden expectations can be to a child's growth.

Give yourself a period of time during which you will make a commitment not to be overly concerned about your child's academic progress. You can determine this time span according to your own desires, but I suggest you make it as broad as possible, extending to at least age eight and better yet to age nine or ten. Then, if your child still hasn't learned to read, write, spell, or do math in spite of your best efforts to gently support and nurture the process, you can begin to worry. All too often, parents push the panic button much too early, when their children reach age six or seven—and sometimes even earlier. Louise Bates Ames wrote of one child whose parents brought him to the Gesell Institute because they were worried he might be learning disabled. Their belief was based on the fact that the little chap wasn't so good at writing his letters and numbers. He had just turned four years old!

Recognizing a Blossom When You See One

Think of late blooming in broader terms than just reading, writing, and arithmetic. People like A. S. Neill's Jack, who don't learn to read until adulthood, do bloom—but not necessarily academically. Some parents may need to stop equating blooming with success in the 3 Rs. For a few children, especially kids who are highly developed in bodily-kinesthetic and/or spatial intelligence, blooming in life may have more to do with achieving success in artistic, mechanical, or athletic areas. Blooming also may involve learning to acquire the 3 Rs in alternative ways. The child who has problems with arithmetic may learn to use a calculator. The nonreader may learn to use a tape recorder, typewriter, or computer. Norman and Margaret Silberberg have suggested that schools set up a "bookless curriculum" for these kids. By establishing a different criterion to define blooming, we can make it easier for certain children to grow and develop along the pathways that are most in tune with their inner capabilities.

Provide models of late blooming for your child. If your child is young, read her *Leo the Latebloomer,* a charming story about a little lion who came into his own after a long period of waiting. Older children might enjoy hearing about famous people who bloomed late, including Albert Einstein, Thomas Edison, and Winston Churchill. Adolescents could perhaps relate better to contemporary celebrities such as Cher, Bruce Jenner, and Tom Cruise—individuals who achieved success in a certain field yet had great difficulty with academic skills.

Respecting the Garden of Childhood

Provide your child with plenty of opportunities to enjoy childhood. Reading, writing, math, and other abstract activities hurry kids out of the garden of childhood with its carefree games, wonderful imaginative life, and spontaneous play. Several books, including David Elkind's *The Hurried Child,* Marie Winn's *Children without Childhood,* and Neil Postman's *The Disappearance of Childhood,* suggest that we're rushing children prematurely into the tasks and responsibilities of adulthood. Anthropologist Ashley Montagu observed in his book *Growing Young* that it may be to our advantage biologically to retain as much of our youth as possible into adulthood. As long as late-blooming children aren't going to be reading early anyway, you might as well let them enjoy these golden days while they last. Don't schedule lots of readiness activities for them. Let them choose their activities themselves but provide them with the right environmental supports: playgrounds, nature experiences, art supplies, puppets and costumes, and toys and games of all kinds. They will often instinctively be drawn to the materials that help them prepare for the skills of literacy.

Realize that a child's natural course of development does not follow a predictably even path. Children typically grow in fits and spurts, through periods of stagnation and periods of discovery, times of flare-up and times of quietude. Our schools generally do not provide environments that are sensitive to the ups and downs of growth. Schools tend to identify children as problem learners when they are in their "down" times—intervening in such a way that they are identified for many years to come on the basis of what might more likely have been a fleeting phase in the entire pattern of their development. If your child happens to be in a valley right now, it's entirely possible that a mountain is just around the corner.

Even if your child is an "on-time bloomer" or an "early bloomer," you still should be concerned about the current educational trend to push children prematurely into academic learning. Such early pressures on children to achieve may cause stresses that can result in emotional or physical problems later on down the line. In *The Hurried Child,* David Elkind describes the fate of gifted children pushed beyond their limits at too early an age, only to burn out before they even reach adulthood. This doesn't mean that if your child eagerly takes to reading as a four-year-old you should be alarmed and hide the books. I once asked progressive educator John Holt what he thought about Rudolf Steiner's belief that children shouldn't read until they're at least seven, and he emphatically replied: "Children should read when they want to." The important word here is when *they* want to, not when *you* want them to. If reading, writing, and math skills come out of a child's own exhuberance about learning, then it's clearly time for him to bloom academically. However, what we see happening across the country with current attempts at early education looks too often like parents and teachers attempting to foist academic learning on children because of their own concerns about keeping up with the Joneses or enhancing their prestige as super-parents. Children become victims of our own self-importance when we push them in this way.

Finally, I want to repeat that you not simply throw up your hands and say "Okay, I'll leave my child alone until he's seven years old." In the chapter on relationships, I pointed out how you are *always* educating your child, whether you know it or not. It's extremely important for parents to provide *appropriate* learning experiences for their children based on their interests and needs. During the first seven years of life that especially means lots of opportunities to engage in sensory exploration. In the next chapter, we'll examine how the education of the senses should provide the basis not only for learning during the first seven years of life but also for much of a child's formal academic learning during the years that follow.

The Doors of Perception

Helping Children Come Back to Their Senses

Part of the two-year-old's passionate "Whazzat, Mamma?" is the desire to have his experience verified. This reality check with parents occurs throughout childhood ... If the child asks for a name and, for whatever reason, does not get it, the child senses that the parent does not share that experience or give it sanction. The concept of that event will not be filled in; it will remain shallow and eventually disappear. Selective inattention results.

JOSEPH CHILTON PEARCE,
Magical Child

The senses pervade our lives just as they permeate our language: "Can you *hear* what I'm trying to say?" "I *see* what you mean . . ." "Let me *touch* on that issue for a moment . . ." "I can almost *taste* victory." "He's trying to *sniff* out the competition." In fact, the senses serve as the bedrock of our entire existence. As adults, our feelings and ideas often seem far away from the sensory world, yet if we traced the origins of thought back far enough, as Piaget and others have done, we would come back to the senses as the raw material of far more complex forms of consciousness.

For the infant, the senses are everything. Unlike the interior world of the adult, whose hours are filled with subjective ramblings, each moment of an infant's life is lived on the outside, as it were, in direct contact with the textures, timbres, and tessellations of the sensual world. Learning takes place in the midst of this perceptual universe. Only by seeing, touching, tasting, smelling, and hearing the objects of the external world can the infant construct a model of reality that will serve as a basis for more abstract learning later on in life.

The Unified Senses Theory

Most children before the age of five or six do not experience five clearly distinct senses. Instead, the senses tend to flow into each other. This phenomenon—known as *synaesthesia*—is far more common in childhood than is currently believed. Heinz Werner, one of the country's pioneering developmental psychologists, suggested that "instances of synaesthesia can be found in almost any carefully written diary of observations on child behavior." He offers examples, including a six-year-old's description of "light and dark-red whistling" and the "gold and silver striking of the hour." This mixing of the senses drops off considerably as children grow older, with one study measuring about 13 percent of an adult population to be gifted with chromatism—or color hearing—whereas 50 percent of children measured had this capacity.

The senses also appear to be highly fused to feeling and dynamic action in the young child. Werner called this form of holistic sensory experience *physiognomic perception*. He wrote: "All of us, at some time or other, have had this experience. A landscape, for instance, may be seen suddenly in immediacy as expressing a certain mood—it may be gay or melancholy or pensive. This mode of perception differs radically from the more everyday perception in which things are known according to their 'geometrical-technical,' matter-of-fact qualities." He illustrated this form of perception by citing the case of a boy who at two and a half years of age called a towel hook a "cruel thing" and at three and a half years old thought that the number 5 looked "mean" while the number 4 appeared to be "soft." A four-year-old girl, upon seeing some cards on which certain angular pictures were drawn, exclaimed, "Ugh! What a lot of prickles and thorns!" and refused to pick up the cards, fearing she would be injured by them. The world to young children is alive with vital energy, purpose, and drive. As children grow up, they usually abandon this rich sensory experience. Adults begin to give children labels for things, and the verbal name of an object overshadows its vivid perceptual immediacy. Parents caution, "Don't touch," "Don't stare," "Don't be an eavesdropper," and in other ways discourage children's highly active sensory exploration. Teachers focus greatest attention in school on pure auditory and visual information, while providing few opportunities for smelling, tasting, touching, or experimenting in ways that combine all of the senses.

Most children silently submit to this socialization process. Five distinct senses emerge after a few years that operate in isolation from emotion and physical action. Children learn to emphasize hearing and seeing over feeling, touching, smelling, and tasting. They are forced to confront a world of abstract symbols and learn how to accommodate their blunted perceptual organs to these new requirements.

Some children don't make this transition quite as easily. Children with unique combinations of their multiple intelligences often perceive the world in multisensory, synaesthetic, or physiognomic ways. Their sensory apparatus hasn't fragmented into separate perceptual channels. You may recall Billy from chapter 1, who described his thought processes as a combination of music and architecture, or the boy at the beginning of chapter 6 who needed to move and listen at the same time. Actually, each and every child has his or her own unique perceptual style. Regardless of the specific pattern, most youngsters' senses are organized in ways different from the expectations of society, and often parents or teachers don't have a clear idea of how to reach and teach them in their own way.

Sacrificial Lambs: Giving Away One's Ears and Eyes

As a result of their unique sensory capacities, some children get diagnosed as having special learning and attention disorders. Neurologists, psychologists, and special educators create "learning sicknesses" for them ("dyslexia," "learning disabilities," "attention deficit hyperactivity disorder," and so on). These kids are supposed to be seeing twisted symbols, backward letters, and have attention spans that can't be controlled. The reality is that most of these children perceive the world just fine—*from their own point of view.* What trips them up is the collision of their personal way of looking at the world with the expectations that others have about how they are to see and attend to the world.

What people call a learning disability or attention deficit might really be more of a *perceptual mismatch.* This idea occurred to me when I was reading about an experiment in R. L. Gregory's classic book on perception, *Eye and Brain.* In this experiment, a subject was instructed to complete a tracing task—staying within the boundaries of a double-lined star—and to write several words. In the first trial, he simply did the tasks normally. In the second trial, he did the tasks with his writing hand obscured so that he could only see what he was doing by looking at a television monitor. In the final trial, the television was tape delayed so that there was a half-second interval between writing and seeing what was written on the monitor.

In the first two trials, performance was more or less satisfactory. In the final trial, however, the performance was virtually illegible—looking very much like the work of a person labeled as a severe dyslexic. This experiment beautifully illustrates the internal state of many individuals labeled learning disabled or ADHD. Like the subject in the experiment, so-called learning disabled or ADHD people experience a conflict between two situations—their own immediate experience and one imposed from without. Caught between the two, a severe perceptual dissonance results, and performance and attention disintegrates.

Many children with unique combinations of multiple intelligences encounter a similar situation. They enter school only to find that their original perceptions about things are not acknowledged or accepted, and they soon learn to mistrust them. In their efforts to adjust to the demands of a traditional curriculum, they give away their eyes, ears, and mind to parents and teachers who they feel know more than they do. Yet their sacrifice ultimately works against them when they confront a persistent gap between what they actually see and hear and what others tell them they must perceive. This conflict creates anxiety—or perhaps it would be better to say that this conflict *is* the anxiety—and it results in the chaos that specialists regard as the warning signs of hidden learning disability or attention deficit disorder.

School stress may be responsible for many learning and attention problems affecting children nationwide. We now know that stress has a major impact on the senses—dulling and distorting them in many ways. Ray Gottlieb, a California optometrist and psychologist, suggests that "a major cause of nearsightedness and other visual problems is the tension generated by current methods of education." He cites a Connecticut study where myopia was reduced by 50 percent when multisensory education and anxiety reduction techniques were used in classrooms. Helmer Myklebust, a well-known authority on the role of hearing in learning, points to what he calls "psychic deafness" in certain children, stemming from emotional trauma. In each case, demands placed upon children that are beyond their control serve to distort perceptual abilities that are crucial to academic success.

It's rather easy to create learning disabilities or attention deficit disorder in a whole population of schoolchildren by establishing a conflict between perception and expectation. This was actually done when an instructor asked a group of elementary schoolchildren to make paper airplanes as a part of an experiment. Everyone got to work and after ten minutes of intense activity made many different kinds of planes—all working just fine. Then the instructor asked them to put their planes away and to follow *his* directions. He led them through a step-by-step method for creating a paper airplane. After a few minutes, most of the class was totally confused, and the floor was littered with botched attempts at plane making. In this experiment, children were presented with an official version of doing something that conflicted with their own personal knowledge. The result was frustration and failure. Tim Gallwey, author of several books on peak performance in sports, puts it more succinctly: "The more 'how-to-do-it' a learner receives, the likelier he is to get in his own way."

Beyond Short Circuits and Crossed Wires: Some Guidelines

Children must be allowed to experience their *own* perceptions—not someone else's expectations for how they are to perceive—in order to fully realize their true potential. Parents and teachers should put aside much of the foolishness they've heard about learning disabilities or ADHD and their relationship to short circuits, crossed wires, and malfunctioning neurological pathways. It equates kids with machines and reminds me of the science cartoons I used to watch as a child that showed a little man inside the brain at a switchboard controlling all the nerve impulses and brain functions.

The human brain is far more flexible, adaptable, and complex than these elementary models lead us to believe. Even more important than human neurology is the human spirit—that part of our being that Arthur Koestler called "the ghost in the machine"—which has suffered neglect in all the hue and cry about remediation of learning and attention problems. Each child is a human being with a unique set of perceptions about the world. If we're ever going to help kids find their own competencies, we must start taking their own way of looking at things more seriously. Instead of trying to change them with all the latest remediation techniques, we need to find out more about the sensory world in which they live and then help them to learn according to their own unique perceptions.

Education Through All the Senses

Provide your child with plenty of opportunities for multisensory learning. Children are in their element when surrounded by things they can simultaneously hear, see, touch, taste, and smell. Maureen Murdock, a California therapist and educator, writes: "Some people find, to their great surprise, that they can 'see' an entire page that they were studying if they smell the scent of the flowers present in the room while they were studying. Or a complex math formula may be recalled by its thorny texture!"

Supply your child with brightly colored paper for writing assignments. Buy her scratch-and-sniff books or books with unusually textured paper. Mix up pudding or other creamy foods to use as finger paint in writing words and numbers or help her create letters out of bread dough. Use Cheerios, raisins, or peanuts as counters in doing math. Vicki Cobb's book *Science Experiments You Can Eat* suggests many delicious ways of learning about the properties of the physical world. Act as a "guide" for your blindfolded child during walks in nature where she can attend to the sounds, smells, and textures of the outdoors. Provide a sensory-rich play environment; with optical illusions; smell bottles (little film containers with different scents inside); texture boards (plywood with rug swatches, silk, rubber, felt, and other tactile materials attached to its surface); and sound boxes (sealed boxes with mystery sounds inside). Allow kids to engage in natural multisensory experiences, including cooking, building dams and forts, water play, creative movement, dramatic improvisation, and such tactile art activities as clay sculpting or making three-dimensional collages.

"Mistakes" May Be Misunderstandings

When your child perceives something in a different way than you do, before correcting her, ask her to tell you a little about it. We're so quick to correct children's errors that often their real meaning—reflecting an inner perception of children's personal reality—evades us. It's important to keep in mind that Jean Piaget began his illustrious career as a child researcher in the Paris laboratories of Alfred Binet when he became fascinated with the meaning behind the *errors* children made on early intelligence tests.

An Alabama mother wrote me once about her son's own curious brand of sensory logic: "When Adam was almost three he told his father, 'My cold leg hurts.' His dad asked, 'Is your leg cold?' Adam said, 'No! My cold leg has a scratch on it.' If you don't understand the logic of what he was trying to say, go to the bathroom sink and turn on the cold water. Our bathroom is right by the hot water heater, and it is very important to know which hand turns on which faucet. At times when he can't understand right and left, we use 'hot side' and 'cold side.' He gets it every time."

The mother went on to tell me about her own confusion as a child in school when asked to raise her right hand. She held up her *write* hand (she was lefthanded) and couldn't understand why people laughed at her.

Similarly, when children reverse letters and numbers, there may be an underlying perceptual reason why they do this. John Holt suggested that for many youngsters who reverse, it simply doesn't make any difference which way the letter is pointing. Holt commented: "To be told that a 'backward P' that they have drawn is 'wrong' or that it isn't a P at all, must be very confusing and even frightening. If you can draw a horse, or dog, or cat, or car pointing any way you want, why can't you draw a P or B or E any way you want?" In fact, these kids may be using a perfectly legitimate spatial strategy (where directionality is not crucial to the recognition of an object) to accomplish a linguistic task. Children who reverse letters need to be carefully initiated into the realization that letters are different from pictures. But this can only happen *after* you acknowledge that your child's own perceptions are legitimate. And it certainly doesn't help things to tell them that they do this because they suffer from a special learning or attention disease.

Sensory Obstacles to Learning

Make sure your child is free from specific perceptual impairments that can block his learning. Children who can't see the front of the classroom or hear the teacher's instructions won't learn what is being taught. Symptoms to watch out for include eye rubbing, squinting, looking with one eye, straining to hear, watching the teacher's lips, asking for directions over and over again, and headaches or eye strain after short periods of reading. If you suspect that your child may have minor hearing or seeing problems affecting his or her school performance, consult with your family physician or a qualified optometrist or audiologist to have him evaluated. Sometimes eyeglasses or a hearing aid will correct the problem.

Often the problem may be more subtle, involving choppy eye movements that make it hard for a child to follow words across a page, or hearing loss at specific frequencies that affects his ability to tell the difference between certain sounds in language—for example, "bit" and "bet." Behavioral optometrists can help eliminate some visual problems through the use of specially designed optical training exercises that coordinate and relax eye muscles. Audiologists or speech and language therapists can engage children in activities designed to increase their sensitivity to subtle auditory changes in the language.

Here are some simple exercises that your child can do at home to unblock and de-stress the senses for academic learning. To help his eyes focus and move quickly across a printed page, have him select an old book or magazine and, beginning at the top of the page, circle or color in all the "o"s (or three-letter words, letters with stems pointing downward, capital letters, or words beginning with "m") *in order* for a specific period of time—let's say, three minutes. When doing this activity—or when reading for meaning at any time—allow him to use his finger or a pencil to follow words across the page. Some parents and teachers still think that "word pointing" is a bad thing, but speed-reading teachers will tell you that the use of the finger to guide the eye—with the finger always moving faster than the eye—is a key to rapid reading.

If your child experiences fatigue after reading, have him do the following exercise to relax his eyes.

Palming
- Take off glasses, hats, or other obstructions around the eyes.
- Sit upright in a straight-backed chair with relaxed posture and a straight spine and neck.
- Rub your hands together until they are warm.
- Cup the palms of your hands and place one over each eye, palms inward, so that the heels of your palms touch your cheekbones. *Do not press or rub up against the eyes at any time.*
- Close your eyes and begin gently massaging the muscles around your eyes. Use a table as a support for your elbows if your arms get tired. Feel the spaces behind and around your eyes getting loose and relaxed. Let your jaw and shoulders drop a bit as you relax them, too.
- When you feel ready to stop, open your eyes slowly and continue to feel the relaxation in and around your eyes as you return to your reading.

To heighten auditory awareness, read passages that have unusual sound patterns or changes in inflection, including nonsense poetry by Lewis Carroll, Ogden Nash, and Shel Silverstein. Bill Martin's *Sounds of Language* is an excellent reading series that focuses on playfulness with the auditory patterns of language.

Work out auditory codes for communicating messages around the house. For example, three long whistles might mean come to dinner, or a short whistle and a long whistle could indicate time for bed. Turn off the television and suggest that your child listen to the radio, or tell stories and sing songs together as a family. Each of these activities will help your child become more sensitive to the auditory dimensions of language.

Whatever means you choose to use in enriching your child's sensory world, it's important to keep in mind that you aren't trying to *change* the way in which he perceives, but to help him use the sensory abilities he already possesses in a way that helps rather than hinders him. Too many children suffer from learning frustration not because of their own sensory dysfunction, but because inappropriate educational methods and cultural influences rip them away from their perceptual roots. When we bring these kids back to their senses, their learning capacities really begin to unfold. Of course, adverse environmental influences sometimes cloud the senses and impair learning. Such factors as improper food, polluted air, and excessive noise may distort sensory information pouring into a child from the outside world. We'll look at the important question of learning ecology in the next chapter.

Chapter

13

The Ecology of Learning

Providing Your Child with a Nurturing Environment

The developing child is a psychosocial and biological entity that requires optimal nourishment for optimal functioning. Nourishment is obviously derived from many sources: these include vision, hearing, touch, movement, companionship, love, and food.

RAY C. WUNDERLICH JR., M.D., AND
DWIGHT K. KALITA, PH.D.

Mrs. Carlson got the news on Thursday. Her son Paul had just gotten his report card—liberally sprinkled with Cs, Ds, and even a couple of Fs. On Friday she received a call from his teacher. Paul was being considered for testing because of his poor performance. During the weekend, Mrs. Carlson thought things over. Why was Paul doing so badly at school? Had she failed him as a parent? Was it his teacher's fault? Did he have a learning disability or ADHD?

The answer may be none of the above. In fact, during the next week, as Mrs. Carlson looked more carefully at Paul's learning environment, she began to get a better picture of why her son might be doing so badly in his schoolwork. On Monday she noticed that Paul only had a donut for breakfast, and she remembered something she'd read about how a protein-poor breakfast can make it harder to pay attention during the day. On Tuesday she kept track of how Paul was spending his after-school hours and realized that television was winning out over homework five hours to one. On Wednesday she visited his classroom and discovered one helpless teacher and thirty-five noisy kids trying to learn in a room with chalk dust everywhere, drab green carpets, and the noise of jets taking off and landing overhead every five minutes—the school was next to the municipal airport. On Thursday Mrs. Carlson took stock of her investigations, and it became very clear to her that the *environment,* as much as anything else, was in need of restructuring if Paul was to be helped in his efforts to become a better learner.

There's been a lot of research undertaken over the last twenty years in the area of the learning ecology, yet the field itself is still relatively unknown in educational circles. While the media frequently report on the influence of nutrition in learning, few parents, teachers, and school administrators seem to be aware of the impact of other ecological factors, such as air, sound, space, and time on attention, motivation, and behavior in educational settings at home and at school. The material on learning ecology presented here applies to all children, but it may be particularly relevant to those youngsters who are experiencing problems in learning or attention at home or in school. Research suggests that some of these children may be highly sensitive to environmental influences that make traditional classroom learning a chore.

What's Eating Johnny Is What Johnny's Eating: The Role of Diet in Learning

My visits to candy stores and fast-food outlets as a youngster were more like pilgrimages to sacred temples than trips to commercial establishments. For many children today this continues to be true. However, certain children can no longer afford to make the journey. The refined carbohydrates, colas, and synthetic substances that go into their bodies when they visit these places affect their ability to concentrate, remember, and behave. With breakfasts of sugar-laden cereals and syrupy pancakes, lunches of white bread and chemically treated meats, and dinners of minimal protein and maximum dessert, home and school environments often do little to improve the situation.

Some children seem to do just fine with whatever goes into their mouths at the table. Other youngsters, however, appear to be biochemically vulnerable—for whatever reason in nature or nurture—and develop any number of symptoms including red, swollen, or baggy eyes; headaches or stomachaches; restless behavior a couple of hours after eating; specific cravings for foods; chronic fatigue; and constant coughing, sneezing, or sniffling. These symptoms can affect school performance by clogging up children's eyes and ears, fogging their brains, and kicking up their bodies' energetic systems to a frenzied pitch or dragging them down to the depths of lethargy. Naturally, you should consult a medical doctor when any of these symptoms persist. However, if no clear-cut medical problem can be detected after a thorough exam, then consider the following possibilities.

Food Allergies

Certain children are allergic to foods they eat every day. In fact, some doctors suggest that allergenic foods are often a person's favorite foods. The most common culprits include wheat, milk, corn, beef, chocolate, cola, eggs, coffee, and tea. In order to determine whether your child is allergic to a given food or set of foods, it's best to work with a medical specialist called a *clinical ecologist.* These doctors help parents set up "elimination diets." Diets of this type remove all potentially offending foods for several days while the doctor observes the child's behavior for signs of improvement. After a time, the doctor systematically reintroduces selected foods into the diet one at a time, with parent and doctor monitoring the child for any sign of a recurrence of the symptoms. Finally, after the doctor identifies the specific food allergies, she sets up a "rotation diet" that allows the child to eat selected foods that he can tolerate. To prevent new allergic reactions from forming, the child is allowed these foods only every few days.

Chemical Additives

While specific foods may trigger problems for certain kids, in other cases it may be what's been put into the food by manufacturers to preserve it, color it, or enhance its flavor. While chemical additives are not new (wine was adulterated back in ancient Greece and Rome), the large-scale processing of food for a whole culture goes back only a few decades. And while the Food and Drug Administration has helped to cut back on some of the nastiest of these industrial ingredients (for example, Red Dye No. 3 has been banned in some foods because of its links to causing cancer in test animals), there are still thousands of other additives that are still out there, some of which may affect the attention, behavior, and learning abilities of a selected group of chemically sensitive kids. The dietary approach that has focused the most attention on this problem is the Feingold Diet. The diet was developed in the 1960s by Dr. Ben Feingold, a San Francisco Bay area allergist who saw improvement in many of the hyperactive children in his practice when they were placed on a diet free of artificial flavorings, synthetic dyes, and three preservatives (BHA, BHT, and TBHQ), as well as foods containing naturally occurring salicylates (for example, apricots, cherries, grapes, oranges, and tomatoes). While the Feingold Diet has come under fire by the food industry (several research studies funded by food groups showed no effectiveness of the diet), there have been several well-designed scientific studies in reputable medical journals showing that the diet can have a dramatic impact on the hyperactive behaviors of certain kids.

Protein-Poor Breakfasts

A third approach to learning ecology that involves food is an intervention that is quite easy to implement compared to the two dietary methods described above. It is simply to make sure that your child has a balanced breakfast—including proteins and carbohydrates—before going off to school. The idea of having a balanced breakfast sounds like good common sense to many people, but for certain kids it may spell the difference between a day of unfocused, erratic behavior and a day of calmness and concentration. In one study done at the George Washington University School of Medicine in Washington, D.C., groups of children labeled "hyperactive" and "nonhyperactive" were given two different kinds of breakfast: a high-carbohydrate breakfast (two slices of toasted and buttered bread) and a high-protein breakfast (two eggs scrambled in butter). Groups were also given, on alternate days, a non-nutritive orange drink sweetened with either aspartame or sucrose. Results indicated that the "hyperactive" group who ate the carbohydrate breakfast and the sugar drink did more poorly on a test of attention span compared to the other kids in the study. However, when they ate the protein meal and the sugar drink, they actually did better on the attention task than even the "nonhyperactive" group. Studies like this emphasize the importance of making sure that your child's breakfast includes a balance of protein (e.g., eggs, milk, yogurt, cheese, beans, etc.) and complex carbohydrates (e.g., cereals, bread, pasta).

Your child may not suffer from food allergies, food additive sensitivities, or vulnerability to protein-poor breakfasts, but you would still do well to ensure a high-quality diet, especially if there are learning or attention problems in the background. That means eliminating candy and colas; substituting whole grains such as brown rice and whole wheat bread; for white rice and white bread; having lots of fresh fruit and vegetables available at breakfast, lunch, and dinner; and providing several high-protein sources every day. Satisfy your child's sweet tooth by giving him desserts prepared with nuts, fruits, and other whole foods.

Room to Move: Space as an Ecological Variable

Perhaps you're familiar with scientific experiments on crowding where animals were packed together in a small space for a long period of time. These environments appeared to increase aggression, distress, and disease among the animals. We can draw some parallels with human populations—in this case, children in school. As Carole S. Weinstein, assistant professor of education at Rutgers, aptly put it some years ago: "Nowhere else [but in schools] are large groups of individuals packed so closely together for so many hours, yet expected to perform at peak efficiency on difficult learning tasks and to interact harmoniously." Weinstein's research revealed a number of factors associated with density in the learning place, including nervousness, less social interaction, increased aggressiveness, and dissatisfaction.

It could be that these crowded learning conditions have more than a little to do with our recent epidemic of children diagnosed with attention deficit disorder and learning disabilities. The traditional elementary school is a masterpiece of architectural boredom: rectangular blackboards and bulletin boards surround straight rows of desks. This bureaucratic and bland environment sets the tone for the kind of minds that inhabit its spaces. Most youngsters willingly comply with this unnatural order of things, but a few either cannot or will not follow along. These are often the highly bodily-kinesthetic learners in class who need to move their bodies, touch things, and dynamically interact with the spaces they inhabit. In a static and linear classroom, kids with proclivities in bodily-kinesthetic intelligence all too often end up being physically frustrated and exhibit hyperactive or aggressive behaviors. At home, too, many of these kids find themselves in environments where they have no space they can really call their own. There's simply no place for running, climbing, jumping, playing, or in other ways using space in creative ways. The most successful classrooms and home learning environments have a number of spatial alternatives to allow for a broad spectrum of activity levels and styles, including open spaces for creative movement, physical games, and vigorous exercise; solo spaces where kids can go for privacy; and social spaces for interpersonal interaction, game playing, and group projects.

Making Time for Learning: The Temporal Factor

Children experience time in a different way than adults. Jean Piaget and his colleagues observed that for the child age seven and younger, time passes much more slowly than for older people. A day is an eternity in the lives of young children, filled to the brim with activity and not segmented into minutes or hours. For some, this way of experiencing time persists past seven years of age. These youngsters have a lot of trouble fitting into a school environment where time is divided up into forty-minute periods, punctuated by a ringing bell. Many of them just start warming up to an activity when the period ends and it's time to move on to something new. They often have trouble remembering homework assignments, not because they're trying to be nasty or have poor memories, but because they operate according to C.S.T. (Children's Standard Time), which is essentially life in the present tense.

Children also have different temporal rhythms. The new field of chronopsychology provides us with information about the way in which human beings respond to internal patterns of time, including the daily circadian rhythms that regulate our sleep and waking cycles. We now know there is a biological basis for the common belief that certain people seem to be more active and alert in the morning ("larks"), while others take several hours to warm up and often don't reach their peak until late afternoon or evening ("owls"). The larks of the world have an easy time of it in school because they're all fresh and perky when the teacher is doing most of the instruction. The owls, on the other hand, reach their peak of alertness and concentration after school is out for the day. They may be the ones to end up identified as "tuned-out," underachieving, ADD or ADHD, or learning disabled. We also know that there are ninety-minute cycles of attention in each individual, which alternate between poles of rest and activity.

Pay attention to the time cycles of your child. See if you can identify peaks and valleys in attention during the day. Then build homework periods or other times of focused work around the peaks. If your child is an owl, afternoons or evenings may be the best time for learning. Author and educator Tony Buzan suggests that a study period last no longer than twenty to forty minutes. After forty minutes a person's learning curve begins to decline significantly. If study periods need to last longer than this, they ought to be punctuated by short breaks, perhaps using one of the relaxation exercises suggested in chapter 8. Of course, if children are fully absorbed in an activity, they ought to be allowed to complete it, no matter how long it takes. Maria Montessori described this intense absorption of children as "the great work" and implored educators and parents to leave them alone when they are creatively engaged in this way.

Sound Mind, Sound Body: The Impact of Environmental Noise on Learning

Imagine a girl bent over her homework in the bedroom. Outside you hear her parents quarreling. Inside, a television in the corner blares out the latest sitcom while a radio in the next room thumps in time to a rock beat. Down the street, the jackhammers noisily work on the city streets while trucks, buses, and cars go whizzing by. You wouldn't call this child learning disabled, underachieving, or suffering from attention deficit disorder because she couldn't produce acceptable work in this environment. You'd call her heroic for just trying.

Many children are similarly handicapped at home and school by the noises that surround them twenty-four hours a day. Dr. Sheldon Cohen and his associates at the University of Oregon studied elementary schools near Los Angeles International Airport. They discovered that students in these schools had higher blood pressure and more difficulty solving mathematical problems and logical puzzles than control groups in nonairport areas. These children also were more likely to give up in frustration on school tasks earlier than the control groups.

Become aware of the different levels of background noise at home and at your child's school. Work to filter out harmful or distracting stimuli. At the same time seek to build in harmonious environmental sounds. This is especially true if your home or school is near an airport, a busy traffic intersection, or a noisy factory. Yet, even in a tranquil setting, there are internal noises to contend with—the constant low humming or buzzing of appliances, the activities of family members, the sounds of stereos, TVs, and radios. Where noises can't be eliminated, your child might wear soft foam earplugs available in most drugstores or hearing protectors similar to those used by airport and construction workers. Bring soothing background sounds into the learning environment, including relaxing music, recorded environmental sounds, and white-noise generators. These efforts will provide your child with the "sound barrier" he needs to focus on learning tasks without interruption.

Clearing the Air for a Better Learning Atmosphere

We've learned a lot over the past few years about the negative short- and long-term effects of air pollution on physical health. Less well known is the impact of air pollution on learning. Lead, for example, may be implicated in the failure of some children to learn. Children absorb lead more easily than adults, one reason that lead exposure from crumbling paint chips in old buildings poses such a vicious threat to many children in this country. Smaller quantities of lead enter children's bodies through factory and car emissions and drinking water from leaded pipes. Because children ingest this lead in such minute quantities, its effects are not immediately obvious. Yet one study suggested that lead and other metallic contaminants may be responsible in part for lower cognitive functioning in some children.

Other contaminants, such as tobacco smoke, ozone from smog, asbestos, formaldehyde from walls and insulation, natural gas fumes from ovens and heaters, and outgassing from plastics and synthetic fibers in clothes and furniture can plague a chemically sensitive child, leading to many of the same kinds of symptoms and problems described in the food allergies section of this chapter. Clinical ecologists can test the influence of these factors by eliminating each potentially offending substance from the environment and then systematically reintroducing it while looking for changes in behavior or learning performance.

You may find that you need to create a "chemically free oasis" for an especially sensitive child, setting up a bedroom or study room atmosphere that has hardwood floors or cotton scatter rugs instead of synthetic carpets, unvarnished wood furniture, and natural fabric clothes, pillows, and mattresses. You also may want to introduce an air purifier into your child's principal place of study, especially if there is a smoker in the house or you live in an area near heavy traffic or industrial pollution.

You have less control over air quality in your child's school but should be on the lookout for any obvious sources of pollutants. Check to see that the school has been examined for asbestos and make sure that the art supplies are safe. Legislation in some states has outlawed certain art materials because of their potentially harmful effects on students. Try to determine whether your child is allergic to chalk dust, copier fluid, or other common educational nuisances. Some of these items can be checked by a clinical ecologist. While many of the above suggestions may seem unnecessary or impractical, "clearing the air" could represent one solid way that you can improve your child's learning climate.

Other ecological influences on learning include stress, expectation, and social interaction—factors taken up in earlier chapters. Still other influences remain to be discussed, including temperature and such technological stressors as television, computers, and video games (see my book *The Myth of the A.D.D. Child* for more about high-tech hazards). Your own approach to your child's eco-education will depend upon the unique factors of your environment. Putting together a positive program of environmental change may represent only a small contribution to the ecological problems of the world, but it could make a big difference to your child's learning life, transforming a turned-off or failing student into a happy learner. Isn't it worth a try?

Afterword

The Learner of
the Future

> *All education springs from some image of the future. If the image of the future held by a society is grossly inaccurate, its education system will betray its youth.*
>
> ALVIN TOFFLER

Our public schools still look to the past for solutions to their educational dilemmas even as we pass into the new millennium. Locked within a still-archaic structure, they struggle to make learning relevant to today's youth by leaning on past achievements yet discover to their dismay that millions of youngsters have already moved into the future and left them far behind. The emergence of a new kind of learner has been taking place across the country over the past three decades, and the schools appear to be all but blind to this plain fact. Rather than taking the time to discover something about the phenomenon, the schools choose instead to label millions of these youngsters as disabled learners or ADHD students and ignore the learning potential in millions of others.

Three decades ago Marshall McLuhan pointed out that our culture had moved from a linear, print-oriented mode of learning to an electronic, space-age style where information is available instantaneously to everyone. The schools still operate according to the old orientation, while the child has moved swiftly into the new. McLuhan wrote, "Today's television child is attuned to up-to-the-minute 'adult' news, inflation, rioting, war, taxes, crime . . . and is bewildered when he enters the nineteenth-century environment that still characterizes the educational establishment where information is scarce but ordered and structured by fragmented, classified patterns, subjects and schedules." McLuhan wrote this thirty years ago, but except for the addition of computers in education, his words still ring true in tens of thousands of classrooms across the country. Trapped in an obsolete setting, many children simply tune out.

Today's kids appear to be processing information in a very different way than yesterday's children. Perhaps as a way of coming to grips with the sheer volume of information that enters their lives every day, they've rejected the linear, classifying, and categorizing methods of parents and teachers and embrace instead a learning style based on quick, multisensory scanning strategies. Tony Schwartz, author of *The Responsive Chord,* observed, "The educator would like his students to understand fully something they see or hear, and not miss any information. In an age of information overload, this is a death warrant. The student must learn to scan to live." And many students do scan in the classroom. They scan the walls, the ceiling, their peers, their imagination— anything but the lesson at hand!

It's ironic that the youngsters who appear to be most suited to the new demands of information overload could well be the so-called learning disabled or attention deficit disordered. Many kids labeled ADHD possess a sort of "hyper-mind" that is actually being emulated by "hypertext" formats in computer software and the Internet. "Dyslexics are the wave of the future," proclaims Charles Drake, headmaster of the Landmark School in Prides Crossing, Massachusetts. Drake points out that as the requirements of society become increasingly complex, "the world's going to demand people who see relationships and who have problem-solving potential." We saw in the first chapter of this book how many so-called learning disabled kids possess superior creative and visualization abilities. Norman Geschwind wrote: "There have been in recent years an increasing number of studies that have pointed out that many dyslexics have superior talents in certain areas of nonverbal skill, such as art, architecture, engineering, and athletics." Other studies suggest that many of these kids process information holistically. They see the whole more than the parts.

These global abilities are sorely needed in today's society. It's said that there are 500,000 scientists worldwide working on weapons production. These scientists possess well-articulated and highly developed skills. They are products of some of the finest schools. However, even as they work intently on the technical requirements of their craft, they appear to be oblivious to the deeper consequences of their collective actions—the potential destruction of the planet. They see the parts but not the entire picture.

With so many other problems besetting humankind—pollution, racism, poverty, disease, and overpopulation among the most pressing—we need citizens who have vision, integrity, intuition, flexibility, creativity, and wisdom, not simply people who are good with numbers, words, and logic. Tragically, the schools may be writing off many children as school failures, underachievers, or disabled learners who possess these badly needed qualities. These youngsters may be the people Jonas Salk called the "evolvers" of the society, the change-agents who do things in a different way—their own way—and, as a result, transform culture.

It's not surprising to look into the past and discover that many of the people who changed the way we live suffered from *schoolitis*. Albert Einstein didn't read until he was eight or nine and Woodrow Wilson until he was nearly eleven. Thomas Edison once said: "I remember I used never to be able to get along at school. . . . I almost decided that I was a dunce." Teachers described Auguste Rodin, the sculptor, as "the worst pupil in school." Friedrich Nietzsche's parents thought he was retarded. Giacomo Puccini, the opera composer, consistently failed examinations. Teachers criticized Marcel Proust for writing disorganized compositions. Amy Lowell, the poet, was an atrocious speller. A thirteen-year-old tried unsuccessfully to teach Ludwig van Beethoven basic arithmetic. Many other great people, transplanted into contemporary society, would also probably have ended up in classes for the learning disabled or attention deficit disordered, including Winston Churchill, Pablo Picasso, Sergey Rachmaninoff, Leonardo da Vinci, Henry Ford, William Butler Yeats, Agatha Christie, Hans Christian Andersen, and Gamal Abdel Nasser. Each of these talented people possessed an ability—scientific, artistic, musical, political, literary—that was irrelevant or even bothersome in a school setting but vital to the betterment of civilization.

In the same way, many children in our culture have abilities that put them at a disadvantage in the classroom but may be just what we need if our planet is to survive. I'm not just talking here about the gifted, the dyslexic, the ADHD, or the learning disabled, but ultimately about each and every child who has something to contribute to society—if only someone would recognize their ability and help them develop it. With schools focusing most of their attention on the good test-taker, the expert fill-in-the-blanker, and the hand-raiser who always has the "right answer," we're left with a situation in which 99.9 percent of the country's natural human resources could go undeveloped. A greater national tragedy could scarcely be envisioned.

But now you know that there are many ways of developing children's potential in and outside of the classroom. You should have a sound grasp of the range of their abilities based on Howard Gardner's theory of multiple intelligences and a good, practical sense of how those abilities can be cultivated. You know now that these abilities can't be forced or speeded up, but they can be gently guided and nurtured. You should have a greater appreciation for the influence of "learning ecology" in children's lives and realize that your own expectations can have a tremendous impact—for good or ill—on their learning potential. You know that you have several options for schooling children. Finally, you've seen, in spite of the gross malpractice of many public and private schools, the existence of numerous positive efforts among parents and teachers across the country to improve the conditions for learning among our children.

The Resources section that follows provides a wealth of materials that will help you implement some of this book's suggestions. Using these resources, you can construct inviting programs for children that draw upon the spectrum of learning abilities—linguistic, logical-mathematical, spatial, bodily-kinesthetic, musical, interpersonal, intrapersonal, and naturalist. By creating an environment tailor-made to their needs, you will help them really begin to learn—perhaps for the first time—in their own way.

A Parent's

Guide to

Multiple

Intelligences

Questions Parents and Teachers
Ask About Multiple Intelligences

The following are some of the most commonly asked questions that parents and teachers raise during my workshops around the country on the theory of multiple intelligences. Obviously, there is much more that could be said in response to each question, but my comments should help to answer some frequent misunderstandings about the model, allay some concerns, and provide parents and teachers with ways to dialogue with individuals who are new to the theory.

Q. *How is the theory of multiple intelligences related to learning styles?*

A. In the early stages of my own understanding about the theory of multiple intelligences, I considered the model to be another learning style model (in fact, the original subtitle to *In Their Own Way* was *Discovering and Encouraging Your Child's Personal Learning Style*). However, I now consider it very different from learning styles. Most learning style theories are concerned with identifying a specific learning style for each person. For example, in the visual/auditory/kinesthetic learning style theory, parents may decide that their child has a "visual learning style." Multiple intelligences theory, however, is not concerned with identifying only one intelligence in a child, since everyone has all eight intelligences. In fact, there is a danger that if parents or teachers label a child as, say, a "spatial learner," that the other intelligences may be neglected and the child may never learn to develop to his or her full potential.

Q. *I'm concerned that if my child gets involved in multiple intelligences at school—drawing, dancing, playing music, and such—that this will take valuable time away from academics, and my child stands to lose in the process. After all, the tests he has to take are mostly linguistic and logical-mathematical—so shouldn't he spend most of his time on these two intelligences to get ready for those tests?*

A. The experiences of schools that have been using multiple intelligences for several years indicate that standardized test scores do not suffer as a result of this new approach to learning. On the contrary, recent research suggests that they improve; see, for example, the book by Linda and Bruce Campbell, *Multiple Intelligences and Student Achievement: Success Stories from Six Schools,* or visit the website of Harvard Project Zero (http://www.pz.harvard. edu./SUMIT/OUTCOMES.HTM.) to see the results of an analysis of over forty schools using multiple intelligences theory in their curriculum: "Project SUMIT "Outcomes."

The reason that so many schools using multiple intelligences improve in their test scores is, I believe, due to the fact that students now have many more ways to process information than in a traditional school setting. Instead of just a math formula or some verbal memories to rely on in the testing room, students have a variety of multiple intelligences test-taking strategies to draw upon, including visualization, personal memories related to the curriculum, musical mnemonics, and more. In fact, many students will simply not be able to pass their standardized tests unless they have alternative ways of learning that information, and multiple intelligences provide a rich collection of new learning strategies to help them.

Q. *I have another question about tests in the schools. Aren't teachers really sending students a double message if they spend lots of time during the semester doing multiple intelligences activities, and then at the end of the term say to the students: "Okay, we had a lot of fun this year, but now get out your number two pencil and let's find out what you really know on this standardized test!"*

A. Yes. As I've pointed out in chapter 3, standardized testing and other formal tests have done much to paralyze real learning in the schools. Giving students standardized tests after a multiple intelligences curriculum sends the wrong message to them about what parents and teachers value (e.g., that test results are more important than the nontestable discoveries the student made during the term). That's why it's very important for teachers to develop multiple intelligences assessments, which give kids an opportunity to tell us what they know about the curriculum through the different intelligences. A students may not be able to tell us what he knows about the Civil War, for example, through a paper-and-pencil test but could do so if he could create a miniature three-dimensional battlefield with tiny soldiers and show the movements of soldiers during the war. Such an approach may be more time consuming, but it is far more rich a source of assessment information than a computer printout. See my book *Multiple Intelligences in the Classroom* for ways to structure these new kinds of assessments (available at www.ascd.org).

Q. *How did you come up with the eight intelligences for this book?*

A. I didn't actually come up with the eight intelligences. The theory is the creation of Dr. Howard Gardner, a professor of education at Harvard University. Dr. Gardner applied a set of very specific criteria to a number of candidate intelligences, and the eight described in this book were the only ones that consistently met the criteria. Briefly, the criteria includes the following:

- *Each intelligence can be symbolized in some way.* For example, linguistic intelligence can be symbolized through words, musical intelligence through musical notation, and spatial intelligence through color, form, line, and shape. Dr. Gardner says that humanity's ability to symbolize (to represent things that are not immediately present to the senses through a mark on a page, a speech sound, a gesture, and so on) is a true indicator of what it means to be intelligent.

- *Each intelligence relates to certain areas of the brain.* For example, spatial intelligence is linked to areas at the back of the head (the occipital lobe), while inter- and intrapersonal intelligences are related more to the frontal lobes of the brain. Musical intelligence tends to be associated more with the right hemisphere of the brain, while linguistic intelligence is generally more of a left-hemisphere activity. These observations help explain why a person can have a stroke in a linguistic area of the brain and have their speaking or writing ability damaged yet still be able to sing or draw (since the musical or spatial areas may have been unaffected by the stroke). This new model for how the brain works helps us better understand the variations that exist between intelligences in each person.

- *Each intelligence has examples of exceptional people who show high levels of ability.* We can look at examples of eminent people from history to show what Dr. Gardner calls the "end-states" (the highest levels of achievement) in any given intelligence. For example, for linguistic intelligence we might cite Shakespeare, for logical-mathematical intelligence, Einstein, and so forth. Dr. Gardner also suggests that there are certain exceptional individuals who show great ability in one intelligence but are severely underdeveloped in most of the others. These individuals have been called "savants." A well-known example is the character of Raymond in the movie *Rain Man*, who was a logical-mathematical savant. There are also individuals who might be considered "mentally retarded" or "developmentally challenged" yet can draw incredibly well, sing opera in twenty-five languages, or read encyclopedias. Multiple intelligences help explain how this is possible.

- *Each intelligence can be traced back to the early history of humanity (e.g., Stone Age) and to other species.* For example, we can see evidence of early spatial intelligence in the cave drawings of prehistoric man, interpersonal intelligence in the evidence of social organization in Paleolithic ruins, and logical-

mathematical intelligence in the precise astronomical placement of the rocks at Stonehenge. In other species, we see musical intelligence in bird song, spatial intelligence in the way
in which bees go about building hives, and interpersonal intelligence in the bonding and attachment behaviors of a baby
chimpanzee to his mother. The bottom line of these observations is that these intelligences weren't just invented by
Howard Gardner twenty years ago, but have been around for
a very long time.

There are a number of other criteria. To read about Dr. Gardner's
use of these criteria, see his *Frames of Mind*, pp. 59–70.

Q. *Are there any other intelligences waiting in the wings to be incorporated
into this model?*

A. Recently, Dr. Gardner added an eighth intelligence to his original list of seven—the naturalist—which has met his criteria as
described above. This intelligence has been incorporated into
the body of this revised edition of *In Their Own Way*. He also has
been considering a possible ninth—the existential—or the intelligence of concern with ultimate life issues (e.g., life, death, jus-
tice, truth). This would be the intelligence of the theologian, the
monk, the imam, the rabbi, the scientist or artist working with major life themes, or other individuals who are grappling with life's
big questions. However, as of this writing, Dr. Gardner has not included it in his list, and so as of this date (2000) there are only
eight intelligences in the model.

Q. *Aren't qualities like creativity, intuition, and humor intelligences?*

A. Many people have considered these possibilities, but it remains to explore how these qualities meet Gardner's specific criteria as described above. For example, are there specific areas of
the brain that are tied directly to creativity or to intuition? Thus
far, the evidence is not very supportive. Dr. Gardner has suggested
that qualities like creativity, for example, are intelligence-specific.

That is, a scientist may be highly creative logically but not show that creativity in working with words. Similarly, a cartoonist might be very humorous in his or her drawings, but not when she tries to perform a stand-up comedy routine that demands more linguistic competence. These are certainly highly important qualities and deserve to be nurtured in our children and in ourselves. However, they appear to require other theories or models to account for their functions and benefits.

Q. *I'm a Christian educator, and I'm concerned that multiple intelligences may not be in harmony with my religious beliefs. I don't want to expose my child to something that may be spiritually harmful.*

A. There is nothing in multiple intelligences that Christians, or individuals of any other religious faith or creed, could not find compatible with their own beliefs. The Bible, in fact, is filled with examples of multiple intelligences: in the communal life of the disciples (interpersonal), the elaborate measurements of the Tabernacle of the Hebrew Bible (logical-mathematical), the visually rich teaching parables of the New Testament (spatial-linguistic), the role of music throughout the scriptures, and the physical endurance of many of the prophets.

There is a wonderful passage in Romans 12:6–8 that expresses the essential belief of Paul the Apostle that we all have different gifts given to us in life: "The gifts we possess differ as they are allotted to us by God's grace, and must be exercised accordingly: the gift of inspired utterance, for example, in proportion to a man's faith; or the gift of administration, in administration. A teacher should employ his gift in teaching, and one who has the gift of stirring speech should use it to stir his hearers. If you give to charity, give with all your heart; if you are a leader, exert yourself to lead; if you are helping others in distress, do it cheerfully." Multiple intelligences have been used and applied in many faiths worldwide, from Judaism and Catholicism to Buddhism and Islam. As one religious educator put it: "That's how the Creator made us."

Q. *I'm a member of a minority culture, and I want to make sure that my child receives an education that respects and celebrates his own culture. Can multiple intelligences help me do that?*

A. Yes. One important way you can do this is by sharing with your child role models from your culture who exemplify each of the eight intelligences. Examples from different minority cultures in the United States might include the following:

African American: Toni Morrison (linguistic), Benjamin Banneker (logical-mathematical), Elizabeth Catlett Mora (spatial), Jackie Joyner-Kersee (bodily-kinesthetic), Mahalia Jackson (musical), Martin Luther King, Jr. (interpersonal), Malcolm X (intrapersonal), George Washington Carver (naturalist)

Asian and Polynesian American: Amy Tan (linguistic), Yuan Lee (logical-mathematical), I. M. Pei (spatial), Kristi Yamaguchi (bodily-kinesthetic), Midori (musical), Daniel K. Inouye (interpersonal), Suzuki Roshi (intrapersonal), Nainoa Thompson (naturalist)

Hispanic American: Isabel Allende (linguistic), Luis Alvarez (logical-mathematical), Frida Kahlo (spatial), Roberto Duran (bodily-kinesthetic), Linda Ronstadt (musical), Xavier L. Suarez (interpersonal), Cesar Chavez (intrapersonal), Severo Ochoa (naturalist)

Native American: Vine de Loria (linguistic), Robert Whitman (logical-mathematical), Oscar Howe (spatial), Jim Thorpe (bodily-kinesthetic), Buffy Saint-Marie (musical), Russell Means (interpersonal), Black Elk (intrapersonal), Wilfred Foster Denetclaw, Jr. (naturalist)

When helping your child understand his or her own culture using multiple intelligences, remember that every cultures values *all eight of the intelligences.* The questions to ask about your culture, then, would be: How does my culture value words? (linguistic); how does my culture value numbers and logical systems? (logical-mathematical); how does my culture value pictures and images? (spatial); how does my culture value musical expression (musical); how does my culture value physical expression and skill? (bodily-kinesthetic); how does my culture value social relations? (interpersonal); how does my culture value inner-experience? (intrapersonal); and, finally, how does my culture value nature? (naturalist).

Lesson Plans and Guidelines for Teaching Your Child Anything Through Multiple Intelligences

Whether you're helping your child with homework or simply engaged with your child in a learning activity around the home, there are some simple strategies you can use based on the theory of multiple intelligences that can make the difference between frustration and fulfillment in your child's ability to learn something new. Whatever the topic or skill, here are several ways that you can assist your child in approaching the material using each of the intelligences.

Linguistic: read about it, write about it, talk about it, listen to information about it

Logical-mathematical: quantify it, think logically about it, conceptualize it

Spatial: see it, draw it, visualize it, color it, chart it

Bodily-kinesthetic: build it, act it out, touch it, dance it

Musical: sing it, rap it, listen to it

Interpersonal: teach it to someone else, collaborate with others on it, interact with others with respect to it

Intrapersonal: connect it to your personal life, feelings, or memories; make choices with regard to it

Naturalist: connect it with the natural world in some way

So, for example, if your child is reading a textbook passage about Washington's crossing of the Delaware during the Revolutionary War and not understanding much or caring much about it, here are some strategies you might use to ignite his interest and learning capacity based on the eight intelligences.

Linguistic: Read the passage outloud, taking each sentence or paragraph and individually discussing it. Underline specific key words that assist in understanding the material. Ask your child to explain in his own words what he does and doesn't understand about the material.

Logical-mathematical: Consider questions of number (How many people were in each boat? What were the dimensions of the boats? What would be the maximum capacity of each boat? Did each boat exceed its capacity?). Consider logical strategies (Was Washington smart to attack German mercenaries in the nighttime? What could have gone wrong? What would have been some other approaches?).

Spatial: Show your child a picture of Emanuel Leutze's famous painting *Washington Crossing the Delaware* and talk about it. Have your child draw his or her own picture of the crossing. Have him close his eyes and visualize the crossing.

Bodily-kinesthetic: Act out the crossing of the Delaware in your backyard, using household items as props (for example, a sled might substitute for one of the boats). Pantomime the crossing and the events that occurred along the way. Build a miniature replica of the river crossing (with boats, water, soldiers, etc.). Your child can act out the crossing by manipulating the miniature figures.

Musical: Have your child create sound effects that attempt to replicate what the crossing of the Delaware might have sounded like (e.g., gunfire, water rushing, etc.). Go to the library and find music of the Revolutionary War that might contain information about the crossing (or at least create a musical climate of the times). At the very least, sing "Yankee Doodle Dandy"!

Interpersonal: Set up a study party where your child's classmates can meet together to read and discuss the material. Match your child up with a younger child that he can teach the material to (it will require him to study the material more closely in order to be able to teach it to someone else). Match your child up with an older child (or adult) who can help him understand the material.

Intrapersonal: Ask your child to think about a time in his life when he crossed a river or to consider how *he* would feel if he were in Washington's place (a military general taking a risk).

Naturalist: Ask your child to think about the natural phenomena in the scene (what kinds of trees, horses, ice formations, etc. were part of the scenery). Were horses treated with care? What other animals might have been affected by the crossing (including fish)? What does war in general do ecologically to the landscape?

Naturally, you do not have the time to go through each of these activities (although you can see how the material contained in a textbook can give rise to a wealth of explorations that could well fill an entire semester with fruitful study). Put together what you know about your child's multiple intelligences with the strategies that seem most likely to have a big impact on him. If your child is artistically inclined, then drawing or visualizing the event may make the most sense. If your child enjoys dramatic activity, then role-playing the crossing may be most effective. Don't make the mistake of labeling your child with one kind of intelligence and limiting yourself to only these strategies. Try different strategies over a period of several weeks or months, keeping the ones that seem to work best and dropping the ones that appear to create apathy or active resistance from your child. Here are a few more examples to show you how this works for different topics at different age and grade levels:

Grade Level: Preschool, kindergarten

Topic: Pre-reading (to learn the letter sound "s").

Linguistic: With your child, come up with as many words that begin with the "s" sound as possible. Print and show the words to your child and point out how each has the same letter beginning the word.

Logical-mathematical: Make a game with your child to count the number of times during a given period (say 10 minutes) when she hears a word that has the "s" sound in it (give her a grocery store counter for this purpose or have her mark it down on a piece of paper).

Spatial: Tell a story about a snake (emphasize the "hisssssing" of the snake in the story), and draw a few pictures of the coiled snake for your child. Gradually make the shape of the snake look more and more like the letter S.

Bodily-kinesthetic: Show your child how to create the S shape from coils of clay (or other malleable materials) and together come up with words beginning with the "s" sound as she works.

Musical: Sing a song (or make one up) that has lots of "s" sounds in it.

Interpersonal: With a group of six to eight people, make the shape of the letter S and all together say the sound or say words that have the "s" sound in them.

Intrapersonal: Have your child list her favorite things to do (or favorite foods, favorite animals, favorite toys, etc.) and then discover together which ones begin with the "s" sound and print them on a special list.

Naturalist: Together with your child, look for the S shape in nature (in plants, animals), and whenever you see it, say the "s" sound.

Note: Many of these activities also will work well with other letter sounds.

Grade Level: Second grade

Topic: Geography (learning the names of the seven continents).

Linguistic: Using a map of the world, have your child read the names of the continents on the map and memorize their names.

Logical-mathematical: Have your child rank the seven continents according to different properties (e.g., geographic size, population, etc.) on a chart that he creates.

Spatial: Find (or make) a puzzle of a map of the world that includes each of the seven continents. As your child puts the puzzle together, ask him to say the name of each continent puzzle part.

Bodily-kinesthetic: Using an inflated globe of the world with the continents listed and labeled, throw the ball to your child. When he catches it, he should give the name of the continent on which his left thumb rests (if on a body of water, he simply says "water").

Musical: Collect samples of music indigenous to each of the seven continents (for Antarctica try the sounds of penguins). Then play the samples randomly and ask your child to point on a map to the continent that he believes the music comes from. Alternatively, make up a little song that includes the names of the seven continents.

Interpersonal: Together with your child, find people who have visited each of the seven continents and talk with them about their experiences.

Intrapersonal: After having gotten information about each of the seven continents, ask your child to rate the continents from most favorite to least favorite, letting him give his reasons for the choices.

Naturalist: Use different animals and plants native to each continent as symbols for each of the continents in learning their names (e.g., a kangaroo for Australia, a buffalo for North America, etc.).

Grade Level: Fourth grade

Topic: Grammar, to learn the function of, and differences among four punctuation marks: the question mark (?), period (.), comma (,), and exclamation point (!).

Linguistic: Explain to your child the functions of the different marks and then have your child read sentences with the different punctuation marks in them. Stop at each one and say verbally what mark it is and what function it has in that position in the sentence.

Logical-mathematical: Have your child count the number of punctuation marks in a given reading passage and categorize them by type (e.g., 14 commas, 12 periods, 3 question marks, 1 exclamation mark), and then ask about reasons for the given proportion (for example, Why might there be so many commas and so few exclamation marks? Could this vary according to the type of reading material? And so forth).

Spatial: Create graphic images (or have your child do this) that correspond in meaning and form to each mark (e.g., a question mark might be a hook because questions "hook" us into requiring an answer; an exclamation point might be a staff that you pound on the floor when you want to exclaim something; a period might be a point since you've just made your point; and a comma might be a brake pedal since it requires you to temporarily stop in the middle of a sentence). Then your child can write something using these picture symbols in place of the ordinary ones.

Bodily-kinesthetic: Have your child create a special body posture for each of the punctuation marks. Read something with a variety of different punctuation marks in it and ask your child to put his body into a specific "punctuation posture" each time he thinks a mark is needed in the passage.

Musical: Have your child make up different sounds that mimick the punctuation marks (Victor Borge used to do something like this in his novelty musical acts), and then ask your child to read something and put in the musical punctuation marks as part of his reading.

Interpersonal: With three other friends, suggest that your child and the others each take responsibility for being a specific punctuation mark. While you read a passage with a variety of punctuation marks in it, have each of them jump up from a sitting or lying position whenever their particular punctuation mark is called for in the passage.

Intrapersonal: Have your child write on topics of great personal interest to him using the different punctuation marks; he might write on a question he'd like someone to answer (?), a statement he feels strongly about (!), a fact he'd like other people to know (.), or a list of favorite things (using a string of commas).

Naturalist: Suggest that your child think of animals to represent each of the punctuation marks (e.g., a lion for an exclamation mark because it's so emphatic; a monkey for a question mark because it's always scratching it's head quizzically, etc.). Then, he could act out the different gestures of the animals to represent each punctuation mark when it is called for in a passage that you read.

Grade Level: Seventh grade

Topic: Algebra (to understand the function of "x" in an equation).

Linguistic: Provide a verbal description of x (e.g., "x is an unknown—solve for x in the equation").

Logical-mathematical: Write down an equation (e.g., $2x + 1 = 5$) and show how to solve for x in a step-by-step fashion.

Spatial: Use a visual metaphor to explain the role of x (for example, "x is like a masked outlaw that needs to be unmasked").

Bodily-kinesthetic: Act out the role of being an "unknown" that people have to discover.

Musical: Chant the following musical mnemonic several times:

> *x is a mystery*
> *you've gotta find a way*
> *to get him all alone*
> *to that he's gotta say his name*

Interpersonal: With a group of friends, create a "people equation," with each person representing a different part of the equation and holding up a sign that explains their function (e.g., for 2x + 1 = 5, you might have two people holding signs with "x" on them, a person with a +1 sign, a person with an = sign, and then five people with +1 signs). Then solve the equation (e.g., removing a +1 person from each side of the equation, to create 2x = 4, then taking half of the people away from each side of the equation, leaving x = 2). The people with the x signs might cover their faces with them until the final step when x is revealed to be 2.

Intrapersonal: Mention that "x is an unknown" and ask your child, "What are the unknowns in your own life that you'd like to solve?"

Naturalist: Use (or modify) an example that Einstein's Uncle Jacob used with young Albert: "We go hunting for a little animal whose name we don't know, so we call it x. When we bag our game we pounce on it and give it its right name" (Ronald W. Clark, *Einstein: The Life and Times*, New York: Avon, 1984, pp. 29–30).

- -

Grade Level: Eleventh grade

Topic: Chemistry (to learn the concept of "Boyle's Law").

Linguistic: Provide the verbal definition (for a fixed mass and temperature of gas, the pressure is inversely proportional to the volume) and discuss it with your child.

Logical-mathematical: Provide the equation ($P \times V = K$, where P = pressure, V = volume, and K = a constant) and do some examples (e.g., 4 atm x 2 cm^3 = 8; 2 atm x 4 cm^3 = 8; 1 atm x 8 cm^3 = 8; etc.).

Spatial: Give your child a picture metaphor: "Imagine that you've got a big ugly boil on your hand and you start to squeeze it. The pressure starts to increase. Then you let go a little bit and the pressure goes down. Then you squeeze harder and the pressure goes up, and you keep squeezing harder and harder, and the pressure goes up and up until finally it bursts and pus goes squirting all over the room!" (This image is also designed to stimulate the "emotional brain"!)

Bodily-kinesthetic: Have your child do a little "mouth experiment." "Put some air into your mouth so that it is about half filled up with air—so that your cheeks are a little rubbery. That air is now gas in the chamber of your mouth. Boyle's law says a fixed mass of gas so don't let the air out or swallow it because that would change the mass. Now, take that gas and put it over on one side of your mouth so that it is in a smaller volume. What's happened to the pressure? (Ask your child to point in the right direction; note: it's gone up.) Now, take the gas and put it back in both sides of your mouth so that there's more volume. What's happened to the pressure? (It's gone down). That's Boyle's law!"

Musical: Have your child memorize the following musical mnemonic to a rhythmic beat (perhaps he can put it to a rap beat!):

When the volume goes down
The pressure goes up
The blood starts to boil
And a scream erupts.
I need more space
Or I'm going to frown!
The volume goes up
And the pressure goes down.

Interpersonal: Have five or more people milling around randomly in a delimited area (a hallway works well for this demonstration). These individuals are now molecules of gas in a chamber (the space that they're moving around in). Have two more people on either end begin to enclose the group (thus decreasing the volume of space available for the group's movement). What happens to the pressure? (It increases: the group comes closer and closer together.) Then have the two end people begin to move away from the group, thus increasing the volume available for moving. What happens to the pressure? (It decreases: the group has more space to move.) That's Boyle's Law! (Note: Boyle's law says there must be a fixed mass and temperature of gas. That means that the group cannot leave the "chamber" because that would change the mass, and they must all move at the same rate with respect to each other, since temperature is movement of molecules, and this keeps the temperature of the gas steady.)

Intrapersonal: Ask your child to think of a time in his life when he was under a lot of pressure. Ask him if, during that time, he had lots of psychological "space." (Chances are, he didn't.) Then ask him to think of a time in his life when he was under very little pressure and whether during that time he had lots of psychological space. (He probably did.) So, under lots of pressure he had little space, and under little pressure he had lots of space. That's the "Boyle's Law" of his life!

Naturalist: Suggest that scuba divers are emphatically told never to go down into the ocean, hold their breath, and then go up to the surface. Point out why this is so damaging (high pressure conditions in deep water, expanded lungs from holding the breath; then going up to lower pressure conditions causes, through Boyle's Law, further expansion of volume in the lungs, causing air to go into the blood stream with sometimes fatal consequences).

I've intentionally included examples from middle school and high school (even though much of this book has been designed for parents of elementary-aged children) to make the point that there is nothing in MI theory that prevents it from being used just as comprehensively at the upper levels of education. Too often, parents and educators have the misconception that multiple intelligences activities are for younger children and that, as kids move up the grades, these types of experiences disappear and are replaced with traditional linguistic and logical-mathematical approaches (mainly lectures, worksheets, and textbooks). This may be what in fact happens, but my point is that it needn't happen; that one can take highly sophisticated ideas and concepts and teach them through the different intelligences.

To help you continue the process of thinking of ideas, activities, and strategies for learning about different topics using the eight intelligences, I'd like to suggest that you use the following brainstorming tool. On a blank sheet of paper, put a square in the middle and eight arrows radiating out from the center. Label each arrow with the initials of a different intelligence. It should look something like this:

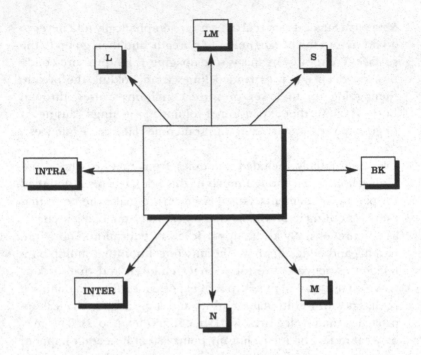

Put in the center box the objective or topic that you'd like to generate multiple intelligences strategies for (e.g., the factors leading to the destruction of the rain forest, multiplication of two-digit numbers, the three states of matter [solid, liquid, gas], writing a topic sentence, etc.). Then ask the following questions to help generate strategies.

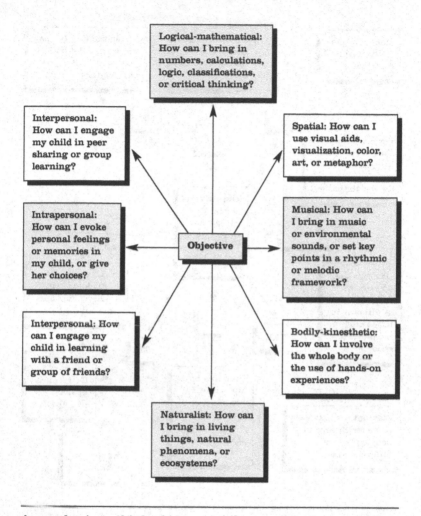

As you begin to think of ideas, put them next to the appropriate intelligence. (Many ideas may use several intelligences; don't worry about where to put it, just put it somewhere on your map.) If you're particularly interpersonally developed, you may find it very helpful to do this activity with some of your own friends (and also involve your child). Eventually, you should be able to come up with fifteen or more activities. Your brainstorming map may look something like this.

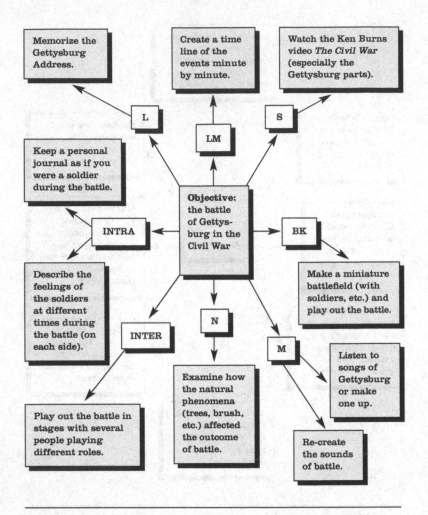

Put down as many ideas as you can think of, even if they seem far-fetched or impractical. You can always throw the ideas out later. After you have at least fifteen to twenty ideas, begin to sort through them and decide which ones might seem most interesting, practical, and effective. Involve your child in the decision making too, since he will be far more involved in activities that he's helped to design and choose. Then try out the ideas. Over time, you'll be able to see which types of activities work best.

Multiple Intelligences and Your Child's School

Unlike Montessori schools, Waldorf schools, or other specialized educational systems, there are no "official" multiple intelligences schools and no accrediting body for certifying that a school using the multiple intelligences approach is following any set of approved standards. Different schools apply multiple intelligences in different ways. The Key Renaissance Learning Community in Indianapolis, Indiana, perhaps the school with the longest-running experience in using multiple intelligences, uses many different kinds of organizational structures to weave MI theory into the curriculum. Teachers develop two themes each year on a variety of topics that engage all the intelligences, including "Journeys," "Heritage," "Working in Harmony" "Inventions," and "Here and Now, in Other Cultures." Students participate in interdisciplinary "pods" (elective classes based on specific areas of interest and intelligences) with names such as "Big Mac Pod" (computers), The Dance Pod, Cinemaniac Pod, and The Key Economists. The Key School assesses student progress using the multiple intelligences as well, having students prepare portfolios of their work through the intelligences and using a special progress report that addresses the eight intelligences. The school also integrates elements of school reform from other educational theorists as well.

Other schools and classrooms around the country that use multiple intelligences may have elements similar to the Key Renaissance Learning Community, but each has its own distinctive qualities. At Cascade Elementary School in Marysville, Washington, teacher Bruce Campbell created special activity centers in his classroom dedicated to specific intelligences. He gave them names based on famous people who excelled in each area including the Mother Teresa Center (interpersonal intelligence), the Emily Dickinson Center (intrapersonal intelligence), the William Shakespeare Center (linguistic intelligence), and the Pablo Picasso Center (spatial intelligence). In the course of a year, students had an opportunity to engage in activities in all the centers (and activities within each center would also change according to the needs of the curriculum). At the Kent Gardens Elementary School in McLean, Virginia, K–6 students flock to a hands-on discovery room called "The Think Tank" for explorations in multiple intelligences. Students develop special projects that draw upon different intelligences (for example, in a project called "Watch the Drop" students created pathways for marbles to drop with PVC tubes on a Velcro backboard, experimenting with logical predictions and spatial design, and relating their findings to other parts of the curriculum).

These are just a few examples of the many ways in which multiple intelligences can be integrated into a school or classroom program. (For a list of schools using multiple intelligences, see pages 219–222.) Dr. Howard Gardner, the originator of the theory of multiple intelligences, has been quoted as saying, "Let one hundred multiple intelligences schools bloom," meaning that there are many ways to take his theory and apply it in various settings. This does not mean, however, that anything goes in an MI school. There are many ways that multiple intelligences can be used in name but misapplied in spirit. A school or classroom might look like a multiple intelligences program, with lots of MI posters, songs, and activities going on, but not really be reaching into the heart of the theory. Here are some misapplications of MI theory and reasons why these approaches are not appropriate for children.

Misapplication: The school or classroom tests kids for their multiple intelligences using paper-and-pencil MI tests and inventories and then labels the kids as "spatial learners," "body-smart learners," or similar terms, and groups them according to their "preferred intelligence."

What's wrong with this: Every child has *all* the intelligences, not just one, and by labeling a child as having only one, that student is limited in her capacity to develop in all eight. Teachers cannot discover a student's multiple intelligences through paper-and-pencil tests. A broad range of assessments are necessary that use words, music, hands-on experiences, social interactions, and more, over a period of time, in order to put together a total picture of a child's multiple intelligences.

Misapplication: The school or classroom has kids filling out all kinds of "multiple intelligences worksheets" during the day that purport to develop all eight of their intelligences.
What's wrong with this: Worksheets cannot develop much of a student's multiple intelligences since they are limited to very specific linguistic skills for the most part. Children should be interacting, singing, building, problem-solving in real situations, and engaging in other rich natural learning contexts.

Misapplication: The school or classroom has kids engaging in generic "multiple intelligences activities," such as swimming around the classroom like fish (to "develop" bodily-kinesthetic intelligence), holding discussions on random topics (to "develop" interpersonal intelligence), engaging in free drawing (to "develop" spatial intelligence), and so on.
What's wrong with this: None of the learning is directed toward any specific educational goals or objectives. The value of multiple intelligences is that it enables teachers and parents to help kids learn more effectively things that are important for them to learn, such as reading skills, math skills, history, geography, science, goal-setting, social skills, and more. A good teacher has in mind in advance what specific objectives he or she wants to achieve (e.g., "to help students understand factors leading to the destruction of coral systems worldwide") and then uses selected multiple intelligences activities to help reach that objective. In this context, using an activity like swimming around the classroom (where the teacher points out various coral formations, students as fish find they cannot obtain food in the destroyed environment, etc.) may

have value. But simply having kids engage in an activity because it somehow seems like it will develop an intelligence is nonsense.

Misapplication: Schools or classrooms have kids sing spelling words, the times tables, and history facts to musical rhythms or "raps" and declare that they are using multiple intelligences.
What's wrong with this: Nothing is specifically wrong with this approach, but it's not enough. Simply to use multiple intelligences to help kids master rote material (or lower-order thinking skills) is not a very deep application of this theory. Also, to use one or two multiple intelligences strategies during a term, and to say that they are using multiple intelligences, is a cop-out. Multiple intelligences should not just be limited to a few teaching tips or tricks but should interpenetrate the entire teaching and learning environment.

When looking for a school that embraces multiple intelligences principles, a parent should look for the same kinds of qualities in the classroom, teachers, and administrators as those outlined earlier in chapter 1. It may be wiser for a parent to choose a school that *doesn't* specifically embrace multiple intelligences but is an exciting learning place, over a school that does call itself an MI school but lacks that vitality. In the broadest sense, multiple intelligences isn't really a new concept. It's what good teachers have always done to help their students succeed in life. Any school that accomplishes this is a multiple intelligences school in spirit even if it doesn't call itself one.

A Few Schools Using MI Theory

The following list is just a few of the more than 500 schools that are implementing multiple intelligences in some way into their school programs in the United States. These schools are not necessarily exclusively multiple intelligences schools (in most cases they implement other school reforms as well) and are not specifically recommended over other schools that might use MI theory.

Briarcliff Elementary School
Briarcliff Rd.
Shoreham, NY 11786-9745

Centennial Elementary School
3306 W. Berry Ave.
Littleton, CO 80123

Champlain Valley Union High School
RR 3, Box 160
Hinesburg, VT 05461

The Claremont School
1537 Washington St.
Bronx, NY 33157

Cloud Elementary School
1205 W. 26th St., N
Wichita, KS 67204

Dover School
3035 Nelson Ave.
Dover, FL 33527

Edgemont Montessori School
20 Edgemont Rd.
Montclair, NJ 07042

Elk Elementary Center
3320 Pennsylvania Ave.
Charleston, WV 25302

EXPO for Excellence Elementary Mofnet School
540 Warwick
St. Paul, MN 55116

Fawcett Center for Year-Round Learning
126 E. 60th St.
Tacoma, WA 98404

Freeman School
120 Filmore St.
Phillipsburg, NJ 08865

Fuller School
4 School House Rd.
Gloucester, MA 01930

Glenridge Elementary
19405 120th Ave., SE
Kent, WA 98058

Governor Bent School
5700 Hendrix Rd., NE
Albuquerque, NM 87110

Jessie Wowk Elementary School
5380 Woodswards Rd.
Richmond, BC
Canada V7E 1H1

Josiah Quincy School
885 Washington St.
Boston, MA 02111

Kennedy Elementary School
Foggintown Rd.
Brewster, NY 10509

Key Renaissance School
222 E. Ohio
Indianapolis, IN 46204

King's Park Elementary School
5400 Harrow Way
Springfield, VA 22151

Liberty Elementary School
1919 Tenth St.
Marysville, WA 98270

Limona School
1115 Telfair Rd.
Brandon, FL 33510

Lincoln High School
6844 Alexandria Place
Stockton, CA 95207

McCleary Elementary School
Holmes St. at McCandless
Pittsburgh, PA 15201

McWayne Elementary School
328 West Wilson St.
Batavia, IL 60510

Madrona Non-Graded K–8 School
9300 236th St.
Edmonds, WA 98020

Moore Alternative School
451 Knollwood St.
Winston-Salem, NC 27103

Mountlake Terrace High School
21801 44th Ave., West
Mountlake Terrace, WA 98043

The New City School
5209 Waterman Ave.
St. Louis, MO 63109

Russell Elementary School
201 West St.
Lexington, KY 40508

Searsport Elementary School
Mortland Rd.
Searsport, ME 04974

Sharon School
4330 Foxcroft Rd.
Charlotte, NC 28111

Skyview Junior High School
21404 35th Ave., SE
Bothell, WA 98201

Southhampton Elementary School
30 Pine St.
Southhampton, NY 11968

Spectrum School
2909 N. Main St.
Rockford, IL 61103

Stanton Elementary School
P.O. Box 367
Appalachia, KY 40380

Tuscan School
225 Harvard Ave.
Maplewood, NJ 07040

Union School
102 East Broadway
Maumee, OH 43537

Valerie Elementary School
4020 Bradwood Rd.
Dayton, OH 45405

West Boylston Middle High School
125 Crescent St.
West Boylston, MA 01583

Wheeler Elementary School
5410 Cynthia Dr.
Louisville, KY 40921

Whitfield Elementary School
2601 Grandview Blvd.
West Lawn, PA 19609

Teaching Your Child About Multiple Intelligences

Probably the most important thing you can do to help nurture your child through multiple intelligences is to teach him or her about the theory. If you teach your child about the eight kinds of intelligences, then they will begin to understand how they learn best. This information will help them for the rest of their lives. If they are in school and having trouble with a reading assignment, for example, instead of thinking, "I'm dumb" or "The teacher hates me!" they can instead think, "I learn best through pictures and images—I need to find some pictures that go along with the material I'm reading to help me understand it better." It also can help them begin to think about career aspirations. A child who realizes that he or she learns best through hands-on experiences or nature experiences may want to begin, for example, to explore careers in mechanics or ecology.

One of the neatest things about this theory is how easy it is to teach to children. I've found that I can go into a second grade classroom and teach a group of students the theory of multiple intelligences in ten minutes (below first grade, kids are likely not to benefit much from actually being taught about the intelligences, though they certainly will be influenced profoundly by being surrounded by the many different ways of learning). Here are some pointers for teaching your child about multiple intelligences:

- *Use simple language.* I've found it useful to change Dr. Gardner's academic-sounding terms for the intelligences to simpler, more direct words that kids can more readily relate to (word smart [linguistic], number smart [logical-mathematical], picture smart [spatial], body smart [bodily-kinesthetic], music smart [musical], people smart [interpersonal], self smart [intra-personal], and nature smart [naturalist]. You might even have your child make up his own words to describe the intelligences (for younger children, sometimes "we smart" [interpersonal intelligence] and "me smart" [intrapersonal intelligence] work best).

- *Relate the intelligences to the child's own world.* When explaining the eight kinds of intelligences, make sure you use examples drawn from your child's experience. Instead of giving a text-book definition ("Linguistics is the ability to process words through oral or written channels"), provide explanations closer to home ("Remember when you made up that funny word yesterday—*biggieboo*—to describe the monster in the story we read? You were very word smart! You were also word smart when you knew many of the words in the book!").

- *Emphasize that your child has all the intelligences.* Some people make the mistake of thinking that a child has only one of the eight intelligences, and then attempt to drill the child on how they are good in that way. ("You know how you love to play basketball? That means you're body smart!") There are many ways to be intelligent in each category, and every child has positive things going on in each area, so be sure as you're go-ing through the eight intelligences with your child to point out aspects of his or her life that relate to each one.

- *Point to role models in your child's life.* Provide your child with ex-amples of famous people they know and admire in each of the eight intelligences or let them tell you who they admire in each area (for example, children's book writers [word smart], scientists or computer people [number smart], children's book illustrators [picture smart], athletes [body smart], musi-cians [music smart], politicians [people smart], entrepre-neurs [self smart], ecologists or nature explorers [naturalist]). This might be an opportunity for you to study the lives of great individuals in each intelligence area. You might even create a display area somewhere in the house with your child that has pictures of his or her heroes and shows which intelligences they display (remember, the heroes will often display *several* intelligences, so mention them all).

- *Visit places where the intelligences are valued.* So that your child can see that these intelligences are not just school-related or somebody's empty theory, go on field trips to places where the intelligences are actively used (for example, a library [word smart], an accountant's office [number smart], a graphic artist's office [picture smart], a sculptor's studio [body smart], a business manager's office [people smart], a counselor's office [self smart], and a park rangers place of work [nature smart]). In this way, your child sees that these intelligences are a vital part of the real world.

- *Use creative ways to present multiple intelligences to your child.* It would be rather hypocritical to say to your child, "There are eight ways of being smart!" and then proceed to use only one of those ways to explain it to him or her (e.g., lecture). Here are some different ways you can present the theory to your child that actually draws upon the different intelligences:

   Songs. Music is a wonderful medium for summarizing all the intelligences in a fun way. Here, for example, is a little song you can sing to the tune of "Frère Jacques" ("Are You Sleeping, Brother John?").

I am smart
I am smart
Eight great ways
Eight great ways
Numbers, words, and pictures
Body, music, people
Self and nature smart
Eight kinds of smart.

Your child may want to make up his own song about the eight kinds of smart (older kids can create raps or put the information into other musical genres).

Stories. You can make up a tale about a group of eight kids, each of whom has a special ability in an intelligence area, who don't get along very well, but who are forced into an adventure that requires them to travel to distant magical lands. In each land, they run into challenges or problems that require the talents of each child in turn. For example, perhaps the children come to a land where, in order to be understood, they have to communicate through singing, so the child with a wonderful singing voice guides them through this land. In another land, they fall into a hole and get out through the help of a child who has the body-smart gift of rock climbing. And so forth. At the end of the story, they are able to accomplish their quest (perhaps to retrieve a golden jewel or something else of great value) because they have cooperatively drawn upon the intelligences of all the kids.

Art activities. You might want to provide a picture symbol for each of the eight intelligences (e.g., the letters "ABC" [word smart], "123" [number smart], some geometric shapes [picture smart], a musical note [music smart], a figure kicking a ball [body smart], two figures shaking hands [people smart], a person working alone [self smart], and a tree [nature smart]). See the "MI Pizza" on page 227 for an example of graphic representations of each intelligence. Once your child learns about the eight intelligences, he or she may want to make up their own picture symbols. Also, as your child begins to learn about the intelligences, invite her to draw pictures of things in each intelligence she especially enjoys.

Gestures and pantomime. Create specific hand signals or mime gestures as bodily-kinesthetic symbols for each of the intelligences (e.g., a talking hand [word smart], fingers displaying "1, 2, 3," in turn [number smart], gesturing drawing or painting [picture smart], pantomiming the act of singing [music smart], two hands "talking to each other" [people smart], a finger pointing to "me" [self smart], making a tree with arched hands [nature smart]). Again, your child can have fun with this activity and may want to express their fa-

MI PIZZA

vorite (and least favorite) intelligences through more active pantomime, role-play, or drama.

Board games or scavenger hunts. Create a list of simple activities that involve the different intelligences (e.g., "Make up a story" [word smart], "Do this math problem: 6 + 9 = __" [number smart], "Draw a picture of a horse [picture smart], "Sing a song" [music smart], "Do a cartwheel" [body smart], "Tell a friend something you like about him" [people smart], "Share something you really like about yourself" [self smart], "Find a bird outside and give its name" [nature smart]). Then make a simple board game with cardboard, magic markers, dice, and miniature figures as game pieces (e.g., something that looks like the game CandyLand, with a long trail). On each square, write the activity and a symbol for which intelligence it belongs to. Then kids take turns shaking the dice, landing on squares and doing the activity involved in order to move up the trail to the winner's circle.

Most important, you can teach your child about the eight intelligences by making sure they are available in some form around the house during the day. As you go about your activities, make sure to point out the intelligences that you are using in everyday life (e.g., while working on paying the bills, you might comment, "Whew! This sure is taking all my number smart today!" or while watching TV, saying "That singer is so very music smart!"). I can't overemphasize how important it is for you to teach your children about the theory of multiple intelligences. Remember the maxim: "Give me a fish and I eat for a day. Teach me to fish and I eat for a lifetime." By teaching your child about the eight kinds of smart, you will indeed provide them with nourishment that will last them for the rest of their lives.

Books for Parents

How to Use This Section

The books and videos listed here are organized according to Gardner's eight types of intelligence and by the following major categories: developmental issues; ecological issues; alternatives to ADD, LD, Ritalin, and labeling; perspectives on creativity and learning; and options in educating children. Many of the books referred to in the text of *In Their Own Way* can be found here. All the books listed are in print as of 2000.

General Resources on Multiple Intelligences

Armstrong, Thomas. *Multiple Intelligences in the Classroom*, 2d ed. Alexandria, VA: Association for Supervision and Curriculum Development, 2000.

Armstrong, Thomas. *Seven Kinds of Smart: Identifying and Developing Your Many Intelligences: Revised and Updated with Information on 2 New Kinds of Smart*. New York: Plume, 1999.

Bower, Bert, Jim Lobdell, and Lee Swensen. *History Alive! Engaging All Learners in the Diverse Classroom*. Menlo Park, CA: Addison Wesley, 1994.

Campbell, Bruce. *The Multiple Intelligences Handbook*. Tucson, AZ: Zephyr Press, 1994.

Campbell, Linda, and Bruce Campbell. *Multiple Intelligences and Student Achievement: Success Stories from Six Schools*. Alexandria, VA: Association for Supervisory and Curriculum Development, 1999.

Campbell, Linda, Bruce Campbell, and Dee Dickinson. *Teaching and Learning through Multiple Intelligences.* Boston: Allyn and Bacon, 1995.

Fogarty, Robin, and Judy Stoehr. *Integrating the Curriculum with Multiple Intelligences.* Palatine, IL: Skylight Publications, 1995.

Gardner, Howard. *Frames of Mind: The Theory of Multiple Intelligences.* New York: Basic Books, 1983.

Gardner, Howard. *Intelligence Reframed: Multiple Intelligences for the Twenty-first Century.* New York: Basic Books, 1999.

Gardner, Howard. *Multiple Intelligences: The Theory in Practice.* New York: Basic Books, 1993.

Haggerty, Brian. *Nurturing Intelligences.* Menlo Park, CA: Addison Wesley, 1994.

Lazear, David. *Seven Ways of Knowing: Teaching for Multiple Intelligences.* Palatine, IL: Skylight Publications, 1991.

New City School. *Celebrating Multiple Intelligences* (order from New City School, 5209 Waterman Avenue, St. Louis, MO 63108).

"Teaching for Multiple Intelligences," Special issue of *Educational Leadership,* September 1997 (periodical available through the Association for Supervision and Curriculum Development, 1-800-933-2723).

Wahl, Mark. *Math for Humans: Teaching Math through Seven Intelligences.* Langley, WA: LivnLern Press, 1997 (416 Fourth Street, Langley, WA 98260).

Linguistic Intelligence

Ashton-Warner, Sylvia. *Teacher.* New York: Simon & Schuster, 1986. The "organic method" for teaching reading using a child's oral language.

Calkins, Lucy McCormick. *Lessons from a Child: On the Teaching and Learning of Writing.* Portsmouth, NH: Heinemann, 1983.

Koch, Kenneth. *Wishes, Lies and Dreams: Teaching Children to Write Poetry.* New York: Harper & Row, 1980.

McGuire, Jack. *Creative Storytelling: Choosing, Inventing and Sharing Tales for Children.* New York: McGraw-Hill, 1985.

Rico, Gabriel. *Writing the Natural Way.* New York: Tarcher Putnam, 2000.

Smith, Frank. *Insult to Intelligence: The Bureaucratic Invasion of Our Classrooms.* Portsmouth, NH: Heinemann, 1988.

Trelease, Jim. *The Read Aloud Handbook* 4th ed. New York: Viking Penguin, 1995. Suggests that reading is learned in the lap of a trusted adult.

Zahler, Kathy A. *50 Simple Things You Can Do to Raise a Child Who Loves to Read.* Foster City, CA: IDG Books Worldwide, 2000.

Zavatsky, Bill, and Ron Padgett, eds. *The Whole Word Catalogue 2: A Unique Collection of Ideas & Materials to Stimulate Creativity in the Classroom.* New York: Teachers and Writers Collaborative, 1987.

Logical-Mathematical Intelligence

Baratta, Mary. *Mathematics Their Way: 20th Anniversary Edition.* Menlo Park, CA: Addison Wesley, 1995.

Burns, Marilyn. *The Book of Think: Or How to Solve a Problem Twice Your Size.* Boston: Little, Brown and Co. (Brown Paper School Books), 1976.

Burns, Marilyn. *The I Hate Mathematics Book.* Boston: Little, Brown and Co. (Brown Paper School Books), 1975.

Furth, Hans, and Harry Wachs. *Thinking Goes to School: Piaget's Theory in Practice with Additional Thoughts.* New York: Oxford University Press, 1974.

Jacobs, Harold. *Mathematics: A Human Endeavor: A Book for Those Who Think They Don't Like the Subject* 3rd ed. San Francisco: W.H. Freeman, 1994. Grades 9–12.

Kohl, Herbert. *Math, Writing and Games in the Open Classroom.* New York: Random House, 1974.

Spatial Intelligence

Brooks, Mona. *Drawing with Children*. New York: Tarcher/Putnam, 1996.

Demille, Richard. *Put Your Mother on the Ceiling*. New York: Viking Penguin, 1976.

Edwards, Betty. *The New Drawing on the Right Side of the Brain*, rev. ed. New York: Tarcher Putnam, 1999.

McKim, Robert H. *Experiences in Visual Thinking*, 2nd ed. Boston: PWS Pubs, 1980.

Samples, Robert. *The Metaphoric Mind: A Celebration of Creative Consciousness*. Rolling Hills Estates, CA: Jalmar Press, 1993.

Silberstein-Storfer, Muriel, and Mablen Jones. *Doing Art Together*. New York: Abrams, 1980.

Singer, Jerome L., and Ellen Switzer. *Mind-Play: The Creative Uses of Fantasy*. Englewood Cliffs, NJ: Prentice Hall, 1980.

Bodily-Kinesthetic Intelligence

Cobb, Vicki. *Science Experiments You Can Eat*. New York: HarperCollins Children's Books, 1994.

Feldenkrais, Moshe. *Awareness through Movement: Easy-to-Do Health Exercises to Improve Your Posture, Vision, Imagination, and Personal Awareness*. New York: Harper San Francisco, 1991.

Gelb, Michael. *Body Learning: An Introduction to the Alexander Technique*. New York: Delilah Books, 1981.

Gilbert, Anne G. *Teaching the 3 Rs through Movement Experiences*. Englewood Cliffs, NJ: Prentice Hall, 1986.

Griss, Susan. *Minds in Motion: A Kinesthetic Approach to Teaching Elementary Curriculum*. Portsmouth, NH: Heinemann, 1998.

Masters, Robert, and Jean Houston. *Listening to the Body: The Psychophysical Way to Health and Awareness*. New York: Dell, 1979.

Mettler, Barbara, ed. *Materials of Dance as a Creative Art Activity*. Tucson, AZ: Mettler Studios, 1979.

Patterson, Marilyn Nikimaa. *Every Body Can Learn: Engaging the Bodily-Kinesthetic Intelligence in the Everyday Classroom*. Tucson, AZ: Zephyr Press, 1997.

Spolin, Viola. *Theater Games for the Classroom*. Evanston, IL: Northwestern University Press, 1986.

Musical Intelligence

Bonny, Helen, and Louis Savary. *Music and Your Mind*. Barrytown, NY: Station Hill Press, 1990.

Brewer, Chris Boyd, and Don G. Campbell. *Rhythms of Learning*. Tucson, AZ: Zephyr Press, 1991.

Halpern, Steven, and Louis Savary. *Sound Health: Music and Sounds That Make Us Whole*. San Francisco: Harper and Row, 1985.

Judy, Stephanie. *Making Music for the Joy of It*. Los Angeles: Jeremy P. Tarcher, 1990.

Lingerman, Hal A. *The Healing Energies of Music*. Wheaton, IL: Theosophical Publishing House, 1995.

Macldover, Wilma, and Marienne Uszler. *Sound Choices: Guiding Your Child's Music Experiences*. New York: Oxford University Press, 1996.

Merritt, Stephanie. *Mind, Music, and Imagery: Forty Exercises Using Music to Stimulate Creativity and Self-Awareness*. New York: NAL/Plume, 1990.

Suzuki, Shinichi. *Nurtured By Love: New Approach to Education*. Pompano Beach, FL: Exposition Press of Florida, 1982. By the founder of the Suzuki method of musical instrument playing.

Wallace, Rosella R. *Rappin' and Rhymin': Raps, Songs, Cheers, and SmartRope Jingles for Active Learning*. Tucson, AZ: Zephyr Press, 1992.

Interpersonal Intelligence

Baldrige, Letitia. *More Than Manners!: Raising Today's Kids to Have Kind Manners and Good Hearts*. New York: Scribners, 1997.

Ginot, Haim. *Between Parent and Child*. New York: Avon, 1976.

Gordon, Thomas. *P.E.T.: Parent Effectiveness Training: The Tested New Way to Raise Responsible Children*. New York: Plume, 1975.

Johnson, David W., Roger T. Johnson, and Edythe Johnson Holubec. *The New Circles of Learning: Cooperation in the Classroom and School.* Alexandria, VA: ASCD, 1994.

Orlick, Terry. *The Cooperative Sports and Games Book.* New York: Pantheon, 1978.

Sobel, Jeffrey. *Everybody Wins: 393 Noncompetitive Games for Young Children.* New York: Walker and Co., 1983.

Wade, Rahima Carol. *Joining Hands: From Personal to Planetary Friendship in the Primary Classroom.* Tucson, AZ: Zephyr Press, 1980.

Weinstein, Matt, and Joel Goodman. *Playfair: Everybody's Guide to Noncompetitive Play.* San Luis Obispo, CA: Impact, 1980.

Intrapersonal Intelligence

Armstrong, Thomas. *The Radiant Child.* Wheaton, IL: Quest, 1985. Explores "peak experiences" in the life of the child.

Berends, Polly Berrien. *Whole Child Whole Parent,* 4th ed. New York: HarperCollins, 1997.

Briggs, Dorothy Corkille. *Your Child's Self-Esteem.* Garden City, NY: Doubleday, 1975.

Dreikurs, Rudolf, and Vicki Stolz. *Children: The Challenge.* New York: Plume, 1991.

Elkins, Dov Pieretz. *Glad to Be Me: Building Self-Esteem in Yourself and Others,* rev. ed. Rochester, NY: Growth Assoc., 1989.

Goleman, Daniel. *Emotional Intelligence.* New York: Random House, 1996.

Holt, John. *How Children Fail.* New York: Dell, 1981.

James, Muriel, and Dorothy Jongward. *Born to Win.* New York: NAL Dutton, 1978.

Lansky, Vicki. *101 Ways to Make Your Child Feel Special.* Lincolnwood, IL: NTC/Contemporary, 1991.

Oaklander, Violet. *Windows to Our Children.* Gestalt Journal, 1989.

Zack, Linda R., and Pamela Espeland. *Building Self-Esteem through the Museum of I.* Minneapolis, MN: Free Spirit Press, 1989.

Naturalist Intelligence

Beame, Rona. *Backyard Explorer Kit.* New York: Workman Publications, 1989.

Cornell, Joseph. *Sharing Nature with Children.* Nevada City, CA: Dawn Publications, 1998.

Lingelbach, Jenepher R., ed. *Hands-On Nature: Information and Activities for Exploring the Environment with Children.* Vermont Institute of Natural Science, 1989.

Marina, Lachecki et al. *Teaching Kids to Love the Earth.* Duluth, MN: Pfeifer-Hamilton Publications, 1990.

Roth, Karen. *Naturalist Intelligence: An Introduction to Gardner's Eighth Intelligence.* Palatine, IL: Skylight Publishers, 1998.

The Young Naturalist Kid Kit. EDC Publications, 1998.

Developmental Issues

Dodson, Fitzhugh. *How to Parent.* New York: NAL/Dutton, 1971.

Elkind, David. *The Hurried Child: Growing Up Too Fast, Too Soon.* Reading, MA: Addison Wesley, 1988.

Erikson, Erik. *Childhood and Society.* New York: Norton, 1993. Includes Erikson's famous "Eight Ages" model of human development.

Miller, Alice. *The Drama of the Gifted Child: The Search for the True Self.* New York: Basic Books, 1997.

Montessori, Maria. *The Secret of Childhood.* New York: Ballantine, 1982.

Pearce, Joseph Chilton. *Magical Child: Rediscovering Nature's Plan for Our Children.* New York: NAL/Dutton, 1992.

Piaget, Jean, and Barbel Inhelder. *The Psychology of the Child.* New York: Basic Books, 1972. Perhaps Piaget's clearest introduction to his child development model.

Ecological Issues (Diet, TV, Computers, Stress, Etc.)

Anderson, Joan, and Robin Wilkins. *Getting Unplugged: Take Control of Your Family's Television, Video Game, and Computer Habits.* New York: John Wiley & Sons, 1998.

Axelrod, Lauryn. *TV-Proof Your Kids: A Parents Guide to Safe & Healthy Viewing.* New York: Carol Publishing Group, 1997.

Chen, Milton, and Andry Bricky. *The Smart Parent's Guide to Kids' TV.* San Francisco: KQED, 1994.

Crook, William G. *Tracking Down Hidden Food Allergy.* Jackson, TN: Professional Books, 1980.

Crook, William, and Laura Stevens. *Solving the Puzzle of Your Hard to Raise Child.* New York: Random House, 1987.

Dadd, Debra Lynn. *The Nontoxic Home and Office: Protecting Yourself and Your Family from Everyday Toxics and Health Hazards.* Los Angeles: Putnam Publishing Co., 1992. Excellent survey of potential toxic substances around the home and what to do about them.

Deqaetano, Gloria, Kathleen Bander, and Jane M. Healy. *Screen Smarts: A Family Guide to Media Literacy.* Boston: Houghton Mifflin, 1996.

Feingold, Ben. *Why Your Child Is Hyperactive.* New York: Random House, 1985.

Ferber, Richard. *Solve Your Child's Sleep Problems.* New York: Simon & Schuster, 1986.

Healy, Jane M. *Endangered Minds: Why Our Children Don't Think.* New York: Simon & Schuster, 1991.

Healy, Jane M. *Failure to Connect: How Computers Affect Our Children's Minds—for Better and Worse.* New York: Simon & Schuster, 1998.

Hersey, Jane *Why Can't My Child Behave?* Alexandria, VA: Pear Tree Press, 1996 (P.O. Box 30146, Alexandria, VA 22310).

Kuczen, Barbara. *Childhood Stress: How to Raise a Healthier, Happier Child.* New York: Dell, 1987.

Mander, Jerry. *Four Arguments for the Elimination of Television.* New York: Morrow, 1978.

Moran, Barbara, and Kathy Trens. *Internet Directory for Kids and Parents.* IDG Books Worldwide, 1998.

Papert, Seymour A., and Nicholas Negroponte. *The Connected Family: Bridging the Digital Generation Gap.* Marietta, GA: Longstreet Press, 1996.

Polly, Jean Armour. *The Internet Kids and Family Yellow Pages,* 2d ed. New York: Osborne/McGraw-Hill, 1997.

Rapp, Doris J. *Is This Your Child? Discovering and Treating Unrecognized Allergies.* New York: William Morrow, 1992.

Salzman, Marian, and Robert Pondiscio. *Kids On-Line: 150 Ways for Kids to Surf the Net for Fun and Information.* New York: Avon/Camelot, 1995.

Smith, Lendon. *Feed Your Kids Right.* New York: Dell, 1981. Includes many recipes.

Traverso, Debra Koontz. *TV Time: 150 Fun Family Activities That Turn Your Television into a Learning Tool.* New York: Avon, 1998.

Winn, Marie. *The Plug-In Drug: Television, Children and the Family.* New York: Viking, 1985.

Youngs, Bettie B. *Stress in Children.* New York: Avon, 1986.

Alternatives to ADD, LD, Ritalin, and Labeling

Armstrong, Thomas. *ADD/ADHD Alternatives in the Classroom.* Alexandria, VA: Association for Supervision and Curriculum Development, 1999.

Armstrong, Thomas. *The Myth of the ADD Child: 50 Ways to Impove Your Child's Behavior and Attentin Span without Drugs, Labels, or Coercion.* New York: Plume, 1997.

Biklen, Douglas. *Schooling without Labels.* Philadelphia: Temple University Press, 1992.

Block, Mary Ann. *No More Ritalin: Treating ADHD Without Drugs.* New York: Kensington Publishing Corp., 1997.

Breggin, Peter R. *Talking Back to Ritalin: What Doctors Aren't Telling You About Stimulants for Children.* Common Courage Press, 1998.

Davis, Ronald D., and Eldon Braun. *The Gift of Dyslexia: Why Some of the Smartest People Can't Read and How They Can Learn.* New York: Perigee, 1997.

Dixon, John Philo. *The Spatial Child.* Springfield, IL: Charles C. Thomas, 1983.

Fleming, Elizabeth. *Believe the Heart: Our Dyslexic Days.* LF Pub VA, 1984. Dyslexia needs to be recognized as a hidden strength.

Freed, Jeffrey, and Laurie Parson. *Right-Brained Children in a Left-Brained World: Unlocking the Potential of Your ADD Child.* New York: Simon & Schuster, 1997.

Garber, Stephen W., Marianne Daniels, and Robyn Freedman Spizman. *Beyond Ritalin: Facts About Medication and Other Strategies for Helping Children, Adolescents, and Adults with Attention Deficit Disorders.* New York: HarperCollins, 1997.

Hartmann, Thom. *Attention Deficit Disorder: A Different Perception.* Lancaster, PA: Underwood-Miller, 1993.

Kurcinka, Mary Sheedy. *Raising Your Spirited Child.* New York: HarperCollins, 1991.

Merrow, John. *Attention Deficit Disorder: A Dubious Diagnosis* (Video). The Merrow Report, 588 Broadway, Suite 510, New York, NY 10012; 212-941-8060 (phone); 212-941-8068 (fax).

Schwartz, Judy. *Another Doorway to Learning.* New York: Crossroads, 1992.

Taylor, Denny. *Learning Denied.* Portsmouth, NH: Heinemann, 1991.

Welsh, David J. *The Boy Who Burned Too Brightly.* Fort Worth, TX: Alisam Press, 1997. (Alisam Press, 6040 Camp Bowie, Suite 52, Fort Worth, TX 76116)

West, Thomas G. *In the Mind's Eye: Visual Thinkers, Gifted People with Learning Difficulties, Computer Images, and the Ironies of Creativity,* Buffalo, NY: Prometheus, 1991.

Different Ways of Learning

Alvino, James. *Parents' Guide to Raising a Gifted Child: Recognizing and Developing Your Child's Potential.* New York: Ballantine, 1996.

Buzan, Tony. *Use Both Sides of Your Brain.* New York: NAL/Dutton, 1991.

Diamond, Marian, and Janet Hopson. *Magic Trees of the Mind: How to Nurture Your Child's Intelligence, Creativity, and Healthy Emotions from Birth through Adolescence.* New York: Dutton, 1998.

Dunn, Rita, and Kenneth Dunn. *Teaching Students through Their Individual Learning Styles*. Boston: Allyn & Bacon, 1993.

Dunn, Rita, Kenneth Dunn, and Donald J. Treffiner. *Bringing Out the Giftedness in Your Child: Nurturing Every Child's Unique Strengths, Talents, and Potential*. New York: John Wiley & Sons, 1992.

Gallas, Karen. *The Languages of Learning: How Children Talk, Write, Dance, Draw, and Sing Their Understanding of the World*. New York: Teachers College Press, 1994.

John-Steiner, Vera. *Notebooks of the Mind: Explorations in Thinking*. New York: HarperCollins, 1985.

Kennedy, Marge. *50 Ways to Bring Out the Smarts in Your Kid*. Princeton, NJ: Petersen's, 1996.

Perry, Susan K. *Playing Smart: A Parent's Guide to Enriching, Offbeat Learning Activities for Ages 4–14*. Minneapolis, MN: Free Spirit Publishing, 1990.

Rich, Dorothy. *MegaSkills*. Boston: Houghton Mifflin, 1992.

Tobias, Cynthia Ulrich. *The Way They Learn*. Colorado Springs, CO: Focus on the Family, 1994.

Vitale, Barbara Meister. *Unicorns Are Real: A Right-Brained Approach to Learning*. Rolling Hills Estates, CA: Jalmar Press, 1982.

Williams, Linda Verlee. *Teaching for the Two-Sided Mind*. New York: Simon & Schuster, 1986.

Options in Educating Children

Anderson, Winifred, Stephen Chitwood, and Deidre Hayden. *Negotiating the Special Education Maze*. Bethesda, MD: Woodbine House, 1997. Practical advice for parents on using special education laws to benefit children.

Colfax, David, and Micki Colfax. *Homeschooling for Excellence*. New York: Warner, 1988.

Collins, Marva, and Civia Tamarkin. *Marva Collins Way, Updated: Returning to Excellence in Education*. New York: Tarcher/Putnam, 1990. A Chicago school principal's prescriptions for learning success in all children.

Holt, John. *Teach Your Own.* New York: Dell, 1982. Discusses schooling your child at home.

Kohl, Herbert. *Thirty-Six Children.* New York: NAL/Dutton, 1988. Alternative education in a large urban public school.

Mothering, P.O. Box 8410, Santa Fe, NM 87504. Quarterly magazine. Focus on birthing and parenting issues but includes regular section on alternative educational approaches.

Neill, A. S. *Summerhill: A New View of Childhood.* New York: St. Martin's Press, 1995.

Pathways to Learning, P.O. Box 328, Brandon, VT 05733. www.greatideas.org/paths.htm. Quarterly magazine on alternative education approaches.

Richards, Mary Caroline. *Toward Wholeness: Rudolf Steiner Education in America.* Middletown, CT: University Press of New England, 1980. Includes a listing of Waldorf Schools in the United States.

Organizations for
the Eight Intelligences

Multiple Intelligences

Association for Supervision and Curriculum Development, 1703 North Beauregard Street, Alexandria, VA 22311-1711; 703-578-9600 or 800-933-ASCD (phone); 704-575-5400 (fax); www.ascd. org. Publishes my book *Multiple Intelligences in the Classroom* and also other materials on multiple intelligences, including *Multiple Intelligences CD-ROM* and *Multiple Intelligences Video Series*.

Harvard Project Zero, Harvard Graduate School of Education, 323 Longfellow Hall, Appian Way, Cambridge, MA 02138; 617-495-4342 (phone); 617-495-9709 (fax); www.pz.harvard.edu. The research and organizational umbrella under which Dr. Howard Gardner created and is developing the theory of multiple intelligences. If you write them and make a specific request, they will send you a catalog listing their various publications.

National Professional Resources, 25 South Regent Street, Port Chester, NY 10573; 914-937-8879. Producer of several videos on multiple intelligences, including Howard Gardner's *How Are Kids Smart?*, Jo Gusman's *MI and the Second Language Learner*, and Thomas Armstrong's *Multiple Intelligences: Discovering the Giftedness in All.*

New Horizons for Learning, P.O. Box 15329, Seattle, WA 98115; 206-547-7936; www.newhorizons.org. An online learning community that includes much information about multiple intelligences and other new learning approaches.

Skylight Publications (division of Simon & Schuster), 2626 S. Clearbrook Drive, Arlington Heights, IL 60005-5310; www.iriskylight.com. Publisher and distributor of many multiple intelligences resources.

University of California, Education Extension. Multiple Intelligences Teacher Certification Program, 1200 University Avenue, Riverside, CA 92507-4596; 909-787-4361 (ext. 1663); steele@ucx.ucr.edu. Runs two week-long summer institutes on multiple intelligences and a variety of other courses during the school year that lead to the only teachers' certificate in multiple intelligences in the world.

Zephyr Press, P.O. Box 66006, Tucson, AZ 85728; 602-322-5090; www.zephyrpress.com. Publisher and distributor of many multiple intelligences resources.

Linguistic

American Speech and Hearing Association, 10801 Rockville Pike, Rockville, MD; www.asha.org.

International Reading Association, Dept. TE, Box 8139, Newward, DE 19714; www.reading.org.

National Council of Teachers of English, 1111 Kenyon Road, Urbana, IL 61801; www.ncte.org.

National Writing Projects, 5635 Tolman Hall, University of California, Berkeley, CA 94720; www-gse.berkeley.edu/research/NWP/nwp.htm.

Teachers and Writers Collaborative, 5 Union Square W., New York, NY 10003; www. twc.org. Many fine publications on reading and writing activities for children, developed by teachers and writers working together.

Logical-mathematical

Cuisenaire Co. of America Inc., P.O. Box 5026, White Plains, NY 10602-5026; www.cuisenaire.com.

Edmund Scientific, 101 E. Gloucester Pike, Barrington, NJ 08007-1380; 609-573-6250 (phone); 609-573-6295 (fax); www.edsci.com. Write for catalog of science kits and other educational science materials.

Math-On-Line Resources for Parents & Families; www.kqed.org/fromKQED/Cell/math/resources/parent.html. Collection of web-links that can assist parents in helping kids with math (working together).

National Council of Teachers of Mathematics, 1840 Wilson Boulevard, Arlington, VA 22201-3000; 703-243-7100; www.nsta.org.

Spatial

American Optometric Association, 243 North Lindbergh Boulevard, Street Louis, MO 63141; 314-991-4100 (phone); 314-991-4101 (fax); www.aoanet.org.

National Art Education Association, 1916 Association Drive, Reston, VA 20191-1590; 703-860-8000 (phone); 703-860-2960 (fax); www.naea-reston.org.

Optometric Extension Program Foundation Inc., 1921 E. Carnegie Avenue, Suite 3-L, Santa Ana, CA 92705-5510; 714-250-8070; www.healthy.net/oep/.

Bodily-kinesthetic

American Alliance for Health, Physical Education, Recreation and Dance (AAHPERD), 1900 Association Drive, Reston, VA 20191; 703-476-3400; 800-213-7193; www.aahperd.org.

American Camping Association, 5000 State Road 67 North, Martinsville, IN 46151-7902; 765-342-8456 (phone); 765-342-2065 (fax);

www.aca-camps.org. Provides list of over 2,000 accredited camps around the United States.

Childlife Play Specialties, Inc., 55 Whitney Street, Holliston, MA 01746; 800-Go-Swing; www.childlife.com. Children's play equipment.

Children's Theater Resources; pubweb.acns.nwu.edu/~vjs291/children.html. State-by-state listing of children's theaters.

Musical

American Orff-Schulwerk Association, P.O. Box 391089, Cleveland, OH 44139-8089; 440-543-5366; www.aosa.org.

Music Educators' National Conference, 1902 Association Drive, Reston, VA 22091; 800-828-0229; www.menc.org.

Organization of American Kodaly Educators, www.music.indiana.edu/kodaly/oake.htm.

Suzuki Association of the Americas, P.O. Box 17310, Boulder, CO 80308; 303-444-0948 (phone); 303-444-0984 (fax); www.suzukiassociation.org.

Personal Intelligences

Free Spirit Publishing Inc., 400 First Avenue North, Suite 616, Minneapolis, MN 55401-1724; 800-735-7323; www.freespirit.com.

National Association for Self-Esteem; www.self-esteemnase.org.

Naturalist

The Nature Company, P.O. Box 6432, Florence, KY 41022-6432; 800-477-8828; www.natureco.com.

Other Learning Organizations

Association for Childhood Education International, 179 Georgia Avenue, Suite 215, Olney, MD 20832-2277; 800-423-3563 (phone); 301-570-2212 (fax); www.udel.edu/bateman/acei/.

Creative Education Foundation, 1050 Union Street, Buffalo, NY 14224; 716-675-3181 (phone); 716-675-3209 (fax); www.cefcpsi. org. Publishes materials on creativity, children, and education.

Feingold Association of the United States, 127 East Main Street, Suite 106, Riverhead, NY 11901; (516) 369-9340 (phone); (516) 369-2988 (fax); www.feingold.org. Provides support for families using the Feingold diet to treat hyperactivity.

Growing without Schooling, 2269 Massachusetts Avenue, Cambridge, MA 02140-1226; 617-864-3100 (phone); 617-864-9235 (fax); www.holtgws.com. Support organization for homeschooling families. Also runs a very fine mail-order book shop, "John Holt's Bookstore."

National Association for the Education of Young Children, 1509 Sixteenth Street NW, Washington, DC 20036-1426; 800-424-2460, ext. 604 (phone); 202-328-1846 (fax); www.naeyc.org.

National Parenting Center; 800-753-6667; www.tnpc.com. Online information on a range of parenting topics (including over fifty short articles by Thomas Armstrong).

Learning Materials for
the Eight Intelligences

The following list provides a range of learning tools, toys, games, projects, processes, and other materials that help develop each of the intelligences. Many, if not most, of the materials listed could be placed in more than one intelligence category but are put in the category that seems most linked to it. To order online, try www.faoschwarz.com or www.toys.com.

Linguistic
writing materials
tape recorder
diary or journal
books
talking books (cassettes and books)
typewriter
word processor
alphabet shapes
stamp set
calligraphy kit
trips to the library
crossword puzzles
anagrams
Scrabble
search-a-word puzzles
decoding kits
sign language instruction
wireless microphone
telephone
letter blocks

Logical-mathematical
brain teasers
calculator
math manipulatives
science kits (e.g., chemistry, electricity, etc.)
math games
logic games (e.g., mancala)
money games (e.g., Monopoly)
card games
sorting and classifying games
clock
play money

Spatial
jigsaw puzzles
globe
maps
video games
Lego kits
drawing, painting, and coloring materials
chalkboard and colored chalk
box of sequins or glitter and glue
how-to-doodle/cartoon books
templates for tracing shapes
3-day View Master
Etch-A-Sketch
optical illusions
pictures
camera
video camera (for movie making)
optical instruments (e.g., telescope, microscope, etc.)
collections (e.g., stamps, baseball cards, etc.)
night-vision goggles
mazes
collage materials (e.g., pictures, paper, scissors, glue)

Musical

musical recordings (CDs, tapes, etc.)

percussion instruments (e.g., drums, tambourine, maracas, bells, etc.)

tape recorder

karaoke machine

sound boxes (containers holding "mystery" sounds)

radio

band or orchestra instrument (e.g. flute, tuba, violin)

singing games

piano

electronic keyboard

musical memory games (e.g., Simon)

kazoo, harmonica, or slide whistle

xylophone or glockenspiel

guitar or ukulele

homemade instruments (e.g., oatmeal box, pots, and pans)

Bodily-kinesthetic

toolbox and carpentry materials

materials to build structures with (e.g., Erector set, Lincoln Logs, Legos, K'Nex, Mega-Bloks, etc.)

Sports equipment (e.g. soccer ball, football, golf clubs, etc.)

mobile-making kit

Play-doh

skateboard or skates

frisbee, horseshoes, or other things to throw

action figures

toy bowling ball and pins or bocce ball

ceramics materials

model kits (e.g., building cars, boats, etc.)

gymnastic equipment

mask-making or face-painting materials

handiwork equipment (e.g., for knitting, macrame, crochet, weaving, etc.)

collection of tactile materials (e.g., velvet, sandpaper, fly paper, etc.)

messy art materials (e.g., clay, finger paint, etc.)
simple costumes (dress-up cast-offs) and props for drama
dollhouse and miniature figures, furniture, etc.
housekeeping toys
puppets
magic tricks
bicycle or tricycle
kites
jump rope
stuffed animals
cooking supplies
machines to take apart and put back together
trampoline
Hula Hoop
train set
miniature soldiers
big cardboard boxes to play in (e.g., house, rocket ship, etc.)

Interpersonal
board games
cooperative learning activities
party supplies
dollhouse and dolls
miniature trucks, cars, etc. for social play
meeting places (e.g., tree house, clubhouse, fort, etc.)
walkie-talkies

Intrapersonal
self-directed hobbies
independent projects
kid businesses (e.g., lemonade stand)
journal-keeping
individualized, self-paced games
secret places
time to engage in reverie and free play
all-about-me type books

makeup kit
fashion kit

Naturalist
rock or shell collecting kit
nature equipment (e.g., binoculars, magnifying glass, etc.)
wildlife study kit
ant farm
aquarium or terrarium
National Geographic's "Really Wild Animals"
ecology games
a pet to take care of
hiking equipment
home planetarium
gardening supplies
miniature toy animals and plants
real plants to take care of

Books for Children in
the Eight Intelligences

Books might strike most parents as pretty much linguistic creations (with the addition in some cases of spatial illustrations). However, a new generation of books has emerged over the past twenty years that combines words with hands-on tools that span the range of intelligences. I've sought to place each book in a particular intelligence category, but, of course, many of these books stimulate several intelligences at once.

Many of the books that I've listed come from three publishers in particular that I'd like to single out who have specialized in creative books for kids: Workman Publishing Co. (708 Broadway, New York, NY 10003; 800-722-7202; www.workmanweb.com), Klutz Press (455 Portage Avenue, Palo Alto, CA 94306; 800-558-8944; www.klutz.com), and Free Spirit Publishing Inc. (400 First Avenue North, Suite 616, Minneapolis, MN 55401-1724; 800-735-7323; www.freespirit.com). Contact these publishers for many additional titles that engage kids in their many intelligences.

Linguistic

Feder, Chris Welles. *Brain Quest: 1,000 Questions and Answers to Challenge the Mind.* New York: Workman, 1992. This popular series is available for different grades and different subject areas.

Kapell, Dave, and Sally Steenland. *The Kids' Magnetic Poetry Book and Creativity Kit.* New York: Workman, 1998. (Ages 8–12)

Price, Roger, and Leonard Stern. *Mad Libs.* New York: Price, Stern, and Sloan, 1998.

Logical-mathematical

Alexander, Ruth Bell. *Number Jugglers: Math Game Book & Game Cards*. New York: Workman, 1998.

Allison, Linda. *Blood and Guts: A Working Guide to Your Own Insides*. Boston: Little, Brown and Company, 1976.

Burns, Marilyn, and Martha Weston. *Math for Smarty Pants*. Boston: Little, Brown and Company, 1982. (Ages 9–12)

Packard, David, and Marshall H. Peck III. *Grow Your Own Crystals*. Troll Associates, 1995. Includes book and crystal kit. (Ages 9–12)

Spatial

Arnold, Tedd. *My First Drawing Book*. New York: Workman, 1987. Full-color board book with laminated write-on, wipe-off pages using clip-on water-soluble pen. (Ages 4–7)

Bennete, Carolyn, with Jack Romig. *The Kids' Book of Kaleidoscopes*. New York: Workman, 1994. Includes plastic safety mirrors, tube and turning end, plastic eyepiece and tube cover, color gels, and a collection of colored beads, gems, chips, and other materials to put in your kaleidoscope.

Caney, Steven. *Steven Caney's Invention Book*. New York: Workman, 1985. Many ideas for the young inventor. Includes information on applying for a patent and marketing the final product. (Ages 8–13)

Editors of Klutz Press. *Draw the Marvel Comics Super Heroes: A Mighty Manual of Step-by-Step Instruction*. Palo Alto, CA: 1995. Can be read, drawn over, colored in. Includes a pencil and four double-nibbed colored markers stored in a vinyl pouch.

Emberley, Ed E. *Ed Emberley's Drawing Box*. Boston: Little, Brown and Company, 1988. Includes 4 drawing books, 5 markers, 1 sketch book, and 75 things to draw. (Ages 4–8)

Koda-Callan, Elizabeth. *The Artist's Palette: A Story & Sketch Book*. New York: Workman, 1998. Integrates a story about the uniqueness of a girl who draws a tree in a different way from her classmates, with a sketchbook to allow the reader to express his or her own uniqueness. (Ages 5–9)

Kostick, Anne. *My First Camera Book*. New York: Workman, 1989. Includes a kid-tested reusable camera. (Ages 4–8)

Wolfman, Ira. *My World & Globe*. New York: Workman, 1991. Lots of information about geography plus an inflatable globe, magic marker, and colorful stickers to personalize information about people, places, cities, etc. (Ages 4–7)

Bodily-kinesthetic

Cassidy, John. *The Klutz Book of Knots*. Palo Alto, CA: Klutz Press, 1985. Comes with color-coded nylon cord for practice in making knots.

Chevat, Richie. *The Marble Book*. New York: Workman, 1996. Includes 30 marbles and 2 shooters in a drawstring pouch. (Ages 5–12)

Cumbaa, Stephen. *The Bones Book & Skeleton*. New York: Workman, 1992. Includes a 12-inch, 25-piece skeleton to put together and display in a clear plastic bell jar. (Ages 6–12)

Henson, Cheryl, and the Muppet Workshop. *The Muppets Make Puppets*. New York: Workman, 1994. Includes eyes, noses, feathers, and fuzzy fur, with instructions on finding items around the house to make puppets. (Ages 3–6)

Loredo, Elizabeth. *The Jump Rope Book*. New York: Workman, 1996. Comes with a 100 percent cotton, seven-foot-long jump rope with wooden handles. (Ages 8 and up)

Ten Eyck, John E. *The Yo-Yo Book*. New York: Workman, 1998. Comes with its own yo yo ready to go! (Ages 5–12)

Musical

Gindick, John. *Country & Blues Harmonica for the Musically Hopeless*. Palo Alto, CA: Klutz Press, 1984.

McComb, Carol, and Barry Geller. *Country & Blues Guitar for the Musically Hopeless*. Palo Alto, CA: Klutz Press, 1988.

Interpersonal

Editors of Klutz Press. *The Book of Classic Board Games*. Palo Alto, CA: 1990. Laminated pages are board games from around the world (includes game pieces).

Erlbach, Arlene. *The Families Book: True Stories About Real Kids and the People They Live with and Love, Fun Things to Do with Your Family, Making Family Trees and Keeping Family Traditions, Solving Family Problems, Staying Close to Faraway Relatives, and More!* Minneapolis, MN: Free Spirit, 1996. (Ages 9–13)

Gainer, Cindy. *I'm Like You, You're Like Me: A Child's Book About Understanding and Celebrating Each Other.* Minneapolis, MN: Free Spirit, 1998.

Lalli, Judy. *Make Someone Smile: and 40 More Ways to Be a Peaceful Person.* Minneapolis, MN: Free Spirit, 1996.

Levine, Michael. *The Kids' Address Book: Over 2,000 Addresses of Celebrities, Athletes, Entertainers, and More . . . Just for Kids!* New York: Perigee, 1994. (Ages 9–12)

Lewis, Barbara. *The Kid's Guide to Service Projects: Over 500 Service Ideas for Young People Who Want to Make a Difference.* Minneapolis, MN: Free Spirit, 1995. (Ages 10 and up)

Lewis, Barbara A. *The Kid's Guide to Social Action: How to Solve the Social Problems You Choose—and Turn Creative Thinking into Positive Action* (Revised, Expanded, Updated Edition), Minneapolis, MN: Free Spirit, 1998.

Maupin, Melissa. *The Ultimate Kids' Club Book: How to Organize, Find Members, Run Meetings, Raise Money, Handle Problems, and Much More!* Minneapolis, MN: Free Spirit, 1996. (Ages 10–14)

Roman, Trevor. *Cliques, Phonies, and Other Baloney.* Minneapolis, MN: Free Spirit, 1998.

Wolfman, Ira. *Do People Grow on Family Trees? Genealogy for Kids and Other Beginners.* New York: Workman, 1991. (Ages 8–12)

Intrapersonal

Barrett, Susan L. *It's All in Your Head: A Guide to Understanding Your Brain and Boosting Your Brain Power.* Minneapolis, MN: Free Spirit, 1992. (Ages 9–14)

Caney, Steven. *Make Your Own Time Capsule.* New York: Workman, 1991. Silver plastic capsule with screw-top lid comes with instructions for deciding what to put in, how to prepare materials, etc. (Ages 7–11)

Kaufman, Gershen, and Lev Raphael. *Stick Up for Yourself! Every Kid's Guide to Personal Power and Positive Self-Esteem.* Minneapolis, MN: Free Spirit, 1990. (Grades 3–7)

Kincher, Jonni. *Dreams Can Help: A Journal Guide to Understanding Your Dreams and Making Them Work for You.* Minneapolis, MN: Free Spirit, 1988. (Ages 8–14)

Kincher, Jonni. *Psychology for Kids: 40 Fun Tests That Help You Learn About Yourself.* Minneapolis, MN: Free Spirit, 1995. (Ages 10 and up)

Kipfer, Barbara Ann. *14,000 Things for Kids to Be Happy About.* New York: Workman, 1994. Leaves space for kids to write in their own happy things as well.

Kraus, Robert. *Leo the Latebloomer.* New York: HarperCollins Childrens Books, 1998. A wonderful tale about patience and growth. (Preschool and up)

Preston, Edna. *The Temper Tantrum Book.* New York: Penguin/Puffin, 1976. (Preschool–grade 3)

MacDonald, Suse. *Alphabatics.* New York: Simon & Schuster Children's Books, 1992.

Mayer, Mercer. *There's a Nightmare in My Closet.* New York: Puffin Books, 1992. (Grades K–3)

Schwartz, Linda. *What Would You Do? A Kid's Guide to Tricky and Sticky Situations.* Minneapolis, MN: Free Spirit, 1991. (Ages 8–12)

Sendak, Maurice. *Where the Wild Things Are: 25th Anniversary Edition.* New York: HarperCollins, 1988. (Grades K–3)

Silverstein, Shel. *A Light in the Attic.* New York: HarperCollins, 1981. (Grades 4–6)

Simon, Norma. *I Was So Mad!* Chicago: Albert Whitman, 1974. (Grades K–2)

Simon, Norma. *Why Am I Different?* Chicago: Albert Whitman, 1976. A celebration of learning differences. (Grades K–3)

Stock, Gregory. *The Kids' Book of Questions.* New York: Workman, 1988. (Ages 8–12)

Viorst, Judith. *Alexander and the Terrible Horrible No Good Very Bad Day.* New York: Simon & Schuster, 1987. (Grades K–4)

Naturalist

Beame, Rona. *Backyard Explorer Kit.* New York: Workman, 1989. Focuses on trees and leaves. Includes a heavy plastic collecting envelope for gathering leaves and needles and a collecting album to mount them in. (Ages 5–10)

Bown, Deni. *Nature Explorer.* New York: DK Publishing, 1995. A kit that includes two books, bug bottle, pop-up binoculars, and bird mobile. (Ages 4–8)

Bramwell, Martyn, Ian Jackson, and Alan Suttie. *Rocks and Fossils (An Usborne Guide).* EDC Publications, 1994. Book comes with rocks and magnifying glass in vinyl bag.

Danks, Hugh. *The Bug Book & Bug Bottle.* New York: Workman, 1987. Comes with a safe plastic green-lidded jar perforated with air holes for collecting insects. (Ages 5–10)

Dawe, Karen. *The Beach Book & Beach Bucket.* New York: Workman, 1988. Includes instructions for identifying more than 40 species of saltwater plants and animals, along with a plastic beach bucket topped with a perforated lid suitable for sifting and scooping sand. (Ages 5–10)

Dawe, Karen, and Neil Dawe. *The Bird Book & Bird Feeder.* New York: Workman, 1988. A bird field guide and bird feeder with slide-out tray. (Ages 5–12)

Porter, Wes. *The Garden Book & Greenhouse.* New York: Workman, 1989. This book comes complete with a miniature greenhouse, take-it-home and just-add-water grow-kit. (Ages 5–10)

Games That Develop
the Eight Intelligences

The following list includes many board games and other commercially made games that help stimulate the multiple intelligences. Many of these games stimulate more than one intelligence. In particular, many of the games that I've put under the logical-mathematical umbrella (e.g., chess, checkers, Othello, Connect Four, etc.) also develop spatial intelligence (viz. the ability to remember a variety of visual-spatial patterns). Similarly, many games that fall under other intelligences (such as the Carmen San Diego games) also can develop linguistic intelligences through the reading and talking that go on during the game. Naturally, most of these games—being social in nature—can help nurture interpersonal intelligence. Except for generic editions of games, I've listed the manufacturer and the age range appropriate for each game (though it may serve to remember that some younger children may be developmentally ready for games marked for older participants, and some older kids may not yet be ready for games that are within the official age range). The best advice is to play the game with your child and if he or she doesn't enjoy it, don't force him or her to continue playing. The point of games is not really to stimulate the intelligences (that's a positive by-product) but to have fun!

Linguistic
Scrabble (Milton Bradley, age 8+)
Scrabble Jr. (Milton Bradley, 5+)
Blurt (Patch, 10+)
Boggle (Parker Brothers, 8+)
Boggle Jr. (Parker Brothers, 3–6)
Outburst Jr.: The Game of Verbal Explosions (Parker Brothers, 7+)
Mastermind: Crack the Word Code! (Pressman, 6+)
Mad Gab (Patch, 10+)
Password (England Games, 10+)
Scattergories (Milton Bradley, 12+)

Scattergories Jr. (Milton Bradley, 8–11)
Trivial Pursuit Jr. (Parker Brothers, 8+)
Upwords (Milton Bradley, 10+)
Balderdash (Parker Brothers, 10+)
Bird Brain (Tiger Electronic Games, 5+)
Jeopardy (Tiger Electronic Games, 8+)

Logical-mathematical
poker (10+)
Keeno (10+)
backgammon (10+)
bingo (6+)
dominoes (6+)
chess (8+)
checkers (6+)
Chinese checkers (6+)
Clue (Parker Brothers, 9+)
Clue Jr. (Parker Brothers, 5–8)
Connect Four: The Vertical Checkers Game (Milton Bradley, 7+)
Guess Who (Milton Bradley, 6+)
Monopoly (Parker Brothers, 8+)
Mastermind (Pressman, 8+)
Mastermind for Kids (Pressman, 6+)
Mancala for Kids (Pressman, 6+)
Othello (Pressman, 8+)
Payday (Parker Brothers, 8+)
Parcheesi (Milton Bradley, 7+)
Quarto (Pressman, 8+)
Racko (Parker Brothers, 8+)
Sequence (Jax, 7+)
Triominoes (Pressman, 8+)
30 Second Mysteries (University Games, 12+)
Carmen San Diego Jr. Edition (University Games, 4–8)
Where in the USA Is Carmen San Diego (University Games, 8+)
Where in Time Is Carmen San Diego (University Games, 8+)
Yahtzee (Milton Bradley, 8+)

Spatial
pin the tail on the donkey (3+)
Battleship (Milton Bradley, 7+)

Pictionary Jr. (Milton Bradley, 7–12)
Pictionary (Milton Bradley, 12+)
Myst (University Games, 10+)
Stratego (Winning Moves, 10+)

Musical
Simon (Milton Bradley, 8+)
Pocket Simon (Milton Bradley, 8+)
Henry: Match the Sounds Memory Game (Tiger Electronic Games, 5+)

Bodily-kinesthetic
pickup sticks (5+)
Guesstures: The Game of Split-Second Charades (Milton Bradley, 12+)
Jenga (Milton Bradley, 8+)
Ker-Plunk (Tyco, 5+)
Twister (Milton Bradley, 6+)

Interpersonal
Family Feud (Endless Games, 8+)
Game of the Year (University Games, 8+)
Ouija (Parker Brothers, 8+)

Intrapersonal
Careers (Pressman, 8+)
Life (Milton Bradley, 9+)
Risk (Parker Brothers, 10+)
Judge n' Jury (Winning Moves, 12+)

Naturalist
Jumanji (Milton Bradley, 8+)
National Geographic (University Games, 8+)

Internet Sites for Children
in the Eight Intelligences

The Internet is ever expanding and, with it, the opportunities for kids (under parental supervision) to explore and develop their multiple intelligences. The list below is just a drop in the ocean. For hundreds of other sites, see Barbara Moran, *Internet Directory for Kids & Parents*, Foster City, CA: IDG Books, 1997 (or updated versions).

Linguistic
Inkspot, www.inkspot.com/young/. Online support for young writers.
KidPub WWW Publishing, www.kidpub.org/kidpub./. Publishing site for
    writers under the age of twenty-one.
Kids' Stuff, www.digmo.org/kids/frontpage.html. Articles, links, and a
    newspaper for kids sponsored by the Missouri School of Journalism.

Logical-mathematical
Bill Nye the Science Guy, www.nyelabs.kcts.org/. Based on the television
    show, includes science news, demos, a lab, links, and brainteasers.
Chem-4-Kids, www.chem4kids.com/. Easy-to-understand explanations of
    chemistry concepts for kids.
Electric Origami, www.ibm.com/stretch/EOS/. Lots of logical (and
    spatial) puzzles, brainteasers, and activities.
Mad Scientist Network, 128.252.223.239/~ysp/MSN/. Ask real scientists
    questions (sponsored by Washington University Medical School in
    St. Louis, MO).
Whelmers, www.mcrel.org/whelmers/. Lots of science projects for kids,
    including Balloon in the Bottle and Floating Bubbles.

Spatial
Cartoon Mania, www.worldchat.com/public/jhish/cartoon.html. How
    to create your own cartoon-style animals.
Global Children's Art Gallery, www.naturalchild.com/gallery, and Global

Show-n-Tell, www.telenaut.com/gst/. Kids' online art galleries allow a child to post his or her own artwork.

Kids Corner Puzzle, kids.ot.com/. Create puzzles, send in pictures that can be used for the puzzle page, find keypals, and visit other kid-related links.

Bodily-kinesthetic

American Youth Soccer Organization, www.ayso.org/. Kids can have soccer chats, get info on how to participate in local regions, etc.

Little League, www.littleleague.org/. Includes Little League–related news, leagues in your area, a museum, and a scavenger hunt.

Outside Online, outside.starwave.com/index.html. Includes information on hiking, camping, backpacking, and other outdoor recreations.

Musical

The MIDI Farm, www.midifarm.com. Music for the whole family (download free MIDI files of tunes to play).

Resources for Young Composers, www.geocities.com/Vienna/2095/. Shows how to apply for copyright, enter contests, etc.

Interpersonal

Boys and Girls Clubs, www.bgca.org/index1.html. Link with other boys and girls clubs around the country.

Family Games!, www.familygames.com. Demo play is free (full versions reasonably priced).

Gamekids, www.gamekids.com. Collaborative reviews of games and other topics.

Games Kids Play, www.corpcomm.net/~gnieboer/gamehome.htm. Rules for outdoor and party games that require the child to disengage from the computer and try them out in the real world!

KidsPub KeyPals, www.kidpub.org/kidpub/keypals/. Access to keypals (e.g., penpals via E-mail) from all over the United States and the world.

Scouter's Compass, www.scouter.com/sl/. Lots of information about all types of scouts.

Intrapersonal

Berit's Best Sites for Kids, http://db.cochran.com/li_toc:theoPage.db. This website rates the best sites for kids (on a scale from 1 to 5), covering games, toys, stories, sports, recreation, music, movies, and more.

Kid City, www.sftoday.com/enn2/kidcity.htm. Enter a cybertown and explore the library, science museum, computer lab, town hall, newsstand, and more.

Kids Did This!, Sin.fi.edu/tfi/hotlists/kids.html. Links to sites created by kids in projects related to the environment, the arts, math, news, and other areas.

Naturalist

Bug Watch, www.bugwatch.com/bugindex.html. Click on images of a wide variety of bugs and get detailed information about them.

Electronic Field Trips, http://www.aea11.k12.ia.us/public.html. Lists various science and environmental project websites.

KinderGARDEN, aggie-horticulture.tamu.edu/kinder/index.html. Introduces kids (and families) to gardening through activities and weblinks.

National Geographic.com Kids, www.nationalgeographic.com/kids/. Kids section of the *National Geographic* website involves them in games, puzzles, discussions, and more.

National Wildlife Federation: For Kids, www.nwf.org/kids/. Kids can play games, take quizzes, read articles, take cybernature tours, and more.

New Jersey Online: Yuckiest Site on the Internet, www.nj.com/yucky/index.html. A guide to worms, cockroaches, and other yucky things.

WylandKids Web, www.wylandkids.com. Ocean conservation and art projects.

Computer Software That Develops the Eight Intelligences

There is an increasing selection of educational software programs out there for kids. Unfortunately, many of these programs are simply electronic versions of the worksheets that are boring kids to death in the schools. Many others are "cutsie" merchandising gimmicks based on the latest blockbuster films and should be avoided. In general, when shopping for computer software, parents should look for programs that are open-ended, that allow the child not simply to point-and-click at questions and answers, but to engage in creative thinking, writing, problem-solving, reading, drawing, painting, construction, and/or decision making (beware though: Some manufacturers promise "creative thinking" on their packaging but simply have kids doing electronic worksheets once they start the program). A note about electronic arcade or video games. These are generally very limited in their development of kids' minds. Most of them do stimulate a child's brain, but only a very limited part of it: the primitive "fight-or-flight" parts of the brain involved in killing or being killed! Clearly, there's not much multiple intelligences activity going on under these circumstances, and parents would be well advised to limit their use in the home. The software programs below include age ranges. Generally speaking, I am not in favor of kids below the age of five or six engaging in much computer time. The reason for this is that, for all its seeming educational stimulation, computers still provide relatively little active stimulation for the growing mind-body of the young child. Instead of using a draw-and-paint software program, I believe that the average five-year-old should be working with real paints. Instead of "building" with electronic Legos, young children should be playing with the real thing. Too many young kids today are being shoved in front of computer screens when they should be out playing, exercising their full sensory-motor faculties in a variety of hands-on ways. Research in developmental psychology provides ample support for the view that young children's active exploratory play creates a basis for their later abstract learning (when computer use becomes more appropriate). However, since computers are turning out to be such a huge part of the cultural landscape, it would be unrealistic for me to tell parents to keep their youngsters away from it entirely, so a little exposure to computers for kids six and under (perhaps fifteen to thirty minutes a day) may not be unreasonable. For older kids, these times can be increased accordingly (perhaps an hour a day for elementary school–aged kids [not counting school-related computer time], more for adolescents, who will find a way to take the extra time anyway!). Most of the software programs listed below engage more than one intelligence. And though few programs are listed under the personal intelligences, it should be pointed out that any self-paced computer software program can help nurture the intrapersonal intelligence by giving a child the ability to control their own learning. Some studies have suggested that computer activity may stifle social interaction—creating depression and loneliness—even when there is E-mail or internet interactions. So, make sure that you build in opportunities for real social interaction during computer time. You can help make sure that interpersonal intelligence is brought into play by sitting next to your child as he or she interacts with the computer—serving as a mediator, tutor, or helper—or by encouraging your child to engage in computer play with other kids.

Linguistic
Reader Rabbit (Learning Company, various editions for different ages)
Reading Blaster 2000 (6–9)
Adventures in Typing (Disney Interactive, 6+)
Living Books (Interactive Animated Series; Random House/ Broderbund; various titles for different ages)
Carmen San Diego Word Detective (Broderbund, 8–14)
Dr. Seuss's ABCs (Living Books, 3–6)

Logical-mathematical
Math Rabbit (Learning Company, various editions for different ages)
Zap (Thinkin' Science Series) (Edmark, 8–12)
Thinkin' Things (Edmark, 4–12)
Widget Workshop (Electronic Arts, 8+)
Carmen San Diego Math Detective (Broderbund, 8–14)
The Lost Mind of Dr. Brain (Sierra On-Line, 10+)

Spatial
Tomie de Paola's The Art Lesson (MECC, 5–10)
My Own Paint Set (Learning Company, 4–7)
Disney's Print Studio (Disney Interactive, all ages)
Print Factory (IBM, 5–10)
Kid Pix (Broderbund, 3–12)
Crayola Make a Masterpiece (IBM, 5–12)
Kids Works Deluxe (Davidson & Associates, 6–10)

Bodily-kinesthetic
Tonka Construction (Hasbro, 4+)
Lego (Island, 6–12)
Bricks (Knowledge Adventure, 6–12)
Virtual K'Nex (Fox, 6–12)

Musical
Sim Tunes (Electronic Arts, 8+)

The Personal Intelligences
Action Reading: Kenny Kite to the Rescue (Conexus/Davidson & Associates, 6–10)
Rocket's Tricky Decision (Purple Moon, 8–12 girls)
Oregon Trail, 3rd Edition (Learning Company, 10+)
Amazon Trail (MECC, 9+)
Oregon Trail II (MECC, 10+)

Naturalist
Sim Safari (Maxis Kids, 8+)
The Multimedia Bug Book (Workman/Swifte, 6–10)
The Magic Schoolbus Visits the Ocean (Microsoft, 6–10)
Total Biopark (Computer Curriculum, 10+)

Notes

Notes are referenced by chapter, page, and the first few words of the sentence to which the note refers or a general reference to the issue cited.

Chapter 1: The Worksheet Wasteland

p. 1 "How many thinkers . . ." Jean Houston, *The Possible Human* (Los Angeles: Jeremy P. Tarcher, 1982), p. 139.

p. 2 "Billy shut . . ," Jean Houston, *The Possible Human* (Los Angeles: Jeremy P. Tarcher, 1982), p. 137.

p. 2 "Susan wrote . . ." Charles Meisgeier, Constance Meisgeier, and Dorothy Werblo, "Factors Compounding the Handicapping of Some Gifted Children," *Gifted Children Quarterly* (Fall 1978): 329.

p. 3 "All three of these boys . . ." Susan Baum, "Meeting the Needs of Learning Disabled Gifted Students," *Roeper Review* (September 1984).

p. 4 "Einstein once wrote . . ." Quoted in Victor Goertzel and Mildred G. Goertzel, *Cradles of Eminence* (Boston: Little, Brown and Company, 1962), p. 253.

p. 5 "Less than 3 percent . . ." John Goodlad, *A Place Called School* (New York: McGraw-Hill, 1984), pp. 229–230.

p. 5 "Textbooks . . . structure from 75 to 90 percent . . ." H. Tyson, and A. Woodward, "Why Students Aren't Learning Very Much from Textbooks," *Educational Leadership* 47 (November 1989): 14–17; and H. Tyson-Bernstein, *A Conspiracy of Good Intentions: America's Textbook Fiasco* (Washington, DC: Council for Basic Education).

p. 5 "Sales of textbooks . . ." Doreen Carvajal, "Sales of Textbooks Continuing to Defy Gloomy Predictions," *New York Times*, 26 May, 1998.

p. 5 "U.S. schoolchildren are the most tested students . . ." Monty Neill, "National Tests Are Unnecessary and Harmful," *Educational Leadership* (March 1998): 45.

p. 5 "Individual states that have the most impact upon textbook construction . . ." See, for example, Kathleen Kennedy Manzo, "More States Moving to Make Phonics the Law," *Education Week* (29 April, 1998): 24.

p. 5 "State legislatures are implementing rigid . . ." See Bess Keller, "In Age of Accountability, Principals Feel the Heat," *Education Week* (20 May, 1998): 1+.

p. 5 "Schools are even beginning to get rid of recess . . . " Dirk Johnson, "Many Schools Putting an End to Child's Play," *New York Times*, 7, April 1998, pp. 1A, 18A.

p. 6 Statistics on prevalence of learning disabilities taken from LDOnline website (www.ldonline.org), sponsored by the Coordinated Campaign for Learning Disabilities (funded by the Emily Hall Tremaine Foundation).

p. 6 "He suggested that they . . ." Samuel Kirk, "Learning Disabilities: A Historical Note," *Academic Therapy* 17, no. I (September 1981): 7.

p. 7 "Bob Algozzine, a professor . . ." James Tucker, Linda J. Stevens, and James E. Ysseldyke, "Learning Disabilities: The Experts Speak Out," *Journal of Learning Disabilities* 16, no. 1 (January 1983): 9.

p. 7 "It seems such a shame . . ." Douglas Friedrich, Gerald B. Fuller, and Donald Davis, "Learning Disability: Fact and Fiction," *Journal of Learning Disabilities* 17, no. 4 (April 1984): 209.

p. 8 Statistics on increase in use of Ritalin taken from Lawrence H. Diller, *Running on Ritalin: A Physician Reflects on Children, Society, and Performance in a Pill* (New York: Bantam, Doubleday, Dell, 1998). Statistics on ADD prevalence taken from Dyan Machan, "An Agreeable Affliction," *Forbes*, August 12, 1996, p. 148.

p. 8 For details about the problems with attention deficit disorder as a paradigm for understanding children, see Thomas Armstrong, *The Myth of the ADD Child: 50 Ways to Improve Your Child's Behavior and Attention Span without Drugs, Labels, or Coercion* (New York: Plume, 1997); and Thomas Armstrong, *ADD/ADHD Alternatives in the Classroom* (Alexandria, VA: Association for Supervision and Curriculum Development, 1999).

p. 9 "The horrifying truth is . . ." Mary Poplin, "Summary Rationalizations, Apologies and Farewell: What We Don't Know about the Learning Disabled," *Learning Disability Quarterly* 7 (Spring 1984): 133.

p. 9 "She speculated that . . ." Sara G. Tarver, Patricia S. Ellsworth, and David J. Rounds, "Figural and Verbal Creativity in Learning Disabled and Nondisabled Children," *Learning Disability Quarterly* 3 (Summer 1980): 11–18.

p. 9 "Other authorities affirm . . ." Norman Geschwind, "Why Orton Was Right," *Annals of Dyslexia* 32 (1982): 22.

p. 10 "With regard to attention deficit disorder . . ." Bonnie Cramond, "Attention-Deficit Hyperactivity Disorder and Creativity: What Is the Connection?" *Journal of Creative Behavior,* 28, no. 3 (1994): 193–210.

p. 12 "Their new life in . . ." Quoted in Ernest Schactel, *Metamorphosis* (New York: Basic Books, 1959), p. 293.

p. 13 "In spite of this . . ." Roger Lewin, "Is Your Brain Really Necessary?" *Science* 210 (December 12, 1980): 1232–1234.

Chapter 2: Eight Ways to Bloom

p. 15 "Most people in . . ." James Ellison, "The Seven Frames of Mind: Psychology Today Conversation with Howard Gardner," *Psychology Today* (June 1984): 21.

Chapter 3: Testing for Failure

p. 35 "Emile Zola got . . ." Victor and Mildred G. Goertzel, *Cradles of Eminence* (Boston: Little, Brown and Company, 1962), pp. 247, 252.

p. 36 "Thirty years ago . . ." Banesh Hoffmann, *The Tyranny of Testing* (New York: Crowell-Collier, 1962).

p. 36 "The National Education Association . . ." *National Education Association Handbook, 1984–85* (Washington, DC: National Education Association of the United States, 1984), p. 240.

p. 37 "This test is supposed . . ." Cited in Jerome Sattler, *Assessment of Children's Intelligences and Special Abilities* (Boston: Allyn & Bacon, 1982), p. 160.

p. 37 "According to Harvard professor . . ." Steven Jay Gould, *The Mismeasure of Man* (New York: W.W. Norton, 1981).

p. 38 "And as David Owen . . ." David Owen, *None of the Above: Behind the Myth of Scholastic Aptitude* (Boston: Houghton Mifflin Co., 1985).

p. 38 "We don't know what . . ." Gerald S. Coles, "The Learning Disability Test Battery: Empirical and Social Issues," *Harvard Educational Review* 48 (1978): 313–340.

p. 39 "A New York teacher . . ." Pat Carini, *The School Lives of Seven Chil-*

dren: A Five Year Study (Grand Forks, ND: North Dakota Study Group on Evaluation, 1982), p. 39.

p. 40 "This testing room . . ." Thomas A. Sebeok and Robert Rosenthal, eds., *The Clever Hans Phenomenon: Communication with Horses, Whales, Apes, and People* (New York: New York Academy of Sciences, 1981).

p. 40 "As San Diego State . . ." Hugh Mehan, Alma Hertweck, and J. Lee Meihls, *Handicapping the Handicapped: Decision Making in Students' Educational Careers* (Stanford, CA: Stanford University Press, 1986), p. 100.

p. 49 "George Madaus, director . . ." George Madaus, "Test Scores as Administrative Mechanisms in Educational Policy," *Phi Delta Kappan* (May 1985): 616.

Chapter 4: Dysteachia

p. 51 "Formal education has . . ." Frank Smith, *Insult to Intelligence: The Bureaucratic Invasion of Our Classrooms* (New York: Arbor House, 1986), p. 18.

p. 53 "Whether they actually . . ." P. Kenneth Komoski, "What Do We Need to Improve Instructional Materials?" *Education Digest* (October 1985): 15.

p. 55 "Anne Adams of . . ." Quoted in Craig Pearson, "Reading vs. Reading Skills," *Learning* (November 1980): 29.

p. 55 "Research suggests . . ." Jeannine Oakes, *Keeping Track: How Schools Structure Inequality* (New Haven, CT: Yale University Press, 1985).

p. 56 "As a result . . ." U.S. Department of Commerce, *Statistical Abstract of the United States* (Washington, DC: U.S. Government Printing Office, 1984).

p. 56 "Carl Milofsky, a California . . ." Carl Milofsky, *Special Education: A Sociological Study of California Programs* (New York: Praeger, 1976), p. 106.

p. 57 "Lee Ann Trusdell . . ." "How Pull-Out Programs Can Hurt," *Learning* (March 1980): 17.

p. 57 "Jeane Westin interviewed . . ." Jeane Westin, "Educationally Handicapped: The Social Engineers' Gold Mine?" in *The Coming Parent Revolution* (New York: Rand McNally, 1981), p. 132.

p. 57 "As a federal study . . ." Nicholas Hobbs, *The Futures of Children: Categories, Labels and Their Consequences* (San Francisco: Jossey-Bass, 1975), p. 81.

p. 59 "The rats in the . . ." Mark R. Rosenzweig, Edward L. Bennett, and

Marian Cleeves Diamond, "Brain Changes in Response to Experience," *Scientific American* 226 (February 1972): 22–29.

p. 62 "In their classic book . . ." Peter Schrag and Diane Divoky, *The Myth of the Hyperactive Child* (New York: Pantheon, 1975).

Chapter 5: Learning in Their Own Way

p. 67 "The widespread acceptance . . ." David and Micki Colfax, *Home-schooling for Excellence* (New York: Warner, 1988), pp. 49–50.

p. 72 "Now, forty-five years . . ." Rudolf Flesch, *Why Johnny Can't Read* (New York: Harper & Row, 1986).

p. 83 "This fair included . . ." Linda Robertson, "A Celebration of Learning," *Principal* (November 1985): 28–31.

p. 83 "Suggest that they . . ." See Roger Williams, "Why Children Should Draw," *Saturday Review* (3 September, 1977).

Chapter 6: Bodywise

p. 85 "The words or . . ." Albert Einstein, "Letter to Jacques Hadamard," in Brewster Ghiselin, *The Creative Process* (New York: Mentor, 1952), p. 43.

p. 87 "William James . . ." William James, *Principles of Psychology* (New York: Henry Holt, 1910), p. 61.

p. 87 "When *legere* and *lectio* . . ." quoted in Marshall McLuhan, *The Gutenberg Galaxy* (Toronto, Canada: University of Toronto Press, 1965), p. 89.

p. 89 "Michael Gelb . . ." "Gelb: Freeing the Body to Free the Mind for Learning," *Brain-Mind Bulletin* (2 January, 1984): 2.

Chapter 7: The Inner Blackboard

p. 99 "If a Hopi and . . ." Bob Samples, *The Metaphoric Mind* (Reading, MA: Addison Wesley, 1984), p. 45.

p. 101 "Jerome Bruner . . ." Jerome Bruner, Rose R. Olver, and Patricia M. Greenfield, *Studies in Cognitive Growth* (New York: Wiley, 1966).

p. 101 "George Lakoff . . ." George Lakoff and Mark Johnson, *Metaphors We Live By* (Chicago: University of Chicago Press, 1980).

p. 101 "Titchner came to associate . . ." Rudolf Arnheim, *Visual Thinking* (Berkeley: University of California Press, 1969).

p. 102 "Eugene S. Ferguson . . ." Eugene S. Ferguson, "The Mind's Eye: Nonverbal Thought in Technology," *Science* 197 (26 August, 1977): 827–836.

p. 103 "Research suggests that . . ." Amiram Carmon, Israel Nachshon, and Ruth Starinsky, "Developmental Aspects of Visual Hemifield Differences in Perception of Verbal Material," *Brain and Language* 3 (1976): 463–469.

p. 104 "It's interesting to note that many artists . . . ." See, for example, Ronald D. David and Eldon Braun, *The Gift of Dyslexia: Why Some of the Smartest People Can't Read and How They Can Learn* (New York: Perigee, 1998); and Thomas G. West, *In the Mind's Eye: Visual Thinkers, Gifted People with Learning Difficulties, Computer Images, and the Ironies of Creativity* (Buffalo, NY: Prometheus, 1991).

p. 105 "During the course . . ." Barbara Cordoni, "Teaching the LD Child to Read through Visual Imagery," *Academic Therapy* 16, no. 3 (January 1981): 327–331.

p. 105 "With two alphabets . . ." Kiyoshi Makita, "The Rarity of Reading Disability in Japanese Children," *American Journal of Orthopsychiatry* 38 (1968): 599–614.

p. 105 "They wrote: . . ." Paul Rozin, Susan Poritsky, and Raina Sotsky, "American Children with Reading Problems Can Easily Learn to Read English Represented by Chinese Characters," *Science* 171 (March 26, 1971): 1264–1267.

p. 108 "But if you make . . ." A. C. Harwood, *The Recovery of Man in Childhood* (London: Hodder & Stoughton, 1958), pp. 79–80.

p. 108 "In teaching about . . ." W. J. J. Gordon and Tony Poze, *Strange and Familiar* (Cambridge, MA: Synectics Education Systems, 1972).

p. 109 "Studies indicate that . . ." Ralph Norman Haber, "Eidetic Images," *Scientific American* (April 1969).

p. 109 "E. R. Jaensch, . . ." E. R. Jaensch, *Eidetic Imagery* (New York: Harcourt, Brace & Co., 1930).

Chapter 8: Teaching with Feeling

p. 111 "It seems to me . . ." John Holt, *How Children Fail* (New York: Dell, 1977), p. 91.

p. 115 "When an emotion triggers . . ." quoted in Daniel Goleman, *Emotional Intelligence: Why It Matters More Than IQ* (New York: Bantam, 1995), p. 25.

p. 116 ". . . in one study . . . preschoolers showed the ability to delay gratification . . ." Cited in Goleman, p. 80.

p. 117 "We have been brought up . . ." quoted in Constance Holden, "Paul MacLean and the Triune Brain," *Science* 204 (8 June, 1979): 1068.

p. 117 "He calls these codes . . ." "New Theory: Feelings Code, Organize Thinking," *Brain-Mind Bulletin* 7, no. 6 (8 March, 1982).

p. 117 "Jerome Bruner, author . . ." Jerome Bruner, *Actual Minds, Possible Worlds* (Cambridge, MA: Harvard University Press, 1986), p. 69.

p. 117 "Leslie Hart, an educator . . ." Leslie Hart, "Misconceptions about Learning Disabilities," *The National Elementary Principal* 56, no. 1 (September/October 1976).

p. 118 "Yet, I'm reminded . . ." John Goodlad, *A Place Called School* (New York: McGraw-Hill, 1984), p. 108.

p. 119 "Several ways of releasing . . ." See Neil C. Richter, "The Efficacy of Relaxation Training with Children," *Journal of Abnormal Child Psychology*, vol. 12, no. 2 (1984): 319–344; and Steven W. Le, "Biofeedback as a Treatment for Childhood Hyperactivity: A Critical Review of the Literature," *Psychological Reports* 68 (1991): 163–192.

Chapter 9: The Learning Network

p. 135 "I noticed recently . . ." quoted in *Growing without Schooling Newsletter* 18 (1977): 3.

p. 138 "Nineteenth-century British . . ." Erica Carle, "Children as Teachers," in *Human Learning* (American Society of Humanistic Education, 1970).

Chapter 10: Great Expectations

p. 143 "He hypothesized . . ." Robert Rosenthal and Lenore Jacobsen, *Pgymalion in the Classroom: Teacher Expectations and Pupils' Intellectual Development* (New York: Holt, 1968).

p. 143 "The group informed . . ." Glen G. Foster, Carl R. Schmidt, and David Sabatino, "Teacher Expectancies and the Label Learning Disabilities," *Journal of Learning Disabilities* 9 (1976): 58–61.

p. 143 "Another study had psychiatrists . . ." Eberhard M. Mann et al., "Cross-Cultural Differences in Rating Hyperactive-Disruptive Behaviors in Children," *American Journal of Psychiatry*, vol. 149, no. 11 (November 1992): 1539–1542.

p. 143 "A third study showed . . ." R. Parker, S. Larsen, and T. Roberts, "Teacher-Child Interactions of First-Grade Students Who Have

Learning Problems," *The Elementary School Journal* 81 (1981): 163–171.

p. 143 "It's no wonder . . ." G. Bingham, "Self-Esteem among Boys with and without Specific Learning Disabilities," *Child Study Journal* 10 (1980): 41–47.

p. 143 "Psychologists are now . . ." Lynn Grimes, "Learned Helplessness and Attribution Theory: Redefining Children's Learning Problems," *Learning Disability Quarterly* 4 (Winter 1981): 91–100.

p. 148 "He never drew . . ." Stanley Krippner, "The Ten Commandments That Block Creativity," *Gifted Child Quarterly* (Autumn 1967): 144–156.

p. 149 "She suggests that . . ." Diane McGuinness, *When Children Don't Learn: Understanding the Biology and Psychology of Learning Disabilities* (New York: Basic Books, 1985).

Chapter 11: A Patient Attitude

p. 151 "TEACHER: 'Monitors, are you . . ." Jules Henry, "A Cross-Cultural Outline of Education," *On Education* (New York: Random House, 1971), p. 150.

p. 152 "Forty years ago . . ." Henry, p. 151.

p. 152 "A joint statement . . ." Barbara Vobejda, "Preschools Accused of Pushing Tots Too Hard," *Washington Post*, 15 November, 1986, A1,18.

p. 154 "Anthropologist Edward T. Hall . . ." Edward T. Hall, *The Hidden Dimension* (New York: Doubleday, 1969), p. 132.

p. 154 "Such countries as . . ." John Downing, "How Society Creates Reading Disability," *The Elementary School Journal* 77, no. 4 (March 1977).

p. 154 "The late Dr. Louise Bates Ames, . . ." Louise Bates Ames, "Learning Disabilities Often Result from Sheer Immaturity," *Journal of Learning Disabilities* 1, no. 3 (March 1968): 207–212.

p. 155 "He emphasized that . . ." Eleanor Duckworth, "Either We're Too Early and They Can't Learn It or We're Too Late and They Know It Already: The Dilemma of Applying Piaget," *Harvard Educational Review* 49, no. 3 (August 1979): 297–312.

p. 155 "Steiner observed . . ." Rudolf Steiner, *The Kingdom of Childhood* (London: Rudolf Steiner Press, 1964), p. 40.

p. 156 "A. S. Neill, the founder of . . ." A. S. Neill, *Summerhill* (New York: Hart, 1960), p. 30.

p. 157 "To parents who . . ." Hazrat Inayat Khan, *The Sufi Message* 2 (The Netherlands: Servire Wassenaar, 1976): 173.

p. 157 "He had just turned . . ." Louise Bates Ames, "Learning Disability—Very Big around Here," *Research Communications in Psychology, Psychiatry and Behavior* 10, nos. 1 & 2 (1985): 26.

p. 158 "The nonreader may . . ." Norman E. Silberberg and Margaret C. Silberberg, "The Bookless Curriculum: An Educational Alternative," *Journal of Learning Disabilities* 2, no. 6 (June 1969): 302–307.

p. 158 "Adolescents could perhaps . . ." Desson Howe, "Reaching the Stars: VIPs Who Overcame Dyslexia Honored," *Washington Post*, 31 October, 1985, p. B12.

p. 158 "Anthropologist Ashley Montagu . . ." Ashley Montagu, *Growing Young* (New York: McGraw-Hill, 1983).

p. 159 "In *The Hurried Child* . . ." David Elkind, *The Hurried Child* (Reading, MA: Addison Wesley, 1981), pp. 177–178.

Chapter 12: The Doors of Perception

p. 161 "Part of the . . ." Joseph Chilton Pearce, *Magical Child* (New York: Bantam, 1980), p. 158.

p. 162 "Heinz Werner, one of . . ." Heinz Werner, *Comparative Psychology of Mental Development* (New York: International Universities Press, 1973), p. 88.

p. 162 "He offers examples . . ." Werner, p. 89.

p. 162 "This mixing of . . ." Werner, p. 90.

p. 163 "He wrote . . ." Werner, p. 69.

p. 163 "He illustrated this . . ." Werner, p. 73.

p. 163 "A four-year-old . . ." Werner, p. 74.

p. 164 "This idea occurred. . ." R. L. Gregory, *Eye and Brain: The Psychology of Seeing* (New York: McGraw Hill, 1973), pp. 216–217.

p. 165 "Ray Gottlieb, a California . . ." "School Anxiety May Be Major Cause of Myopia," *Brain-Mind Bulletin* 7, no. 17 (25 October, 1982).

p. 165 "Helmer Myklebust, a well-known . . ." Helmer Myklebust, *Auditory Disorders in Children: A Manual for Differential Diagnosis* (New York: Grune & Stratton, 1954).

p. 166 "Tim Gallwey, author . . ." "How-to Instructions Inhibit Optimum Performance," *Brain-Mind Bulletin* 7, no. 13 (2 August, 1982).

p. 167 "Maureen Murdock, a California . . ." Maureen Murdock, *Spinning Inward* (Culver City, CA: Peace Press, 1982), p. 48.

p. 168 "An Alabama mother . . ." *Growing without Schooling Newsletter* 18 (1981): 11.

p. 168 "Holt commented: . . ." John Holt, *Teach Your Own* (New York: Delta/Seymour Lawrence, 1981), p. 239.

Chapter 13: The Ecology of Learning

p. 173 "The developing child . . ." Ray C. Wunderlich Jr. and Dwight K. Kalita, *Nourishing Your Child: A Bioecologic Approach* (New Canaan, CT: Keats, 1984), p. 4.

p. 176 "Certain children are allergic . . ." For studies on the role of food allergies in learning and behavior, see, for example, Bonnie J. Kaplan et al., "Dietary Replacement in Preschool-Aged Hyperactive Boys," *Pediatrics*, vol. 83, no. 7 (January 1989): 7–17; and J. Egger et al., "Controlled Trial of Oligoantigenic Treatment in the Hyperkinetic Syndrome," *Lancet* (9 March, 1985): 540–545.

p. 177 "While the Feingold diet has come under fire . . ." See, for example, Katherine S. Rowe and Kenneth J. Rowe, "Synthetic Food Coloring and Behavior: A Dose Response Effect in a Double-blind, Placebo-controlled Repeated-measures Study," *The Journal of Pediatrics* (November 1994).

p. 177 "In one study . . . " The George Washington University study was reported in *Science News*, vol. 132, no. 11 (September 12, 1987).

p. 178 "As Carole S. Weinstein . . ." Carole S. Weinstein, "The Physical Environment of the School," *Review of Educational Research* 49, no. 4 (1979): 585.

p. 179 "The new field of . . ." "'Chronopsychology' Links Brain Function to Cycles," *Brain-Mind Bulletin* 7, no. 1 (23 November, 1981).

p. 180 "After forty minutes . . ." Tony Buzan, *Use Both Sides of Your Brain* (New York: E.P. Dutton, 1974), p. 50.

p. 181 "Dr. Sheldon Cohen . . ." S. Cohen, G. W. Evans, D. S. Krantz, D. Stokols, and S. Kelly, "Aircraft Noise and Children: Longitudinal and Cross-Sectional Evidence on Adaptation to Noise and the Effectiveness of Noise Abatement," *Journal of Personality and Social Psychology* 40 (1981): 331–345.

p. 182 "Yet one study . . ." Charles Moon, Mike Marlowe, John Stellech, and John Errera, "Main and Interaction Effects of Metallic Pollutants on Cognitive Functioning," *Journal of Learning Disabilities* 18, no. 4 (April 1985): 217–221.

p. 182 "Legislation in some states . . ." See, for example, *Not a Pretty Picture: Art Hazards in California Public Schools* (Berkeley: California Public Interest Research Group, August 1984).

Afterword: The Learner of the Future

p. 185 "All education springs . . ." Alvin Toffler, ed., *Learning for Tomorrow: The Role of the Future in Education* (New York: Random House, 1974), p. 3.

p. 186 "McLuhan wrote, . . ." Marshall McLuhan and Quentin Fiore, *The Medium Is the Massage* (New York: Bantam, 1967), p. 18.

p. 187 "Tony Schwartz, author . . ." Tony Schwartz, *The Responsive Chord* (Garden City, NY: Anchor Press/Doubleday, 1973), p. 113.

p. 187 "Drake points out . . ." Quoted in Roa Lynn, *Learning Disabilities: An Overview of Theories, Approaches, and Politics* (New York: The Free Press, 1979), pp. 19–20.

p. 187 "Norman Geschwind wrote: . . ." Norman Geschwind, "Why Orton Was Right," *Annals of Dyslexia* 32 (1982): 22.

p. 187 "Other studies suggest . . ." See, for example, John R. Kershner, "Rotation of Mental Images and Asymmetries in Word Recognition in Disabled Readers," *Canadian Journal of Psychology* 33, no. 1 (1979): 39–49; and Sandra Witelson, "Developmental Dyslexia: Two Right Hemispheres and None Left," *Science* 195 (January 21, 1977): 309–311.

p. 188 "Many other great people . . ." See Victor Goertzel and Mildred G. Goertzel, *Cradles of Eminence* (Boston: Little, Brown and Company, 1962); Lloyd Thompson, "Language Disabilities in Men of Eminence," *Bulletin of the Orton Society* 19 (1969); Jan Ehrenwald, *Anatomy of Genius* (New York: Human Sciences Press, 1984); and R. S. Illingworth and C. M. Illingworth, *Lessons from Childhood* (London: Livingstone, 1966).

Index

Ability, grouping by, 55–56
Abstract thinking, 23, 100–101
Accountability standards, 6
Achievement, grouping by, 55–56
Achievement tests, 37
Activities, 46–48, 225–28
  learning from, 134
  misapplication of, 217–18
Adams, Anne, 55
ADD/ADHD (Attention deficit disor-
    der/Attention deficit hyperac-
    tivity disorder), 3, 6–10, 42,
    186, 187
  bodily-kinesthetic
    intelligence and, 27
  diagnostic tests, 39
  and perceptions, 164–66
  special education programs for, 56–
    57
  stress and, 113
Air pollution, 181–82
Algebra, teaching strategies, 207–8
Algozzine, Bob, 7
Alphabatics, MacDonald, 104
Alphabet, teaching of, 104–5
Alternative evaluation methods, 44–
    47
Alternative schools, 63, 155–56
Ames, Louise Bates, 154, 157
Anderson, Winifred, *Negotiating the
    Special Education Maze*, 65
Apprenticeships, 136
Arnheim, Rudolf, 101
Artistic expression, 120–21
Artists, 18

Ashton-Warner, Sylvia, *Teacher*, 124
Assagioli, Roberto, 123
Association for Children with Learn-
    ing Disabilities, 6
Athletic abilities, 26
Attention deficit disorder. *See*
    ADD/ADHD
Attention deficit hyperactivity disor-
    der. *See* ADD/ADHD
Attributes, positive, 147

Barsch, Jeffrey, 89
Beethoven, Ludwig van, 188
Behavior, intelligences and, 81
Behavior modification programs, 114
Bettelheim, Bruno, *Learning to Read:
    The Child's Fascination with
    Reading*, 124
Bigotry, testing and, 37–38
Bodily-kinesthetic intelligence, 18–19,
    26–28, 70
  activities, 46
  and learning, 86–98
  and multiplication tables, 78
  and reading, 74
  and space, 178–79
Body smart. *See* Bodily- kinesthetic in-
    telligence
Books:
  for children, 253–58
  for parents, 229–40
Brain:
  and emotions, 115–17
  environment and, 59
  and intelligences, 196

Breakfasts, protein-poor, 177
Brigham, Carl, 37
Bruner, Jerome, 101, 117
Buzan, Tony, 180

Campbell, Bruce, 215–16
Centering activities, 119–20
Change, positive, examples of, 83
Charades, 91
Chemical additives, 176–77
Chemistry, teaching strategies, 209–11
Childhood:
    enjoyment of, 158–59
    imagination in, 102–3
Children:
    books for, 253–58
    and diagnostic tests, 39–40, 45
    grouping of, 55–56
    individual differences, 21–22
    and information about intelligences, 223–28
    and learning activities, 98
    learning problems, 10–12
    multiple intelligences, 22–34
    problems of, teaching methods and, 52–60
    protection from formal testing, 43–44
    schools and, 4–6
    and stress, 112–14
Children Who Underachieve, Greene, 6
Chitwood, Stephen, Negotiating the Special Education Maze, 65
Choice in learning, 125–26
Chronopsychology, 179–80
Classrooms, 4–6
    changes in, 84
    emotions in, 118
    evaluation of, 60
Clever Hans phenomenon, 40
Clinical ecologists, 176, 182
Cognitive development, 154–55
Cohen, Sheldon, 181
Coles, Gerald, 38
Colfax, David and Micki, 64
    Homeschooling for Excellence, 67

The Coming Parent Revolution, Westin, 57
Computer software, 42, 267–69
Cordoni, Barbara, 105
Counseling, professional:
    needs for, 30, 32
    and stress, 122–23
Cradles of Eminence, Goertzel and Goertzel, 35
Cramond, Bonnie, 9–10
Creative writing, 123–24
Creativity, 10, 197–98
    nonverbal, 9–10
Criterion-referenced testing, 44
Criticism, by teachers, 143
Crowding conditions, 178–79
Cuisenaire rods, 96
Culture, and intelligences, 21

Daydreaming, 25, 99
Deafness, psychic, 165–66
Development, differing rates, 152–60
Diagnostic tests, 38–43
Diamond, Marian, 59
Diet, and learning, 175–78
Disabilities, test makers and, 39–40
Divoky, Diane, The Myth of the Hyperactive Child, 62
Documentation, evaluation by, 45–46
Drake, Charles, 187
The Drama of the Gifted Child, Miller, 159
Dreikurs, Rudolf, 81
Dyslexia, 3, 9, 26, 42, 187
    and imagination, 102–4
    and spatial intelligence, 105

Ecology of learning, 174–83
Edison, Thomas A., 188
Education, 12
    regulation of, 51
Educational environment:
    change of, 62–63
    evaluation of, 60–61
    at home, 68–72
    See also Learning environment

Education for All Handicapped Children Act, 56
Eidetic imagery, 109
Einstein, Albert, 4, 18–19, 85, 92, 146, 188
Elimination diets, 176
Elkind, David, *The Hurried Child*, 153, 159
Emotional brain, 116–17
Emotional intelligence, 115–18
Emotionally handicapped children, 57
Emotions, and learning, 112–27
Empathy, 19, 30
Enactive representation, 101
Enrichment programs, 82
Environment:
  and brain development, 59
  educational, 60–61
    change of, 62–63
    at home, 68–72
  for learning, 58, 130–31
  nurturing, 173–83
  protection of, 33
Erikson, Erik, 144
Eugenics, 37
Evaluative tests, 39–40
  alternative methods, 44–47
Examples of positive change, 83
Existential intelligence, 197
Expectations, and learning, 142–50
Eyes, relaxation exercise, 170

Failure, mental images of, 109
Fantasy, 99
Fassler, Joan, *Helping Children Cope: Mastering Stress Through Books and Stories*, 125
Federal government, and special education, 6, 41, 56
Federal laws, use of, 64–65
Feedback:
  on assessment results, 48
  nonjudgmental, 133
Feingold, Ben, 176–77
Ferguson, Eugene S., 102
Fidgeting, 88

Field trips, 225
Fine-motor coordination, 18, 26
Flesch, Rudolf, *Why Johnny Can't Read*, 72
Food allergies, 176
Frames of Mind, Gardner, 16
Friedrich, Douglas, 7
Friendship, 19
Frontal teaching, 53

Gallwey, Tim, 166
Games, 134, 259–61
Gardner, Howard, 4, 15–17, 34, 195–98, 216
  The Unschooled Mind, 59
Gelb, Michael, 89
Gender differences, 149
Geography, teaching strategies, 205
Geschwind, Norman, 9, 187
Gesell, Arnold, 86
Gifted children, 13
Goal setting, 31
Goertzel, Victor and Mildred G., *Cradles of Eminence*, 35
Goethe, Johann Wolfgang von, 141
Goleman, Daniel, *Emotional Intelligence: Why It Can Matter More than IQ*, 115–16
Goodlad, John, 4–5, 118
  A Place Called School, 52–53, 59–60
Gordon, W. J. J., 108
Gottlieb, Ray, 165
Gould, Steven Jay, *The Mismeasure of Man*, 37
Grammar, teaching strategies, 206–7
Gray, William, 117
Greene, Lawrence, *Children Who Underachieve*, 6
Gregory, R. L., *Eye and Brain*, 164–65
Grouping of children, 55–56
Growing Young, Montagu, 158

Hall, Edward T., 154
Handicapping the Handicapped, Mehan, 40–41
Hart, Leslie, 13, 53, 117
Harwood, A. C., 108

Hayden, Deidre, *Negotiating the Special Education Maze*, 65
Hearing problems, 169–71
Helping Children Cope: Mastering Stress Through Books and Stories, Fassler, 125
Henry, Jules, 151, 152
Herzog, Stephanie, 119
Hilgard, Ernest, 144
Hoffmann, Banesh, 34
Holt, John, 58, 64, 159, 168
　How Children Fail, 111
Home:
　kinesthetic learning in, 97–98
　stress reduction in, 121
Home schooling, 64
Homeschooling for Excellence, Colfax and Colfax, 67
Homework, 80–81, 90–91
　parents and, 132–34
Houston, Jean, 2
　The Possible Human, 1
How Children Fail, Holt, 111
Howe, Elias, 101–2
Humor, 198
The Hurried Child, Elkind, 153, 159

Iconic representation, 101
Ideas, and emotions, 117
Imagination, and learning, 99–110
Impaired senses, 169–71
Individual differences, 21–22, 149–50
　in development, 152–60
　schools and, 4–6
　teachers and, 137
Individualized programs, 82
Informal testing, 44–45
Information processing, 186–87
Insult to Intelligence, Smith, 51, 55
Intelligences, 15–34, 195–97
　differences, 4
　and teaching methods, 79–81
Interests of child, 146, 148–49
Internet sites for children, 263–65
Interpersonal intelligence, 19, 29–30, 71, 196, 197
　activities, 47
　and multiplication tables, 78–79

and peer teaching, 139
and reading, 75
Intrapersonal intelligence, 20, 31–32, 71, 196
　activities, 47
　and multiplication tables, 79
　and reading, 75
Intuitiveness, 31
Inventors, 18
IQ (intelligence quotient) tests, and intelligence, 16

Jaensch, E. R., 109
James, William, 87
Johnson, Mark, 101

Kafka, Franz, 12
Key Renaissance Learning Community, 215
Khan, Hazrat Inayat, 157
Kirk, Samuel, 6
Kkalita, Dwight K., 173
Kock, Kenneth, 123–24
Koestler, Arthur, 167
Komoski, P. Kenneth, 53
Krippner, Stanley, 148
Kuhn, Thomas, 58

Labeling of children, 6–7, 12–13, 57, 82, 143–44, 216–17
　ADD/ADHD, 8
　bodily-kinesthetic intelligence and, 27
　spatial intelligence and, 26
　testing and, 42–43
Lakoff, George, 101
Lancaster, Joseph, 138
Late bloomers, 153, 154–60
Leadership, 30
Lead exposure, 181–82
Learned helplessness, 144
Learning, 51, 58
　body as tool for, 86–98
　differing rates, 152–60
　ecology of, 174–83
　emotions and, 114–27
　multisensory, 167–71
　music and, 29

testing and, 48
Learning abilities, 4
 neglect of, 8–10
Learning behaviors, positive, 145
Learning disabilities, 3, 6–7, 26, 186,
 187
 and developmental rate, 154–55
 diagnostic tests, 38–40
 and perceptions, 164–66
 schools and, 52
 spatial intelligence and, 104
 special education programs for, 56–
 57
 and stress, 113, 117
Learning disability movement, 6–7
Learning Disability Quarterly (LDQ),
 9
Learning environment, 58, 130–31
 destressing of, 118–23
 See also Educational environment
Learning materials, 247–51
Learning styles, 186–87
 multiple intelligences and, 193
Learning to Read: The Child's Fascination with Reading, Bettelheim
 and Zelan, 124
Leclercq, Dom Jean, 87
Lesson plans, 201–14
Letters, reversal of, 103–4, 168–69
Limbic system, 116–17
Linguistic intelligence, 17, 21, 22–23,
 69, 195, 196
 activities, 46
 and multiplication tables, 76, 77
 and reading, 72–73
Logical-mathematical intelligence,
 17–18, 21, 23–25, 69, 196–97
 activities, 46
 and multiplication tables, 76, 77
 and reading, 73–74
Lorber, John, 12
Lowell, Amy, 188

Macdonald, Suse, Alphabatics, 104
McGuinness, Diane, 149
MacLean, Paul, 116–17
McLuhan, Marshall, 186
Madaus, George, 49

The Magic Trees of the Mind, Diamond,
 59
Mathematical intelligence. See Logical-
 mathematical intelligence
Mathematics, teaching techniques,
 95–97
Mehan, Hugh, 43
 Handicapping the Handicapped, 40–
 41
Meier, Deborah, 49
Mental images, 100–101
Menuin, Yehudi, 146
Metaphor, teaching by, 108
The Metaphoric Mind, Samples, 99
Miller, Alice, The Drama of the Gifted
 Child, 159
Milofsky, Carl, 56
Minority cultures, 199–200
The Mismeasure of Man, Gould, 37
Misunderstandings, mistakes as, 168–
 69
Montagu, Ashley, Growing Young, 158
Montessori, Maria, 180
Montessori schools, 63
Motivation of child, 68–72
Movement, and learning, 86–98
Multiple intelligences, 4, 15–34, 193–
 200
 assessment tests, 46–48
 of child, to discover, 21–34
 and perceptions, 165
 teaching children about, 223–28
 teaching methods, 79–81
Multiplication tables, learning aids,
 76–79
Multisensory learning, 167–71
Murdock, Maureen, 167
Musical intelligence, 19, 28–29, 70,
 195, 196, 197
 activities, 47
 and multiplication tables, 78
 and reading, 75
Myklebust, Helmer, 165
The Myth of the Hyperactive Child, Divoky and Schrag, 62

National Education Association, and
 tests, 36

Naturalist intelligence, 20, 32–33, 71–
    72, 197
  activities, 47
  and multiplication tables, 79
  and reading, 75–76
Nearsightedness, 165
Negative suggestions, 144
Negotiating the Special Education Maze,
    Anderson, Chitwood and Hay-
    den, 65
Neill, A. S., 156
Neurological problems, 88
Nietzsche, Friedrich, 188
Noise, environmental, 180–81
*None of the Above: Behind the Myth of
    Scholastic Aptitude,* Owen, 38
Nonverbal creativity, 9–10
Normality, myth of, 149–50
Number smart. *See* Logical- mathe-
    matical intelligence
Nurturing environment, 173–83
Nutrition, and learning, 175–78

Objective tests, 40–41
Observation, evaluation by, 45
Oral learners, 73
Organic reading, 124
Organizations, 241–45
Owen, David, *None of the Above: Behind
    the Myth of Scholastic Aptitude,* 38

Parents:
  attitudes to learning, 135–37
  and diagnostic testing, 43–44
  and education of child, 60–65, 67,
    160
  and homework, 132–34
  and late-bloomers, 155–60
  learning from children, 131–32
  and teachers, 137–38
Parent-teacher conferences, 45
Pearce, Joseph Chilton, 161
Peers, teaching by, 138–39
People smart. *See* Interpersonal intel-
    ligence
Percentile ranking, 41–43
Perceptions, differing, 163–66, 168–
    69

Persistence, 31
Phonics, 72–73
Physical activity, teaching and, 86–98
Physiognomic perception, 163–64
Piaget, Jean, 58, 86–87, 154–55, 168,
    179
Picture smart. *See* Spatial intelligence
A Place Called School, Goodlad, 52–53,
    59–60
Poplin, Mary, 9
Positive experience, assessment as,
    47–48
Positive qualities, 147
The Possible Human, Houston, 1
Potential of individual, 4, 12
Power struggles, 133–34
Poze, Tony, 108
Praise, 133, 143, 148
Preschool:
  education in, 152–53
  teaching strategies, 203–4
Private schools, 63
Proust, Marcel, 188
Psychologists:
  and diagnostic testing, 42–43
  and learning disabilities, 7
Public schools, 186
Puccini, Giacomo, 188
Punishment, and homework, 133
Pygmalion effect, 142–43

Racism, testing and, 37–38
Rational brain, 116
Reading, 20–21, 87–88
  age of learning, 155–59
  aids to learning, 72–76
  teaching techniques, 93–94, 104–5,
    124–25
Relationships, positive, 131–39
Relaxation techniques, 119–20
  for eyes, 170
Religion, multiple intelligences and,
    198
Reptilian brain, 116
Reversal of letters, 103–4, 168–69
Rewards, 133
Ritalin, 8, 27–28
Robertson, Linda, 83

Rodin, Auguste, 188
Role models, 224–25
   parents as, 136
Rosenthal, Robert, 142–43
Rosenzweig, Mark, 59
Rotation diets, 176

Salk, Jonas, 188
Samples, Robert, 108
   The Metaphoric Mind, 99
Savants, 196
Scholastic Aptitude Test, 37–38
Schooling options, 62–65
School records, 43–44
Schools:
   evaluation of, 60–61
   failure of, 52
   and imagination, 102
   and individual differences, 4–6, 9–
      13, 21, 34, 68, 156, 186–89
   and learning, 58–59
   and learning disabilities, 41
   and multiple intelligences, 82–84,
      215–22
   special programs, 11–12
   stress in, 111, 113
School smart, 23, 24
Schrag, Peter, *The Myth of the Hyperac-
      tive Child*, 62
Schwartz, Tony, 187
Sculptors, 18
Self smart. *See* Intrapersonal intelli-
      gence
Self-concept, labeling and, 143–44
Self-help skills, coping with stress, 122
Senses, development of, 162–64
Silberberg, Norman and Margaret,
      158
Skills, 146
   teaching of, 54–55
Slowness, as virtue, 152–53
Smith, Frank, *Insult to Intelligence*, 51,
      55
Spatial intelligence, 18, 25–26, 69–70,
      195, 196, 197
   activities, 46
   and multiplication tables, 77–78
   and reading, 74, 103–4

Speaking ability, 17
   See also Linguistic intelligence
Special education programs, 11–12,
      56–57, 64–65
Spelling, teaching techniques, 95
Spirit, human, 166–67
Standardized tests, 5, 36–38
   multiple intelligences and, 194–95
Stanford-Binet IQ test, 37
State legislatures, and schools, 6
Steiner, Rudolf, 63, 113, 155, 159
Storytelling, 23
   teaching by, 106–8
Stress:
   children and, 111–14
   from evaluative tests, 39–40
   and learning disabilities, 117
   physical, and learning, 89
   reduction of, 118–23
   in schools, 165–66
Success, visualization of, 109–10
Symbolic representation, 101
Synaesthesia, 162–64
Synectics, 108

Talents, 146
Talk, excessive, by teachers, 53
Tarver, Sara, 9
Task analysis, 54
Teachers, 51, 68
   evaluation by parents, 61
   expectations by, 143–44
   and fantasy, 102
   and individual differences, 12
   interaction with students, 53
   and multiple intelligences ap-
      proach, 83
   parents and, 62
   relationships with, 137–38
Teaching methods, 12–13, 79–80
   and children's problems, 52–60
   multiplication tables, 76–79
   reading, 72–76
Teaching strategies, 148–49, 201–14
   bodily-kinesthetic, 89–98
Teaching to the tests, 49
Terman, Lawrence, 37
Tesla, Nikola, 18

Tests:
  formal, 34, 36–44
  manipulation by administrators,
    40–41
  for ADD/ADHD, 8
  for multiple intelligences, 216–17
  standardized, 5, 36–38, 194–95
Textbooks, 5, 53–54
Thematic teaching, 92
Thought:
  and image, 101
  physical aspects, 85, 87
Three-dimensional mind, 103–4
Time for learning, 179–80
Titchner, E. B., 101
Toffler, Alvin, 185
"Tracking" of students, 38, 55–56
Traits, positive, 147
Trelease, Jim, 136
Trusdell, Lee Ann, 57

Underachievers, 3, 6
Unified senses theory, 162–64
Unique learners, 3, 6, 8–12, 13
The Unschooled Mind, Gardner, 59

Vision problems, 165, 169–70
Visualization, 108–10
Volunteering, 84

Waldorf educational system, 63
Weinstein, Carole S., 178
Werner, Heinz, 162–63
Westin, Jeane, *The Coming Parent Revo-*
    lution, 57
Why Johnny Can't Read, Flesch, 72
Wide Range Achievement Test
    (WRT), 41–42
Wilson, Woodrow, 188
Word smart. *See* Linguistic intelli-
    gence
Worksheets, 5, 217
  skills development, 54–55
Writing:
  and emotions, 123–24
  teaching techniques, 94–95
Wunderlich, Ray C., Jr., 173

Zelan, Karen, *Learning to Read: The*
    Child's Fascination with Reading,
    124

For More Information

To contact Dr. Armstrong regarding presentations on multiple intelligences, the myth of ADD, or the natural genius of children, write: P.O. Box 548, Cloverdale, CA 95425; phone: 707-894-4646; fax: 707-894-4474; or e-mail: thomas@thomasarmstrong.com. His website contains information about his other books, videos, weblinks, articles, resources, and other information about multiple intelligences: www.thomasarmstrong.com.